THE LAND AND ISLES
of
GREECE

THE COMPLETE VACATION GUIDE
FOR ALL BUDGETS

by *Philip Deane*

DOUBLEDAY & COMPANY, INC., GARDEN CITY, NEW YORK, 1966

All photographs supplied by the National Tourist Organization of Greece. Pictures numbered 2 and 21 by Voula Papatioannou; 3, 5, 6, 8, 13, 24 and 25 by Nikos K. Kontos; 4 by Man. Diamantis; 7 by Pavlos Myloff; 9 and 16 by Boutsa; 10 by D. A. Harissiadis; 11 by I. Ioannidou and L. Bortziotou; 12 and 22 by Nick S. Stournaras; 14 and 19 by V. and N. Tombazi; 15 by Dimitri; 27 by Ant. Economides; 26 and 28 by Spyros Meletzis.

For General C. Gigantes, who gave so much to Greece

ACKNOWLEDGMENTS

I wish to thank Mrs. Betty Gregoire for her help; and the Royal Automobile Club of Greece for the use of their maps.

CONTENTS

THE LAND AND ISLES OF GREECE

FOREWORD

"Other countries offer you discoveries in manners or lore or landscape; Greece offers you something harder—the discovery of yourself."   LAWRENCE DURRELL

To the question of whether you should visit Greece there can be only one, emphatic answer. Yes.

Greece brings out the latent creativity in all of us. One learns a lot about the joy of living there, and the lesson stays. Greece is not only a treasure house of classical ruins and sumptuous Byzantine art. These are there, of course, unforgettable, drawing you back in memory.

The Greeks of today will also make you want to return. The Greek character has changed little through the centuries; Finlay makes this clear in his *World of Odysseus* (Pelican A570). The Ancient Greeks invented rational science, anticipated nuclear physics, Darwin, Descartes, Newton, psychotherapy, Keynesean compensatory economics (the Parthenon was built to reduce unemployment and get idle cash back into circulation, Plutarch tells us). Greece produced four of the world's few immortal playwrights, sculptors who have never been surpassed, the architects of the Acropolis, the fathers of all philosophical schools . . . the list goes on.

The environment, the conditions in which these men gave us so much are still there. At sunset, when the brilliant contrasts of dark and light melt into each other, the imagination cannot help but take flight, and you can feel the presence of the great ones. Their modern descendants—somewhat brash, argumentative, amorous—talking volubly in the taverns, merely wear different dress. The seeds of a tremendous renaissance are there and some have bloomed, giving the world Kazantzakis, Seferis, Sikelianos, Cavafy, Palamas, Elytis and many others. There is a quality of intellectuality in Greece, a feeling that something exciting is about to happen.

So read the very few initial pages which follow, choose what you will do for the number of days you plan to stay, go there, leave this book in your hotel room during the day (leave the camera there occasionally, too), and enjoy yourself.

HOW TO USE THIS BOOK

The key to this book is Section I, the Capsule Guide. In this section is information everyone should have before embarking on a holiday to Greece:

1. When you should go to Greece.
2. How to get there.
3. How much it will cost to get there.
4. Approximate cost in Greece per day, including hotels, meals and incidentals, per person, as well as a list of holiday camps, and camping sites.
5. Formalities:
    a. Passports
    b. Health certificates
    c. Currency regulations and exchange rates
    d. Customs regulations.
6. What to eat and drink.
7. What to splurge on.
8. A list of essential information on tourist assistance, tipping, medical care, electric current, etc.
9. How to choose what to see in Greece for the time and money at your disposal. There are brief descriptions of places so that you do not have to read the whole book before deciding where you want to go. This part indicates the minimum time required to visit any locality. For what it may be worth, I list what I would choose for any given number of days. Available prepackaged tours and their costs are also included.

The main body of the book begins with Section II and deals

with the "Classical Landscape," the known and loved high-lights of Greece. Section III introduces endlessly varied but less well-known parts of Greece. In these two sections I have given not only all the famed archaeological sites, but a sampling of the Greek scene—its island, mountain, inland and coastal settings and the different ways of life formed by these settings. If you were to visit every place described in this book, you would really know Greece.

In Sections II and III, the passages on each locality include details about hotels, the things to see and do, as well as how to get there from Athens, how long the journey will take, and cost. If you wish to visit any of the places described and you are outside Athens, your hotel, the local tourist police, or travel agent will assist with arrangements on how to get there. For those who wish to save money, I have listed bus and rail fares, cheaper hotels, village lodgings, and a list of camping sites.

Sections IV and V contain additional information needed respectively by the motorist and the yachtsman.

Section VI gives you a brief panorama of Greece that is not a mere recital of events but rather an attempt to extract the essence, the most significant contribution to mankind of various periods in Greek prehistory, history, and culture.

Finally, Section VII contains an indexed list of stores, galleries, theaters, and artists you may want to patronize in Athens; addresses in Greece and the United States of agencies and organizations you may wish to contact (all from lists compiled by the National Tourist Organization of Greece); useful words and phrases; the Greek alphabet.

NOTE ON SPELLINGS. This book gives the spelling of the *New Century Classical Handbook* (Appleton-Century-Crofts, Inc.). Where the *New Century Classical Handbook* gives more than one spelling, the one chosen is either closer to Greek pronunciation or is the more familiar.

Distances are given in kilometers, since this is the measure used on maps and road signs in Greece. Fares and car hire are computed by the kilometer, which equals 0.62 miles.

SECTION I

CAPSULE GUIDE

*Which includes information everyone should have
before embarking on a holiday to Greece*

WHEN YOU SHOULD GO TO GREECE

Swimming begins in April and goes on through October. On the southern beaches of Rhodes or Crete you can swim from March through November.

April through August are the big tourist months and places tend to be crowded. September and October are less crowded. The ideal months are April, May and October. In April and May everything is fresh—the fields aglow with poppies, the green new and tender. In spring, too, you might be lucky enough to witness the glory of the Greek Orthodox Easter—the most brilliant festival of the Church calendar. In 1966 Greek Easter falls on April 10; in 1967 April 30; in 1968 April 21; in 1969 April 13; in 1970 April 26.

WEATHER IN ATHENS. Latitude 37° 59′ N

Temp.	Jan.	Feb.	Mar.	Apr.	May	Jun.	Jul.	Aug.	Sep.	Oct.	Nov.	Dec.
Low	42°	42°	46°	51°	60°	67°	72°	72°	66°	60°	52°	46°
High	53°	56°	60°	68°	77°	85°	90°	90°	83°	74°	64°	57°
Average	48°	49°	53°	60°	69°	76°	81°	81°	75°	67°	58°	52°
Days of Rain	12	11	11	9	7	4	3	3	4	9	12	13

(When it rains, it rains for short spells. A whole day of rain is rare.) Southernmost Greece is warm earlier. Northern Greece grows cold sooner.

Study the weather chart and plan your wardrobe accordingly. It might be useful to note that Athenians wear coat and tie at night even in midsummer for their visits to the tavernas and night clubs.

NOTEWORTHY EVENTS

Greek Easter: (for description see page 322).

March 25: Greek National Day. Nationwide celebrations and military parades.

April to October: "Sound and Light" spectacles at the Athens Acropolis, and the castle of Rhodes.

May 20–23: The Athens Acropolis Rally—an automobile race.

May 21: Festival at Langada near Salonica, where you can see an ancient rite of initiation—men and women walking barefoot on live charcoal.

June to September: Folk dances by Dora Stratou's group, in national dress, Athens.

June 12: At Hydra the Miaoulis festival. Feasting and dancing.

June 20 to July 25: Epidaurus Festival of Ancient Greek Drama. Weekends.

July 15 to August 15: Ancient Greek Drama Festivals at Philippi near Kavalla, and on Thasos, the nearby island.

July to September: Athens Festival. Concerts, ballet, opera by distinguished companies and orchestras from round the world. Ancient drama at the foot of the Acropolis in the theater of Herod of Attica.

August 1 to 15: Festival of Ancient Greek Drama at Dodoni near Ioannina.

August 11: Feast of Saint Spyridon at Corfu. Processions, feasting and colorful folk dances.

August 15: Feast of the Dormition, or the Falling Asleep of the Virgin Mary—exciting religious festival on the island of Tinos.

August 16: The Feast of St. Gerassimos on the island of Cephalonia.

August 15 to 30: Festival of Ancient Greek Drama at Dimitrias near Volos.

September: Wine Festival at Daphni near Athens. All you can drink for less than a dollar. Sixty varieties of wine to choose from. Folk singing and dancing.

September 20 to 26: Greek Film Festival at Salonica.

Carnival festivities are particularly joyous and colorful in Plaka, the old quarter of Athens, and in Patras. The parties and the fun go on for three weeks and end on the seventh Sunday, or forty-nine days before Easter.

HOW TO GET THERE

Book early, especially if you plan to travel in spring or summer, so that you don't miss the best connections. Buy your ticket through a travel agent. It is no more expensive for you than to buy direct. The agent gets a commission from the shipping line. Timetables change. Your travel agent will have the latest. (If you want a tailored tour arranged for you, train reservations, multiple hotel reservations, the travel agent will charge you a fee. Ask him about it in advance).

You can go to Greece from the United States or Canada by ship or airplane, direct or through Europe, or any part of the Middle East. And you can go *from* Greece anywhere. Athens is a communications knot and an excellent jumping off point in any direction.

You can go to Greece by railway. The famous Orient Express runs three times a week through London, Paris, Lausanne, Milan, Venice, Trieste and Belgrade. There is also the Tauern Express from Ostend through Germany and Yugoslavia; the Balkan Express through Austria and Yugoslavia; and the Yugoslav Express. It is wise to take along provisions on any of these train journeys as well as those foil packets of wash and dry tissues. For men, a battery-powered electric shaver would be useful, and mouthwash in case you should run out of water; the queue to the washrooms is too long, especially in second class.

If you hold a valid international driving license you can drive into Greece through Yugoslavia or take the ferry from Italy. To take your car in you need a certificate of free entry which will be given you by the Greek customs officers. It is valid for four months. For longer stays you need documents from the Automobile Club of your country (in the United States the AAA). (See Section IV, the Motorist's Guide.)

If you want to visit Greece in a yacht, your passport will be checked at the first port of call where you will be issued a "Transit Log" with which to sail in Greek waters, buying supplies and fuel at transit prices. You will also be given a map showing yacht service stations and all the necessary information for your radio and for listening in to weather broadcasts. Service stations are strategically located all around Greece. (See Section V.)

HOW MUCH IT WILL COST
TO GET THERE

All fares are approximate and are given to help in the preparation of a rough budget. Fares change, so consult your travel agent.

Round-trip air fares to Athens:

From	1st Class	Tourist
Amsterdam	$351.20	$260.70
Beirut	229.20	166.70
Belgrade	151.70	111.80
Brussels	338.20	250.10
Bucharest	248.80	180.90
Budapest	174.80	146.30
Cairo	191.40	142.40
Copenhagen	440.30	327.20
Damascus	229.20	166.70
Frankfurt	320.20	242.50
Hamburg	385.70	283.30
Istanbul	92.80	70.90
Lisbon	414.10	316.60
London	395.10	298.00
Madrid	355.50	271.40
Moscow	428.30	342.20
Oslo	497.80	377.00
Paris	333.50	250.10
Prague	285.60	207.50
Rome	223.30	165.00
Stockholm	497.80	379.50
Tel Aviv	229.20	166.70
United States (east coast)	1,087.80	776.40
Warsaw	305.90	234.10

Group air fares. If you and your friends organize a charter flight, the costs plummet dramatically; a round-trip charter ticket from New York can cost as little as $300 per person. Olympic Airways (6 Othonos Street, Athens) offer lower than regular fares to groups of ten or more.

Sea transportation. The cost of going by sea is comparable to the cost of air travel for first and second class. The cheaper cabins are appreciably less than tourist class by air. Make sure you know what sort of accommodation you are getting so examine a plan of the ship at your travel agent's. Upon request, Greek shipping firms offer lower fares to groups of ten or more. Your travel agent can help you.

Rail fares from Europe are fairly cheap. See your travel agent for prices. (Students and teachers accompanying groups of students get lower rail fares *inside* Greece by writing to Greek State Railways, 8 Omirou Street, Athens.)

Cars may be driven overland from Yugoslavia. From Italy by ferry, the cost per car ranges from $16 to $35 depending on size, and the cost per passenger from $11 to $40 depending on which class you travel. Gasoline in Greece costs 80 cents a gallon; lubricants and parts are equivalently priced. Mechanics are good and inexpensive.

APPROXIMATE COST IN GREECE
PER DAY

INCLUDING HOTELS, MEALS AND INCIDENTALS, PER PERSON

Conspicuous consumption	*Modest opulence*	*Comfort on a budget*	*The impecunious*
from $20	from $12	from $8	from $2

(These costs can be cut 25 percent in the autumn and winter)

Living in Greece is still remarkably inexpensive and reduces the overall cost of a trip to Europe. A good meal at a modest tavern, for instance, with wine is $1.50. The most luxurious place, with floor show and dancing, will not cost you more than $6.00 per head unless you try very hard.

The impecunious can stay at selected homes in villages where, under the supervision of the National Tourist Organization, rooms are provided for less than $1.00 a night. Students can stay in Youth Hostels for 50 cents a night, a privilege limited to four nights. The impecunious and students should write to the Greek Youth Hostel Association, 4 Dragatsaniou Street, Athens, for information.

HOTELS AND THEIR PRICES

If you go at the height of the season (April to September) book your room in advance. Hotels in Greece are carefully classified.

Category AA hotels have private baths in all rooms, air conditioning and staff that speak your language.

Category A hotels are almost as good, a little less luxurious and perhaps less gifted linguistically, though the staff certainly speak English and French. They may not have air conditioning in every room.

Category B hotels have private baths and telephones in at least half the rooms; all rooms have hot and cold running water; the staff speak one foreign language, almost certainly English.

Category C hotels are not obliged to provide private baths; they have at least one toilet for every six rooms, hot and cold running water in every room and central heating.

Category D and E hotels do not necessarily have hot running water in every room though they have cold water; there is one toilet for every eight rooms.

Prices are subject to certain surcharges, for instance in a hotel that is newly built or renovated, for short stays of one or two days, for air conditioning and heating. Some hotels include breakfast in the price of the room, some include one other meal; avoid this arrangement if you want to try other restaurants and tavernas. Hotel food tends to be less distinctive than the fare of restaurants or tavernas. Check with the management and with your travel agent if you do not want meals included with your bill. Not all the surcharges mentioned above will be applied to your bill but don't be surprised if they are. With these remarks in view, here is what you may have to pay on an average. (All surcharges are given as percentages of basic room price except for the 15 percent service charge which applies to the entire bill.)

Category	Basic room price		Surcharge for new hotels	Surcharge for short stays	Air conditioner per day	Central heating per day	Service charge
	SINGLE	DOUBLE					
AA	$6.00	$8.00	15%		$1.00	$0.66	15%
A	4.00	5.00	10–65%	10%	1.00	0.66	15%
B	3.00	4.00	10–50%	10%	1.00	0.66	15%
C	2.00	2.50	10–40%	10%	none offered	0.66	15%
D & E	1.00	2.00	none	10%	none offered	0.66	15%

During the autumn and winter, you can get reductions of up to 25 percent.

These prices are averages. In Sections II and III the hotels in each place described are listed and local prices given, including all surcharges and taxes. To help you choose the kind of accommodation you want, I indicate the category to which the hotels of each locality belong; I also give two stars to a hotel with private baths for each room, one star for private baths in some rooms and no star for hotels that have no private baths. Hotels that have been built or rebuilt recently are also marked with a capital letter R in parentheses (R); these are more likely to prove satisfactory. I have not used these markings for hotels in category AA since, by definition, they have baths in all rooms and must have first-rate equipment. In other categories, a hotel marked C** (R) is, in my view, a better bargain than one that merely has a B or even a B*.

The hotel prices given for each locality in Sections II and III are for rooms with private baths. Rooms without baths are 30 to 40 percent cheaper.

The name of the hotel and of the island or town is a sufficient address for small locations. The same holds true of phone numbers—you simply ask the operator for the Delphi hotel by name, for example.

CAMPING SITES

Greece does not yet have many organized camping sites. Those that exist are listed below, and they cost 33 cents per person per day, plus 33 cents per tent or caravan space per day. If you wish to pitch a tent elsewhere, the farmers will most probably give you permission—all you have to do is be as courteous to them as they will certainly be to you. Do not trample on crops.

Camping sites are located at:

Daphni: 10 kilometers from Athens at the site of a famous monastery.

Rion: On a lovely beach not far from Patras.

Kourouta: 88 kilometers from Patras on the way to Olympia.

Limni Heraiou: 72 kilometers from the Corinth Canal near Loutraki.

Arachamita: In Central Peloponnesus, 19 kilometers from Tripolis.

Dimitri Mitropoulos: In the mountains, 88 kilometers from Olympia, on the road to Tripolis.

Monis: For tents only. On an islet near Aegina, one hour by boat from Piraeus.

Samothrakis: For tents only. On the island of Samothrace.

HOLIDAY CAMPS

These are available as package deals including transportation to and from Greece and full board. Contact the head offices of the camps listed below for additional information. Living in these is less than at category C hotels.

Club Mediterranee Holiday Village. Near the town of Corfu. 1100 beds in bamboo huts. 8 Academy Street, Athens.

Olympic Beach at Kyllini, 75 kilometers from Patras. 70 beds in villas, 100 in bungalows, and 200 in tents. Olympos Travel Agency, 4 Jan Smuts Street, Athens.

Lambiri at Egion, 27 kilometers from Patras. 800 beds in bamboo huts and bungalows. 8 Academy Street, Athens.

Bamboo Village at Vouliagmeni, 24 kilometers from Athens, 270 beds in bungalows. American Express, 10 Venizelou Street, Athens.

Xylokastron at a lovely beach on the Patras-Athens road. 400 beds in bungalows and 800 in tents. Aegean Lines, Typaldos Bros., Akti Tselepi, Piraeus.

Dream Island at Eretria on the island of Euboea. 50 two-bed bungalows. TEA, 51 Stadium Street, Athens.

The Argonauts on the island of Poros. Argonauts Yachting Center, 70 Adrianou Street, Athens.

FORMALITIES

PASSPORTS

The documents needed for nationals of each country are listed below. In all cases, except where specifically stated, they are valid for three months, and no visa is needed. All visitors who wish to stay longer than the stated period should apply to the Aliens' Department, Athens Police, 9 Halkokondyli Street, Athens (Telephone 622-597) or to the local police in districts outside Athens. If you want to live and work in Greece you will need a special permit. Greek embassies or consulates have the necessary information.

United States citizens need a valid passport for a stay of two months.

Citizens of Austria, Belgium, France, The Federal Republic of Germany, Italy, Luxembourg and Holland need a valid passport or national identity card, or may enter Greece with the following simplified documents:

Austria: A travel certificate for children of twelve and under.

Belgium: A Belgian passport that has expired within less than five years; an identity card issued by Belgian consular authorities outside Belgium; an identity card with photograph issued by a Belgian Communal Authority for minors up to twelve, if the child is accompanied by a parent. A foreigner's identity card issued by authorities in France, Luxembourg or Switzerland stating that the holder is Belgian but lives in one of these countries.

West Germany: A child's travel certificate issued by a West German authority; a valid temporary West Berlin identity card; a minor's certificate issued by West Berlin authorities.

Italy: An identity card with permit for travel outside Italy; a child's birth certificate with photograph and a permit for travel outside Italy.

France: A French passport which has expired within less than five years; a valid identity card issued by authorities of Belgium, Luxembourg, Switzerland, stating that the holder is French but resides in one of these countries.

Luxembourg: A passport which has expired within less than five years; an identity card or travel document issued to children up to fifteen years by a Communal Authority; a valid identity card issued by authorities of Belgium, France, Switzerland or Liechtenstein stating that the holder is from Luxembourg but lives in one of these countries.

Holland: A passport which has expired within less than five years; an identity card issued by a Belgian or Luxembourg authority stating that the holder is Dutch. A tourist identity card issued in Holland—valid for two months.

British subjects need a valid passport or simplified tourist passport. Those who enter with the tourist passport and wish to stay longer should obtain a regular passport before the three months expire.

Citizens of Australia, Canada, Cyprus, Denmark, Finland, Iran, Ireland, Japan, Liechtenstein, Monaco, New Zealand, Norway, Pakistan, Principalities of the Persian Gulf (Kuwait, Bahrain, Qatar, Abdou, Dari, Muscat), Saar, Spain, Sweden, and Switzerland need only a valid passport.

Citizens of the following countries need a valid passport for a stay of two months: Argentine, Bolivia, Brazil, British Honduras, Chile, Colombia, Congo, Costa Rica, Dominican Republic, Ecuador, Gold Coast, Guatemala, Haiti, Honduras, Iceland, Kenya, Mexico, Nicaragua, Northern Rhodesia, Nyasaland, Panama, Paraguay, Peru, Portugal, Salvador, San

Marino, South Africa, Southern Rhodesia, Tanganyika, Uruguay and Venezuela.

Citizens of countries not specified above need a regular valid passport with visa for entry from a Greek consular authority.

HEALTH CERTIFICATES

Valid international certificates of immunization are required for cholera if travelers come from infected areas; for yellow fever if travelers come from epidemic areas; for small-pox, if travelers come from countries of Asia and Africa other than Egypt or Turkey.

CURRENCY REGULATIONS AND EXCHANGE RATES

If you stay less than two months there are no foreign exchange formalities. If you plan a longer stay, you will have to declare your money on entry and will not be allowed to re-export more than $500 in cash without a special permit.

In Greek currency, you may not take in more than 2000 drachmas; but you can take in unlimited amounts in other currencies.

You can take traveler's checks or letters of credit and take them out again provided they are issued in your name.

The Greek currency is the drachma and comes in coins of 50 lepta (half a drachma), 1 drachma, 2 drachmas, 5 drachmas and 10 drachmas, all of which are made of nickel alloy. The 20 drachma piece is silver and approximately the same size as the 5 drachma piece—do not mix them up. Bills are for 50 drachmas (grayish), 100 (red), 500 (green) and 1000 (orange). There are small perforated aluminum coins for 5 lepta (five-hundredths of a drachma), 10 lepta and 20.

(The figures below are rounded off to the nearest tenth of a drachma where possible. Exchange rates fluctuate a few percentage points each day, but not enough to upset your budget calculations.)

Equivalent values

One American dollar	30 drachmas
One Australian pound	64 drachmas
One Austrian schilling	1 drachma
One Belgian franc	0.6 drachmas
One British pound	83 drachmas
One Canadian dollar	27.50 drachmas
One Cypriot pound	83 drachmas
One Dutch florin	8.3 drachmas
One Danish krone	4.3 drachmas
One French franc	6 drachmas
One Italian lira	0.05 drachmas
One Lebanese pound	9.2 drachmas
One Norwegian krone	4 drachmas
One Portuguese escudo	1 drachma
One Spanish peseta	0.5 drachma
One S. African pound	39.5 drachmas
One Swedish krona	5.7 drachmas
One Swiss franc	6.9 drachmas
One Turkish lira	2.6 drachmas
One W. German mark	7.5 drachmas
One Yugoslav dinar	0.3 drachmas

CUSTOMS REGULATIONS

You can take your personal effects in and out freely, whether they come as accompanied or unaccompanied luggage. If luggage is unaccompanied send a list along with your cases. At the point of entry, you will have to declare verbally what new things you are bringing in and what gifts, if any. Anything you intend to sell must be declared separately.

Included in personal effects are clothing, toiletries, jewelry

and ornaments, linen, 22 pounds of sweets, 50 cigars or 200
cigarettes or 200 grams of tobacco, books (one copy of each),
two packs of cards, five boxes of matches, camping equipment,
one portable radio, one portable typewriter, one portable record player and 20 records, one bicycle per person, sporting
goods, one still camera, one small movie camera with a few
rolls of film (you can buy film in Greece).

Take the cat and dog if you wish, but make sure they have
recent, valid health certificates. Parrots are not allowed into
Greece, nor are dope and narcotics. Nor are weapons other
than a shotgun, but you may only hunt after you have spent
six months in Greece and you need a hunting permit from the
police to do so. The limit for cartridges is 50.

If you manage to acquire something like the Hermes of
Praxiteles, you will not be allowed to take it out of Greece.
It is possible to obtain a permit to export a Byzantine icon,
provided the Archaeological Service does not deem it a national treasure.

WHAT TO EAT AND DRINK

If you should worry about Greek food looking rich in the tavernas, you can always order broiled meat or broiled fish. Greek seafood is infinitely varied and tasty, Greek vegetables and fruit delicious, and village bread (served in many restaurants) a joy. Phrases for ordering food are in the vocabulary section.

There are many fine Greek wines, not all flavored with resin, but try Retsina, the resinated wine, anyway, for many foreigners develop a taste for it. Ask for a glass—there is an appropriate phrase in the vocabulary section.

Local beer is good and so are the soft drinks such as apple juice, apricot juice, orange, lemon. There is a cola drink which is a reasonable facsimile and children seem to love it.

In Athens and the major cities there are wonderful pastry shops with all kinds of patisserie, both French and Greek. All Greek pastries are rich but often very good. Forget the calories at least once to try.

American style coffee is not usually well made. However, there is always Nescafé, good espresso and Greek coffee which you should sample. (See vocabulary section.)

WHAT TO SPLURGE ON

Rent a yacht to tour the islands. For an average yachting party of eight, the cost is from $30 per head per day, including charter of boat, fuel, crew and food. There are cheaper yachts, sleeping four, at $20 per head per day.

Furs are a good buy, so are handicraft items and pottery. Ladies staying near Athens for a couple of weeks should consider having next season's wardrobe made there. The workmanship is excellent, so is the cut. Made-to-measure coats, dresses and suits stand comparison with garments costing $500 and up, yet will cost from $50 to $100 if you take along your own material.

Jewelry is good. Athens is an inexpensive place to have old pieces reset or redesigned. Peasant jewelry, especially of silver, is decorative and well made. The work of modern Greek artists is extremely good value.

If you have friends in Greece (and it does not take long to acquire them) let them do some bargaining for you. They enjoy it and often achieve reductions in price.

ESSENTIAL INFORMATION

Assistance will be given to the traveler by Tourist Policemen wearing badges indicating which language they speak. There are tourist police stations in all tourist centers. Your hotel will phone them for you. Addresses are given in Section VII.

Brochures are given free by all travel agents; they are available at the site you are visiting, or at the hotels nearby. They are useful to have, decorative and make fine souvenirs of your trip.

Bus Fares: 0.39 dr. (1.3 cents) per kilometer.

Chauffeur-driven cars: $12.50 a day plus 12 cents per kilometer for European cars; $15.50 a day plus 17 cents a kilometer for American cars.

Checks. Personal checks are not generally accepted in Greece; make sure you have enough traveler's checks, or letters of credit, or, for the larger tourist centers, credit cards.

Credit Cards are accepted by more and more shops every year, especially in Athens and other major tourist centers. But don't rely on them outside Athens.

Dry cleaning may take up to a week. Some hotels have 24-hour service.

Electric current is mostly 220 AC. Some islands have 110 DC.

Haircuts cost less than a dollar including tip.

Hairdressers charge $5 for a permanent in Athens. $1 for setting.

Hours of business in summer—8 A.M. to 1:30 P.M. and 5

P.M. to 8 P.M.; in winter—8:30 A.M. to 1:30 P.M. and 4 P.M. to 7:30 P.M.

Laundry takes 24 hours in hotels.

Medical services are good. If you need a doctor ask at your hotel.

Postage. Within Greece: 8 cents for the first half ounce; 5 cents for each additional half ounce. Mail travels by air wherever possible. Outside Greece: Surface mail, 12 cents for the first half ounce, 8 cents each additional half ounce. Postcards, 8 cents. Airmail: All airmail is subject to a 12-cent surcharge regardless of weight. In addition each half ounce costs 6 cents for Europe and the Middle East, 25 cents for the United States, Canada, India and Pakistan, 30 cents for Latin America, 35 cents for Japan and the rest of Asia, 55 cents for Australia, New Zealand and the Pacific. An extra 12 cents is charged for registered letters, and 18 cents for special delivery.

Rent-a-car: European cars $4 a day plus 8 cents per kilometer; American cars $5 a day plus 9 cents per kilometer.

Taxis: 10 cents per kilometer. Outside city limits you pay for the return journey whether you return or not. The driver will want to be paid for waiting. Always agree on payment in advance. Ask your hotel to help you bargain.

Telegrams: Within Greece—approximately 20 cents for each 10 words, plus 6 percent of the total charge. Night letters are half price. Urgent cables are twice the ordinary price. Very urgent cables are three times the normal price. Outside Greece: All telegrams are subject to a 6 percent surcharge. Here are the costs per word for the country of destination: America (U. S.), 28 cents for New York, 34 cents for other cities; Austria, Italy, 10 cents a word; England, France, Germany, 14 cents a word. Night letters are half the price with a minimum of 22 words.

Telephones: A three-minute call costs 2 cents within ten

kilometers. Charges double as distances double. Overseas calls for three minutes: America (U. S.) $12; England $4.53; France $4.06; Italy from $2.40 to $3.40; Switzerland $3.50; Germany $3.80. All calls have a 6 percent surcharge. Dial 100 on any Athens telephone and your questions will be answered in English.

Time in Athens is two hours ahead of Greenwich Mean Time and seven hours ahead of Eastern Standard Time.

Tips: 10 to 15 percent on large bills, 15 percent on small bills for the waiter and barber. Give another 3 to 5 percent to their assistants. Taxi drivers do not expect to be tipped; however, I usually round off the fare to the next drachma and add from two to five drachmas.

Trains do not run as frequently and do not serve as many areas in Greece as buses do. Except for the train to Salonica and that to Olympia, Greek rail transportation tends to be slow with frequent stops. First-class travel on fast trains is 0.59 dr. or 2 cents a kilometer (without sleeping accommodation) as opposed to 0.39 dr. (1.3 cents) a kilometer by bus. Third-class accommodation, which usually means a slow train, is the same price as the bus. Railways offer substantial reductions to students, accompanying teachers, and journalists.

Water is safe to drink. If you wish, ask for spring water, which is bottled under medical supervision and is delicious. The vocabulary section will give you the proper words.

HOW TO CHOOSE WHAT TO SEE IN GREECE FOR THE TIME AND MONEY AT YOUR DISPOSAL

You could return to Greece year after year, spending more and more time and still not exhaust its delights. The part of Greece most known and loved, however, is small and can be given a once-over during a fairly short trip. It consists of Athens, the islands of the Saronic Gulf to the south of Athens, the Argolis Peninsula, Delphi, Rhodes, Corfu, and two small islands in the Aegean, Mykonos and Delos. The most popular archaeological and Byzantine sites are here, the best transportation schedules, hotels of all categories, and "prepackaged" tours which provide transportation, a guide, board and lodging for an all-inclusive fee. Also within this definition of Greece's known and loved places are the great island of Crete; Olympia, birthplace of the games; Sparta and Mystras; the Meteora, a group of monasteries in central Greece, perched atop pillars of stone; and Mount Athos, a holy mountain devoted entirely to the monastic life. Thumbnail descriptions of these places follow:

ATHENS

The capital of Hellenism today, as it was in the classical era, Athens is a white and pastel city in a nest of mountains by the sea, a lively metropolis, pleasantly cosmopolitan and the repository of the best ancient Greek relics in the world. In the temples and museums of Athens are the marks left on the earth and on our souls by those tremendous Greeks of the Golden Age, who gave us rational science, our conception of beauty in art and the human body, and the democratic form of government. Athens is endowed with the incomparable Acropolis, a fabulous archaeological museum, Byzantine treasures, a major art festival each summer, many theaters and art galleries. It can accommodate the affluent or modest budget. A courteous city, it makes you feel an honored guest rather than raw material for the tourist industry. Its night life is gay, shopping is good and it is only half an hour from golden beaches, forty-five minutes from a hotel perched on a mountain 4500 feet high. A few hours in Athens can give you a view of the various Greek civilizations from the earliest to the present.

ARGOLIS

The southern part of Greece is called the Peloponnesus, a large peninsula shaped like a hand with a finger missing. The thumb of this hand, southwest of Athens, is called the Argolis and contains some of the main archaeological sites of Greece; for instance Old Corinth, the richest, gaudiest city of Ancient Greece; and Epidaurus, the workplace of Hippocrates, the first great physician. In Epidaurus, Asclepius, the god of medicine, was worshiped, games were held and a tremendous amphitheater was built for productions of ancient Greek tragedies—now performed each weekend in late June and early July by the National Theater of Greece. There are extensive ruins of temples and ancient medical installations.

Near Epidaurus is Mycenae, home of Agamemnon, who led the Greeks against Troy and returned victorious, only to be slaughtered by his wife, Clytemnestra. In Mycenae flourished the preclassical civilization celebrated by Homer in his magnificent stanzas; artifacts identical to those described in the Iliad and Odyssey can still be seen. There are the fortress, palace and fabulous tombs of Mycenae to visit.

Also in the Argolis is Nauplion, Greece's first capital after independence was won from the Turks in the last century. A beautiful town, Nauplion, with its enormous medieval fortress, is set around a sparkling bay in which lies a minute island bearing an old castle, once a prison and now a luxury hotel.

THE SARONIC GULF

The Saronic Gulf lies between Athens and Argolis and is dotted with minuscule islands, all of which can be visited in a day, yet each a world in miniature, complete with its own history and character. Hydra, for instance, cluttered with opulent yachts, spectacular as a cubist painting and alive with artists and folk from round the world; Poros, perfumed by its surrounding lemon tree groves; Aegina, once a proud rival of Athens crowned by temples of rare beauty, small indeed to have experienced greatness, and many other islands.

DELPHI

The drive to the city is unforgettable, passing through some of the most beautiful scenery in Greece. Delphi was called the navel of the earth by the ancient Greeks and it is certainly one of the most breath-taking natural sites anywhere, the ledge of an enormous rock face, surrounded by an amphitheater of towering fir-covered peaks, far above a shimmering bay and valleys of olive trees. Delphi was the home of the Apollonian cult, the religion of light and enlightenment that started as a dark exercise in divination and developed into something very like a modern political research institute where worldly

priests analyzed current events and gave sound advice to statesmen and kings.

Delphi's ruins are superb and its museum contains the
Charioteer, one of the most beautiful bronze statues in the
world. Near Delphi are the splendid mosaics and architecture
of Osios Loukas, a charming Byzantine monastery where you
are welcome to spend the night.

RHODES

Rhodes encompasses every period in Greek history, starting
with the classical age and continuing through the Byzantine
era, the Crusades, the Turkish occupation—Doric and Ionian
columns, domes with golden mosaics, medieval castles, minarets dotted about the fertile island, which is blessed with magnificent and numerous hotels and lovely beaches for lolling in
the sun.

CORFU

Shakespeare called Corfu, Prospero's Isle. It is the greenest,
lushest part of Greece, beautiful all over, and very much influenced by Venice, which held the island for centuries. It is gay
with song and costume, and has many excellent restaurants
in superb settings, as well as a quaint town with an imposing
Venetian fortress. You can gamble at a luxurious casino.

MYKONOS and DELOS

Mykonos and Delos, lying side by side, are mere dots, peaks
of mountains long submerged in the blue Aegean. Mykonos,
a breezy island, is dry as bone, finely polished by the sun and
salt air. It is white everywhere, from the many windmills to

the houses and the narrow paths. Its shops display lovely pottery and fine products of the island's looms. The harbor, usually full of cruise ships and yachts, demands to be photographed or painted. Nearby is a beach of fine silver sand and the water seems as transparent as the clearest glass. Many consider it the most picturesque island in the world. Next door, three quarters of an hour by motorboat, lies Delos, ruined but so well preserved that one can see how Greeks of the classical period lived. Delos, like Delphi, was a shrine of Apollo and the traces of his temples are there, rows of preclassical lions guarding the approach to the sanctuary; and homes, sliced by heaven knows what calamity, their mosaic floors exposed to the eye as one passes by.

CRETE

The tourist facilities this island deserves are only now being built. It is worth a visit, though, for it is a world in itself of heroic men and women, of dark brooding passions, great folding mountain ranges and fertile plains, magnificent beaches, some yet to be discovered by the foreigner, an island fit for the legend of the Minotaur and the mystical mother goddess religion of his era. The Minotaur's palace in Knossos is excellently restored and is the best example yet of the Minoan civilization, which flourished on the island two thousand years before Christ, producing exquisite art, craftsmanship and a luxurious way of life. It influenced, among others, the preclassical civilization of Mycenae.

OLYMPIA

In western Peloponnesus lies Olympia, set in olive groves and sheltering a superb museum and magnificent ruins. One of the world's most haunting archaeological sights, Olympia is a must for anyone who wants to know Greece. In the summer the valley can be very hot from 10 A.M. to 5 P.M. So far there are not enough hotels at the site.

SPARTA and MYSTRAS

Sparta is the home of the "three hundred" who stood at the pass of Thermopylae and fought off the entire Persian might in the fifth century B.C. It is now a fairly typical, small, almost sleepy country town in an orchard valley, between two rocky mountain ranges. It is worth visiting because of its neighbor, Mystras, a marvelously well preserved example of Byzantine architecture, a ghost town that seems alive because of the spirit of its founders.

THE METEORA

The Meteora, in central Greece, are huge uneven pillars of stone crowned by monasteries which you reach in a basket hoisted by pulleys; in some cases you can ride mules or donkeys a certain distance. The view over the plain is breathtaking and the monasteries guard priceless icons and illuminated medieval texts. The Meteora are in the agricultural heart of Greece, Thessaly, the ancient home of riders and horse-breeding.

MOUNT ATHOS

Holy Mount Athos, in northern Greece, is completely devoted to the monastic life. On Mount Athos are many monasteries, some of which are superb examples of Byzantine art and architecture. The monasteries are repositories of imperial embroideries, goldsmiths' art, illuminated manuscripts and marvelous icons. Only adult males may visit—even female animals are barred, except for the hen and cat. If you wish to view all the treasures of Mount Athos, you will need at least a week; but a day and night there can give you an idea of the place, its mood and treasures. There are special formalities to enter. See page 155.

MINIMUM TIME NEEDED TO VISIT
THESE PLACES

The foregoing places constitute an initiation to Greece. What follows is the means of organizing your trip, whether you are a leisurely traveler or one who wants to see as much as possible in the shortest time. The *minimum* time needed to visit any of these places is:

Athens, one day. From Athens and back: *Delphi,* by road, one day; *Argolis,* by road, one day; *Saronic Gulf islands,* by boat, one day; *Rhodes,* by air, one day; *Corfu,* by air, one day; *Crete,* by air, one day; *Olympia,* two days; *Sparta,* two days; *Meteora,* two days; *Mount Athos,* two days.

It cannot be emphasized enough that these are bare minimums, with time to breeze in and out, frequently eating a box lunch on your lap. There are prepackaged tours and cruises to all these places. Before listing them with their prices and the time they take, I suggest below, for what it is worth, the way I would apportion my time for any given number of days in Greece.

AUTHOR'S CHOICE

One Day: Athens

Two Days: Athens

Three Days: One day in Athens and two at Delphi. I pick Delphi next to Athens as the spot that one must visit because it probably offers the greatest contrast to the capital city and its coastal region. To reach Delphi you drive through lovely country and across magnificent mountain ranges; you will meet the Greek mountaineer, a very different man to the Athenian, and you will see old shepherds in traditional skirts. You will probably stop at the Byzantine monastery of Osios Loukas to see its great mosaics. The combination of Athens and Delphi offers good variety.

Four Days: One in Athens, two at Delphi and the fourth day, by boat, visiting the islands of the Saronic Gulf so as to get the feel of the Greek isles.

Five Days: One in Athens, two at Delphi, two days in the Argolis Peninsula, pausing long enough to take a schooner to the island of Hydra. Here you add more classical remains and the Mycenaean civilization, enriching the brew.

Six Days: One in Athens, two at Delphi, two cruising the islands of Mykonos and Delos, and the last day in Athens. Because time is available, I have skipped the Argolis in favor of an island cruise. For some, Delos is as fascinating as the Argolis itself. It may be argued that Delos does not offer both classical and rich Mycenaean ruins as the Argolis does but for me a cruise in the Aegean is compensation enough.

Seven Days: One in Athens, two at Delphi, two on the island cruise to Mykonos and Delos to rest from the drive to Delphi, followed by two days in the Argolis.

Eight Days: One in Athens, two at Delphi, two on the Mykonos-Delos cruise followed by two days in the Argolis and one last day in Athens.

Nine Days: One in Athens, two at Delphi, five on a cruise visiting Mykonos, Delos, Rhodes and Crete, as well as other islands, ending with a day in Athens.

Ten Days: One in Athens, three days for Delphi and the Argolis followed by five days on an island cruise and the last day in Athens.

Eleven Days: One in Athens, four for Delphi, the Argolis and Olympia, five days on an island cruise and one last day in Athens. If you wish, you could visit Delphi only, skip the Argolis and Olympia, substituting two days in Corfu or even three, skipping the last day in Athens.

Twelve Days: Two days in Athens, four to visit Delphi, the Argolis and Olympia, five days on an island cruise, and one last day in Athens. Here you could skip two of the three days I have programmed for Athens and fly instead to Corfu.

Thirteen Days: One in Athens, four for Delphi, the Argolis and Olympia, five days on an island cruise, two days in Corfu and one in Athens.

Fourteen Days: Two days in Athens, two days on an island cruise to Mykonos and Delos, four for Delphi, the Argolis and Olympia, then a flight to Rhodes or Corfu for six days' rest, or three days in each as you wish. The choice between Rhodes and Corfu will at first be determined by your interest in archaeology. Rhodes is richer in sites to visit and is likely to be warmer earlier in the year. However, as you get to know Greece more, you will inevitably adopt your own island—it is inescapable—and defend it above all others, drawn back again and again in both body and spirit.

Fifteen Days: Same as for fourteen days with one more day added at the end in Athens.

Sixteen Days: One in Athens, four for Delphi, the Argolis and Olympia, a two-day island cruise, three days for northern Greece, visiting Mount Athos and perhaps the island of Thasos, ending with five days luxuriating in Rhodes or Corfu, as you prefer, and a last day in Athens.

Seventeen Days: One day in Athens, four for Delphi, the Argolis and Olympia, five on an island cruise, three visiting northern Greece, Mount Athos and Thasos, and four days in Corfu. I say Corfu, in this itinerary, because you are taking the five-day island cruise which stops at Rhodes.

Eighteen Days: One day in Athens, four for Delphi, the Argolis and Olympia, five on an island cruise, three visiting northern Greece, four in Corfu and one day in Athens.

Nineteen Days: One day in Athens, five days for Delphi, the Argolis and Olympia, branching off from Delphi to the north and taking in the Meteora, five on an island cruise, three for northern Greece, Mount Athos and Samothrace, four in Corfu and one day in Athens.

From here on I would add one or more days for whatever you like most—if you like Delphi, stay there longer; if you want more rest sit on an island beach. If you enjoy night life give yourself more time in Athens.

On looking over this series of choices, there is one change I am tempted to make—that is to visit Crete whenever possible or substitute Crete for some other place. The palace at Knossos, the home of the Minotaur, is certainly magnificent, though perhaps no more so than other archaeological sites. Crete is definitely not, at this time, sufficiently well equipped with hotels and restaurants, but I have to confess that this austere isle, mother of poets, artists, heroes, is one I prize. I would, moreover, be tempted to visit the less well-known parts of Crete described in Section III.

Otherwise, you might choose to stay in one of the less well-known places described in Section III. Certain prepackaged cruises stop at some of these places, which are listed below. You could arrange to leave the cruise ship at any one of these islands and re-embark a week later. This could be a remarkably inexpensive interlude.

Santorini. The rim of a volcano protruding from the blue Aegean, crowned by a dazzling white village you reach by donkey. Lovely local wine, good seafood, quaint churches and a good category B hotel.

Cos. The birthplace of Hippocrates, father of scientific medicine, this is a mountainous, green, beautiful island with picturesque bays and huge cliffs that plunge into the sea. The islanders are great sailors, fishermen and sponge divers. Women tend the fields, orchards and beehives, producing delicious fruit and fine honey. The city is a model of civic pride, full of trees and parks. There are some ancient ruins and an imposing medieval castle. Two category B hotels, three category C.

Patmos. The Apocalypse was written on this island which is austere and gaunt but full of marvelous beaches. Fishing is excellent. There are interesting ruins of early Christian churches. You can rent a room with shower in a private home for fifty cents a night. There is a category D hotel.

Syros. An old haunt of the Phoenicians, this island had the first astronomical observatory in Greece. Syros was a rich trading, shipbuilding and manufacturing center in the last century and its public-spirited citizens endowed it with imposing theaters, libraries and churches. Good hotels, good food, splendid for leisurely walks to the little tavernas.

Thasos. A most beautiful island, full of small beaches secluded by pine, chestnut and plane trees. The scene of the first major engagement of the Peloponnesian war, it has extensive ruins, a temple of Poseidon, a well-preserved amphitheater and agora, fine ancient walls with many interesting gates and a good museum. Category B hotels, good food. A delightfully cool place to stay.

PREPACKAGED TOURS AND CRUISES AVAILABLE

Listed by the number of days they take with Athens as the point of departure except where otherwise stated. Itineraries, sailing dates and prices may change, so consult a travel agent.

ONE DAY

Delphi by bus, stopping at *Osios Loukas*. $11 per person, including lunch. Organized by the KEY, ABC, CHAT and HELLENIC EXPRESS companies. Functions year round. This tour involves about eight hours of driving, but the bus is comfortable with reclining seats. Fairly strenuous.

Argolis Peninsula. A KEY, ABC, CHAT or HELLENIC EXPRESS bus tour at $11 per head, including lunch, passing through old *Corinth, Mycenae, Nauplion,* and *Epidaurus.* Functions year round and also involves some eight hours of driving. Fairly strenuous.

Crete. A KEY tour by plane, $40 a head, with a visit to *Knossos.* It includes lunch. In my view, this is much too brief a visit, but some may like it. It involves one hour's flight each way, plus half an hour by bus to Knossos and back.

Saronic Gulf Islands. A tour by boat to *Aegina, Poros* and *Hydra* by ABC, CHAT, HELLENIC EXPRESS or KEY from $10 to $11 per person, including luncheon and bus to and from the harbor in Athens.

TWO DAYS

Mykonos, Delos, Hydra. A KEY tour by ship, each Saturday from March 28 to October 26, costing from $27 to $50 per head. This trip is not tiring and is very comfortable in the more expensive cabins. In July and August there could be a fair amount of ship motion which might upset the queasy.

Mykonos, Delos. A CHAT tour by ship, from March 18 to October 31, every Tuesday and Saturday. Costs from $27 to $40 per person and does not include lunch on the day of departure.

Delphi, Olympia. A CHAT tour by bus, $27 per head, including all meals and hotels. The bus crosses the Gulf of Corinth by ferry from Itea, the port of Delphi. Up to fifteen hours in the bus are involved, plus three hours on the ferry.

Delphi and Osios Loukas. Leaving at 8 A.M. and returning at 9 P.M. the next day with an overnight stop at Delphi. This KEY, ABC, CHAT or HELLENIC EXPRESS tour is one I recommend since it involves a stay at Delphi at a lovely hotel and you get a chance to see sunrise and sunset there. A year-round tour leaving daily, costing $22 per person first class and $17 per person second class.

Argolis. Another of the more leisurely two-day tours that I prefer, organized by KEY, ABC, CHAT or HELLENIC EXPRESS leaving 8 A.M. on the first day and returning 9 P.M. the next. A year-round tour leaving daily. $17 second class, $22 first, full board. You visit *Corinth, Mycenae* and stay overnight at *Nauplion* where hotels are good. You visit *Epidaurus* the next day.

Crete. A KEY tour by air, from March 15 to October 31 daily, with an overnight stay at a class A hotel in *Heraklion,* includes a visit to the Minoan palaces of both *Knossos* and

Phaestos. $55 per head. If you are short of time and for you Crete is a must, I recommend this tour. Variations of this tour are offered by the ABC and CHAT companies.

THREE DAYS

Rhodes. A CHAT, KEY or ABC tour by air from March 15 to October 31 every day, $87 full board, first class; $75 second class; $65 tourist class. This seems good value and is leisurely enough to suit me.

Delphi, Meteora. A CHAT, ABC or KEY tour, by bus to *Delphi* and to *Meteora*, with side trips on the way. Eighteen to twenty hours of driving are involved, but you stay one night at Delphi and the next near the Meteora. If you don't mind the drive, this is not bad value at $40 a head. The tour functions from March 8 to November 2, every Tuesday and Friday. On other days there are similar KEY and ABC tours for the same price.

Crete. A three day ABC tour to Crete by boat with an overnight stay ashore in a class A hotel. A leisurely, restful, short cruise at $55 per person.

Argolis, Olympia and Delphi. A daily KEY tour at $50 per head from March 15 to October 31. It involves eighteen to twenty hours of driving plus three hours in the ferry, but if you don't mind that, you see three major archaeological sites, all of which are "musts" if you want to say you have seen Classical Greece.

Crete and Rhodes. CHAT or KEY tours by air from April 1 to October 31, Mondays, Wednesdays and Saturdays, costing $100 per person for first-class accommodations. If you want to see both islands this is a recommended tour. I would prefer two days in each, but you do get an overnight stay in *Crete.*

Island Cruise on the S.S. Delos. Leaving every Monday and Friday from March 26 through October 26 visiting *Mykonos* and *Delos, Rhodes, Crete* and *Santorini.* It takes 70 hours, of which you spend 25 ashore, and costs from $50 per head in an inside cabin you share with three others on lower deck through $250 in a top-deck luxury stateroom all to yourself. Two persons using the luxury cabin pay $145 each, three people pay $120 each. A similar cruise is offered by the M.V. *Kentavros,* on Saturdays and Tuesdays.

Salonica, Kavalla, the island of Thasos. A CHAT tour by boat and air for $83. This includes tours of the magnificent Byzantine churches of Salonica and a trip to the island of Thasos. If you are interested in Byzantine art, this tour is a good one.

FOUR DAYS

Athens, Cape Sounion, Delphi, the Saronic Gulf and the Argolis. An ABC tour from March 15 to October 31, ranging from $84 to $69 per head, depending on the type of hotel you desire. Even at the lowest price you have a private shower. This is a pleasant tour, gives you a fair variety and is not tiring.

Delphi, Meteora, Argolis. A KEY tour from March 15 to October 31, every Thursday and Sunday. From $60 to $48 per person, depending on whether you want class A or B hotels. This involves approximately 36 hours of driving plus 3 hours in the ferry crossing the Gulf of Corinth.

Delphi, Olympia, Sparta, Argolis. A KEY or ABC tour from March 16 to October 31, with time off for swimming on the fourth day. $60 to $47 per head. It involves approximately 20 hours of driving.

Mount Athos and islands on the S.S. Adriatiki, leaving Salonica every Sunday for Mount Athos, Thasos, Samothrace and Lesbos (Mytilene), from $73 to $283. A good way to see Mount Athos.

Rhodes. A CHAT tour by sea leaving every Tuesday from March 17 to October 27. This is a fairly relaxing way to visit Rhodes with about 20 hours at sea. Prices range from $65 for class B hotels to $85 for class AA hotels.

Crete and Rhodes. An ABC tour by air, two days in each island, $115 first class, $108 second class. A good one.

FIVE DAYS

Argolis, Olympia, Delphi, Meteora. A CHAT tour at $75 a head. This is leisurely enough though it involves approximately 35 hours by bus, plus 3 hours in the ferry crossing the Gulf of Corinth. Still, you get a chance to swim. Every Wednesday and Sunday from March 17 to October 31.

Student Tour with approximately the same itinerary as the one above, $20, including transportation, guide, class C or D hotel or hostel, but no food, every Tuesday. VIKING TRAVEL. Student travel center, 7 Karageorgi Servias, Athens.

Delphi, Olympia, Sparta, Argolis. Either KEY or ABC tours run one of these every day from the middle of March to the end of October. $70 a head for class A hotels and $55 for class B hotels. Twenty-one hours of driving, approximately.

Island cruise on the S.S. Semiramis. To *Crete, Rhodes, Delos,* and *Mykonos* and the islands of *Cos* and *Patmos,* leaving every Monday. Prices range from $50 in a four berth, lower deck cabin over the propellers to $300 by yourself in lonely stateroom luxury on the top deck. If two share this stateroom, the cost is $200 each. A similar cruise is offered by the S.S. *Romantica* for prices ranging from $70 to $245.

Island cruise on the S.S. Aegaeon. To *Delos, Mykonos,*

Rhodes, Crete and the islands of *Cos* and *Patmos*, with a stop off in Turkey for two hours. Prices are a little less on this ship, from $42 sharing a four berth cabin to $208 alone in a stateroom on the top deck. Two sharing the stateroom pay approximately $166 each.

Island cruise on the M.V. Rodos. Similar itinerary to that above. From $56 to $348 per person in a stateroom. ($278 if two share the stateroom.)

SIX DAYS

Meteora, Delphi, Olympia, Sparta, Argolis. A KEY tour every Thursday and Sunday, an ABC tour every Tuesday and Friday from the middle of March till the end of October. $85 for class A hotels, $78 for class B hotels, with full board. These tours involve 39 hours of bus travel plus 3 hours in the ferry crossing the Gulf of Corinth, but you do stop two nights at Delphi, one at Olympia and one at Nauplion. You see all the major archaeological sites outside Athens, with the exception of the islands.

Student Cruise to the islands of *Ios, Sikinos* and *Santorini* every Monday, $26.50 per head which pays for deck passage, all side trips by island schooners or donkeys, buses to and from the port of Athens, and a bed in a village home. You buy your own meals. VIKING TRAVEL, 7 Karageorgi Servias, Athens.

SEVEN DAYS

Island cruise on the M.V. Rodos. This takes in *Crete, Rhodes,* a stopover in *Turkey, Delos, Mykonos* and the islands of *Cos* and *Patmos.* You stay two days in Mykonos. Prices per person range from $90 sharing a cabin with three

others, to $493 alone in a top deck stateroom. If two share
the stateroom they pay $398 each.

Island cruise on the M.V. Mykonos. This visits *Delos,
Mykonos, Troy, Istanbul, Kusadasi* (a port roughly halfway
down the coast of Turkey), *Rhodes, Crete* and *Santorini*.
Prices range from $107 for one berth in a cabin for four, to
$591 alone in a private suite on the top deck. If two share the
suite they pay $476 each. The cruise starts every Monday.

Island cruise on the S.S. Stella Maris. Leaves every Friday
for *Crete, Rhodes, Kusadasi, Istanbul, Delos* and *Mykonos.*
A good deal of the sailing is done at night and you have the
daylight hours ashore or near the shore. The cost is from $120
in a four berth cabin, to $370 alone in a stateroom. If two
share the stateroom they pay $230 each. In addition you pay
$25 per person for optional excursions in Crete, Rhodes and
Turkey.

Island cruise on the S.S. Stella Solaris. Same itinerary as
above only in a more luxurious and expensive ship. Prices
start at $165 in a four berth cabin, to $425 alone in a stateroom ($340 each if two share). There is an additional charge
of $25 for various optional excursions.

Island cruises of comparable itineraries are also available
on the *Argonaut* ($200–$450).

Adriatic, Athens and the Greek Islands from Venice to Venice in one week on the *Athinai,* from $104 to $328 per person.

TWO WEEKS

Adriatic, Athens and the Greek Islands. Two ships, the S.S.
Fiesta and the S.S. *Fantasia* leave *Venice* on alternate Sundays for two-week cruises to the *Adriatic,* the *Peloponnesus,
Athens* and the *Greek islands,* from the middle of March to
the middle of November.

The *Fiesta* visits *Corfu, Olympia, Athens, Santorini, Rhodes, Crete, Delos, Mykonos, Nauplion, Hydra,* Athens again, *Delphi,* an Adriatic port, and back to Venice. Prices per person range from $147 for a berth in a three berth cabin without private shower or toilet, to $368 for a top deck cabin all to yourself with private bath. The S.S. *Fantasia* visits *Corfu, Athens, Crete, Rhodes, Cyprus, Israel, Mykonos,* Athens again, *Dubrovnik* on Yugoslavia's Dalmatian coast and back to Venice. This is a less luxurious and less expensive ship. Prices per person start at $108 in a cabin you share with three others and go up to $350 for single cabins on the top deck with private shower. There are very many combinations of luxury and number of berths to share on the *Fiesta* and *Fantasia,* so before deciding which cabin to book, discuss the matter with your travel agent and study his plan of the two ships. Similar cruises, Venice to Venice, are available in the S.S. *Pegasus,* the S.S. *Hermes,* the S.S. *Agamemnon.*

SECTION II

THE CLASSICAL LANDSCAPE

Dealing with the known and loved highlights of
Greece

ATHENS

HOW TO GET THERE (from the airport or harbor)

From the airport or harbor into Athens, a taxi will cost about $3. (There are airport buses for 50 cents.) Taxis are 10 cents a kilometer and if you drive out of the city limits (as in the case of the trip from the airport) you pay for the return journey whether you are returning by the taxicab or not. (Short trips within Athens, to shops or museums, will cost little more than 15 drachmas or 50 cents including tip.)

The drive into town is fast and the drivers tend to be artistic. Europeans generally consider piloting a car a virile art that should be practiced with nonchalance and some disdain for other practitioners. Taxi drivers are good, however—professionals who don't get involved in accidents and know when to back down.

HOTELS

Your hotel should have been booked in advance, especially if you are traveling between April and September. To ensure a booking, pay one day's stay through your travel agent and obtain a receipt.

Tips. Ten drachmas (33 cents) is what you tip each employee who handles your luggage or shows you to your room. On leaving, 20 to 30 drachmas should be the tip for a one-day stay in category A hotels and above. For longer stays, your total tips should be two thirds of the service charge on your bill.

Prices quoted in this section on Athens hotels include all surcharges, taxes and the 15 percent service charge. The prices given hold good for all hotels of the same category with some exceptions such as the Athens Hilton (class AA) which has magnificent public spaces, attractive restaurants, fine modern rooms, a lovely pool. It is also the most expensive hotel in Athens, charging $18 for a single room without breakfast, per day. Double rooms without breakfast are $21.50. These are total charges including air conditioning. Breakfast from $1.15, lunch from $3.20, dinner from $3.50 per person.

The Grande Bretagne (class AA) is less expensive; single room without breakfast $13, double room without breakfast $17. These are total charges including air conditioning. Meal prices same as those of the Hilton. A fine old hotel, it has been featured in numerous novels set in Greece and in hundreds of news dispatches. Its bar, world famous, is where news correspondents are said to gather most of their information.

At the King George a single room without breakfast is $11, a double room without breakfast is $17.25, air conditioning included. Meals cost the same approximately as at the Hilton or the Grande Bretagne. The Acropole Palace Hotel is ranked as AA and some of its rooms deserve this classification, but others do not. If you are booking there, make sure you know what you are getting.

In these hotels you pay less for food if you take full board than if you eat only occasionally in their restaurants. But the full board arrangement commits you to eating in the same place all the time; some people may prefer the regularity and simplicity of full board. Exploring is good for the soul, however, and I recommend no more than half board, if that.

There are excellent luxury beach hotels in category AA and more are being built. Astir, at Glyfada beach, gives you a charming bungalow with one large room, bath, small refrigerator, secluded sleeping porch for $26 a day for two with half board (obligatory). A single person would pay $17. Prices are reduced sharply from October 31 to April 1. This hotel is 16 kilometers from Athens, about a $3.50 taxi ride. A sister hotel bearing the same name has been built at Vouliagmeni, 26 kilometers from Athens, $5.25 by taxi. This is less expensive. Only breakfast is obligatory. The cost is $14 for one person, $19 for two.

Both these hotels have night clubs where dancing goes on till the early hours. The Vouliagmeni beach is more beautiful, the Glyfada beach more fashionable. There is a similar hotel called Xenia, at Lagonissi, 40 kilometers from Athens, with excellent facilities for sailing and fishing, tennis, minigolf, clay pigeon shooting and nine bus trips to and from Athens a day. This is cheaper, from $8.20 per person, half board. This, in theory, is a class B hotel, but belongs with the luxury establishments in my view. Beach hotels are cooler on a summer night than those in Athens. You can sleep comfortably without air conditioning.

There are also some luxury hotels in the foothills north of Athens, where it is always cool at night. Hotel Mont Parnes is on the very top of the mountain, with magnificent pool, and splendid view and no noise except for birdsong. It is twenty miles from Athens and I recommend it highly for those who seek peace or a retreat in which to digest all they have seen. Two people with full board pay $25 a day for luxury accommodation. A regular bus service to Athens is run by the hotel at a nominal fee for guests.

Other hotels in category AA are less expensive (less than $9 for air-conditioned single room with breakfast, less than $12 for a double) because their public spaces are smaller, but they are very comfortable.

In all but AA hotels you are more likely to get better accommodation if the building is new or thoroughly rebuilt; these I mark in the list below with (R).

In category A is a whole range of good hotels. Restaurants are smaller than those in category AA and menus shorter. Fixtures are less expensive, lobbies less luxurious, but they are at most $6 to $7 for a single room with breakfast and air conditioning, $10 for a double. If you want to live near Omonia Square, the business district, the Ambassadeurs Hotel is there, category A and very good value.

If you are not visiting Greece in July and August you may find category B hotels quite comfortable in Athens since you would not need air conditioning. Single room with breakfast in these are at most $4.50 ($5.75 double) with private toilet, shower and telephone, unless they are older hotels, in which case not all rooms have private baths. The rooms will be smaller than in the higher categories and a rug on the floor is unlikely. The staff will not be quite so stylish, though service will not necessarily be slower.

Class C hotels tend to be on less desirable Athens streets. Some of their rooms have private bath and toilet and if you do not want air conditioning—which they do not have—they are good value for the less affluent; about $2.50 for a single room with shower and toilet ($3.25, double), less without a shower. They are fairly spartan of course.

In the following lists, hotels below category AA with private baths in some rooms are marked with an asterisk. Two asterisks mean that the hotel has private bath or shower in every room.

A reliable listing below category C had not been issued by the National Tourist Organization of Greece at the time of writing, so only a few class D hotels are included. They may only have cold water in the room and they cost about $1.25 for a single room, $2 double. (Note: This is a partial list, in-

cluding only those hotels in Athens proper listed by the Greek
National Tourist Organization as "superior" in each category.)

Category	Name	Address	Telephone
AA	Athens Hilton	17 Vassilissis Sophias	720200
AA	Grande Bretagne	1 Vassileos Georgiou	230251
AA	King George	3 Vassileos Georgiou	230651
AA	Acropole Palace	51 Patission	533651
AA	Amalia	10 Leoforos Amalias	237301
AA	Athenee Palace	1 Kolokotroni	230791
AA	King's Palace	4 El. Venizelou	623231
A ** (R)	Alexiou	18 El. Venizelou	624201
A ** (R)	Ambassadeurs	67 Sokratous	534321
A ** (R)	Attica Palace	6 Karageorgi Servias	628581
A ** (R)	Esperia Palace	Stadiou and Edouardou Low	238001
A ** (R)	King Minos	1 Piraeus	531111
A ** (R)	National	57 El. Venizelou	230606
A ** (R)	Olympic Palace	16 Philellinon	225583
B ** (R)	Acadimia	58 Akadimias	629221
B ** (R)	Achillion	32 Agiou Konstantinou	525618
B ** (R)	Alfa	17 Chalkokondili	521253
B ** (R)	Alice	Kapodistriou and Tritis Septemvriou	534315
B ** (R)	Atlantic	60 Solomou	535361
B ** (R)	Diomia	5 Diomias	625471
B ** (R)	El Greco	65 Athinas	533151
B * (R)	Marmara	Patission and Chalko- kondili	140231
B ** (R)	Pan	11 Mitropoleos	233864
C *	Achillefs	21 Lekka	233197
C * (R)	Alma	5 Dourou	522833
C ** (R)	Amarylis	43 Veranzerou	538539
C * (R)	Asty	2 Piraeus	530424
C ** (R)	Attalos	29 Athinas	631854
C *	Carolina	55 Kolokotroni	630625
C *	Elite	23 Piraeus	521523
C * (R)	Evripidis	79 Evripidou	526498
C ** (R)	Nestor	48 Agiou Konstantinou	535576
C ** (R)	Omonia	Platia Omonias	537210
C * (R)	Rea	31 N. Metaxa	813760
C ** (R)	Solomou	72 Solomou	529101
D (R)	Demokritos	40 Kapodistriou	533780
D (R)	Phaedra	16 Herefontos	238461

Beach Hotels

Distance from Athens is given after name of hotel, in kilometers. The taxi ride is 10 cents per kilometer and you always pay for the round trip, since these are journeys outside the city limits. The bus journey is 1.3 cents per kilometer; you only pay for the number of kilometers you ride. You do not pay for the return journey as in taxis. This list is partial, including only those hotels about which the facts could be checked.

Category	Name	Address	Telephone
AA	Astir 17 km.	Glyfada	046461
AA	Astir 26 km.	Vouliagmeni	048284
A ** (R)	Aigaion 70 km.	Sounion	10
A ** (R)	Atlantis 20 km.	Voula	048443
A ** (R)	Belvedere Park 70 km.	Sounion	11
A ** (R)	Congo Palace 17 km.	Glyfada	046711
A ** (R)	Coral 7.5 km.	Phaliron	991441
A ** (R)	Florida 17 km.	Glyfada	045105
A ** (R)	Glaros 31 km.	Varkiza	048778
A ** (R)	Green Coast 26 km.	Vouliagmeni	048224
A ** (R)	Kavouri 26 km.	Kavouri	048461
A ** (R)	Saronis 11 km.	Kalamaki	980365
B ** (R)	Bonavista 17 km.	Glyfada	046902
B ** (R)	Delphini 17 km.	Glyfada	045020
B *	Lido 7.5 km.	Phaliron	981026
B ** (R)	Xenia 40 km.	Lagonissi	048511
B ** (R)	Themis 17 km.	Glyfada	046506
C * (R)	Diethnes 17 km.	Glyfada	04287
C * (R)	Ilion 17 km.	Glyfada	046011
C * (R)	Rex 11 km.	Kalamaki	991156
C * (R)	Glyfada 17 km.	Glyfada	046833
C * (R)	Alimos 11 km.	Kalamaki	981365

Mountain Hotels

Category	Name	Address	Telephone
AA	Auberge Tatoi 19 km.	Varybopi	019402
AA	Mont Parnes 38 km.	Parnes	831011
AA	Pentelikon 15 km.	Kifissia	012837

(not all rooms have private baths)

A *	Apergi 15 km.	Kifissia	013537
A *	Cecil 15 km.	Kifissia	013836
A ** (R)	Grand Chalet 15 km.	Kifissia	014888
A **	Kastri 15 km.	Kifissia	013791
A ** (R)	Mon Repos 13 km.	Amaroussion	010330
A *	Palace 15 km.	Kifissia	013577
	(not all rooms have private baths)		
C	Roussos 15 km.	Kifissia	012551
C	Vretania 15 km.	Kifissia	013101

WHAT TO DO

Two days is the minimum I would allow myself for Athens. If you cannot stay more than one day take the trips recommended for the first morning and afternoon.

I have divided the two days in Athens into four parts which take in both sightseeing and shopping. Meals and entertainment are fitted in between. Take taxis, or better still, walk. Distances are small and there is no better way than a walk to absorb the spirit of a city. If you wish to take a bus, the hotel will help you. Whatever you do please wear flat, comfortable shoes when sightseeing. High heels will get damaged on archaeological sites.

First Morning

On your first morning, visit the Acropolis, the earlier the better in the summer, because the ancient marbles, reflecting the brilliant sun, can make the trip hot. If you do not tan easily wear a hat, since lobster-colored flesh, even brought on by a trip to the Parthenon, is not attractive.

The Acropolis is open from 8 A.M. in the summer until sunset (from 8:30 A.M. till sunset in the winter). The early morning is fresh, and the sun still low enough to cast long shadows that heighten the beauty of the columns. You enter through the Propylaea, the ceremonial gateway that had, in ancient times, five grand entrances leading to a complex of buildings with an art gallery on the left. Pause here to gaze at the Acropolis. Its buildings were arranged to radiate from the entrance

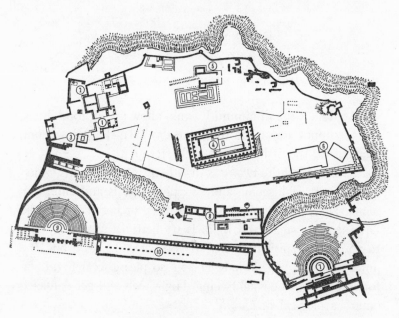

THE ACROPOLIS OF ATHENS

1. Propylaea; 2. Pinacotheque; 3. Temple of Wingless Victory; 4. Parthenon; 5. Erechtheion; 6. Museum; 7. Theater of Dionysus; 8. Asklepeion; 9. Theater of Herodes Atticus; 10. Stoa of Eumenes.

so that their full glory might be captured from the first glance. There is no arbitrary geometric, gridiron plan in their positioning. They were not meant to be seen from above as architects' models. They were positioned to please the eye.

You will find a brief history of ancient Greek art on page 325, but don't read it standing before the Parthenon. Instead gaze long, for this—if there is one—is the symbol of Western civilization, the monument that marks the spot where our culture first took root. There will be distractions, other tourists, for instance (and those who look like caricature Americans are sure to be students from behind the Iron Curtain; the girls with very brief shorts are usually English). There will be photographers and guides. But it will not be hard to ignore them. Inevitably your imagination will take hold. For many, a visit to the Acropolis can have the quality of a mystical experience; surrender to your senses and absorb the mood.

Before you enter the Acropolis Museum you will see the Parthenon, the Erechtheion, the temple of Athena Nike and the view from every side of the hill. All people recognize the Parthenon, shrine of Athena, the patroness of Athens. The Erechtheion has the caryatids—sculptured maidens instead of columns—and is the temple dedicated to Erechtheus, the mythological originator of the Athenians. The temple of Athena Nike is on the right of the Propylaea as you enter, a superb, small structure, a delicate masterpiece.

Now walk to the ramparts for a look at Athens.

The ancient city was a mere hamlet compared with the sprawling metropolis it is today. As it emerged from legend into history Athens was just a settlement huddled at the feet of the Acropolis, and it is alleged that the mythical King Theseus united Athens with the tiny independent states of the region. Later the power of the kings was replaced by aristocratic rule. A first major step toward democracy through justice was taken in 594 B.C. by Solon, the great lawgiver. In 510 B.C. Clisthenes made Athens the world's first true democracy, giving the Athenians a pride of citizenship that enabled them to defeat the vast Persian Empire which invaded Greece in 490 B.C.

After this war Athens emerged as a great naval power leading a confederation of seafaring Greek states, called the Delian

League, which controlled the Mediterranean. This was the fifth century B.C., the Golden Age of Athens when the city developed, in large part, the civilization we call "Western" today. At the end of that century, Athens, having over-extended herself, was defeated by Sparta, her militarist, totalitarian rival Greek state and the city never again was to be a great power, although she remained a major cultural center until the emperors of Byzantium adopted Christianity as the official religion and closed the philosophical academies of Athens.

After the fall of the Byzantine Empire to the Turks in the fifteenth century, Athens became a small provincial town, all but forgotten, a treasure waiting to be rediscovered. When Greece threw off the Turkish yoke in the last century, Athens became the capital of the new state, a renaissance began and with it the ever-growing pilgrimage of travelers to the monuments of Western civilization, bequeathed to the world by those old, great Athenians. (For more see Section VI.)

Athens is no longer distinct from its port of Piraeus or the seaside suburbs where the airport is, or the hillside villas to the north. Athens retains the marks of a queen city, a world capital that forces her people to look outward, if only because the city so abuses itself with the years, as its crowds grow thicker.

Near Omonia Square (due north of the Acropolis—behind the Erechtheion) where the cheaper hotels are located, Athenians pack themselves mercilessly in buses at the end of the working day. Around, the pavement is usually alive with humanity. It is impossible to walk without touching. This is the district where ordinary Athenians live and work. The great groceries are there, the lottery sellers and journeymen lawyers.

Athens has always been a sun-bleached city, on an ocher plain speckled with the green of pine. But the ocher, the faded pastels of the buildings and the strong shadows of the Attic sun mix in a certain proportion that blends with the sea, the gaunt Hymettus, the uncompromising mass of Mount Parnes to the north, and Pendeli with its gaping quarries which provided marble for the Parthenon and are still in use today.

Athens changes color as do the mountains and the sea— with the passage of each hour and the sun's journey along the ecliptic from equinox to equinox. So that each shadow is both pink and blue in the early summer morning, deepening and vanishing through the noon hours of the siesta and moving to violet as the first stars begin to shine. In winter there is less pink, more blue; the violet of the evening grows darker sooner but starts a lighter hue and the sea can look like amethyst, which it never does in summer.

The whole panorama of the city is best seen at night from the church atop the Lycabettus, the sharp, pine-skirted hill northeast of the Acropolis. The climb, not too strenuous, is rewarding. In the distance at night you see the dark sea with fishing boats, acetylene lamps nodding, the great steamers and ships of the fleet. Then comes the land, an apron of light, from the bay to the heart of Athens. The electrical embroidery has grown thick with the years and there has never before been so much color; neon has invaded in force. But it is still beautiful.

At the base of the Lycabettus are apartment gardens of jasmine and gardenias where the affluent can sit at night gazing at the illuminated Parthenon.

Between the Lycabettus and the Acropolis is Constitution Square, dominated by the Parliament building.

From the southern ramparts, toward the sea, and at the foot of the Acropolis can be seen two amphitheaters. The one on the left is the theater of Dionysus. No other theater in existence today can boast the birth of so many masterpieces.

The theater had its beginnings in the sixth century as a natural amphitheater. Around 330 B.C. wooden bleachers were introduced and an elaborate stage. The wood was later replaced with the stone you see today.

This theater was a vital part of ancient Athens whose citizens, dedicated theatergoers, felt personally involved in the stage fortunes of their great playwrights. Here the mighty felt the barbs of ridicule in the bawdy humor of the comedians; here too the great old tragedies were first performed. So obsessed were the Athenians with their theater that they demanded and eventually got free tickets as their birthright, with the state paying for all productions.

In this theater Thespis (sixth century B.C.) changed the recitation of poetry into drama by introducing dialogue and a second actor; later old Aeschylus held sway only to lose out to young Sophocles who, in his turn, lost the prize to Euripides. All Aristophanes' comedies were performed here.

The other amphitheater is called the Odeion of Herodes Atticus, a fabulously wealthy Athenian of the second century A.D. who filled Greece with treasured gifts—the Odeion below the Acropolis where the ancient tragedies are played to this day, a similar one in Corinth, a stadium at Delphi, baths at Thermopylae where the three hundred Spartans once held the Persian army at the pass. Due east of the Acropolis is more of his bounty, the white marble stadium, restored in 1896 for the first modern Olympic games. Between the stadium and the Acropolis stand the graceful pillars of the temple of Olympian Zeus, a building begun by the Greeks and completed by the Romans, an enormous structure then and a handsome ruin now; many of its columns were used by the Turks to make lime.

Due south of the Acropolis there is the small towerlike monument of Philopapous atop a hill, and to the right of that, you will see another hill, the Pnyx, a place of public assembly where Demosthenes addressed his fellow citizens.

Due west of the Acropolis and immediately below it is the Areopagus, the Hill of Ares, god of war. On this hill sat the famous supreme court of Athens, originally a council of elders, later expanded to include all blameless former high officers of the state.

Steps and platforms are hewn into the rock and in ancient times two stones were there: the "Stone of Outrage" on which stood the accuser, and the "Stone of Ruthlessness" for the accused. Legend has it that the goddess Athena voted to acquit Orestes when he argued before the Areopagus that he had killed his mother, Clytemnestra, because she had slain his father, her husband Agamemnon. This legendary trial symbolizes the shift from a matriarchal to a patriarchal society. It also symbolizes the substitution of due judicial process for vengeance, since Orestes' accusers, the Erinyes, goddesses of vengeance, lost.

Northwest of the Acropolis is an ancient temple, the best preserved in Greece and not unlike the Parthenon in design. Called the Theseion, temple of Theseus, it was originally the temple of Hephaistos—the blacksmith god and patron of all artisans—and Athena. Almost a replica, it yet lacks the sublime proportions of the Parthenon.

Between the Theseion and the Acropolis lies the broad, flat expanse of the Agora, or marketplace, the intellectual commercial and political heart of ancient Athens. The Athenian, an intensely public man, spent most of his waking hours with fellow citizens in the Agora, listening to and arguing with the philosophers, questioning travelers, disputing the value of the latest play, or accusing the Parthenon's contractors of theft.

Now you should visit the museum of the Acropolis, to avoid the sun and to see examples of the various periods of

Greek art. Enjoy the works. The posted commentaries on the exhibits are very adequate.

Your first visit to the Acropolis should be over by about noon. At the Propylaea, turn back for one more glimpse of the Parthenon and then, on the climb down, turn left on Dionysiou Areopagitou Street—the street in front of the two amphitheaters—continue to Frinichou Street, the third turning on the left. You will come upon a little square with a church at which you turn left then immediately right to follow Adrianou Street. Don't worry about getting lost. You can always catch a taxi and give the driver the name of your hotel. As you walk along Adrianou Street you will see, off a side street on the right, a very large Greek church next to a very small one. These churches are your destination. If you want further directions, ask any passerby for the Metropolis Athinon. Even if he doesn't speak English he will understand and point in the right direction.

Ignore the big church, if you wish; it is the small one you must see. Called St. Eleftherios (Saint Freedom), patron of women in childbirth, the church is also dedicated to the "Virgin who helps promptly." The church is an eleventh century Byzantine gem, not only because of its delicate proportions, but also because of its decorations and the use of marble fragments from older, ancient Greek and Roman monuments. In the tradition of the Parthenon, the church is decorated with scenes from festivals of Athens, and there are, too, the signs of the pagan zodiac.

The large church is the Athens Cathedral, a modern and remarkably unsuccessful building, but it can show you (though there are better examples) how the Byzantine style has been adapted over the centuries. Note in particular the central dome from which other parts of the church extend in the form of a cross. The screen separating the altar from the body of the church, though more rich and elaborate here than in most churches, is characteristic of all such churches in its set hierarchy of paintings of the prophets, saints and archangels.

After this brief visit to the two churches ask someone for Ermou Street, which is one block north of the Cathedral. Turn right on Ermou and walk toward the large square, Constitution Square (Platia Syntagmatos), a few blocks away.

Ermou is the main shopping street for Athenian women. Here they buy cloth, buttons, thread, toys or have their jewelry reset. The street, in effect, is Athens' department store, with independently-owned departments.

There will not be time to shop before lunch but you can always come back in the evening. For lunch, if you wish to splurge, take a taxi to the Dionysos Restaurant below the Acropolis where, in air-conditioned splendor, you can re-examine the Parthenon while eating really well. Anything on the menu in this restaurant is good.

Equally good is the food at Zonar's one block off Constitution Square on Venizelou Avenue. Everyone knows this place, so simply ask. Here you can sit at a sidewalk table and engage in one of the Athenians' favorite sports: girl watching. Zonar's specialty is a "Chicago special" ice cream. Or for dessert you might try the marvelous patisserie of Floca's, the restaurant next door.

These restaurants, expensive by Greek standards, charge approximately three to four dollars a person for a three-course meal with wine. If you want something more modest, turn back toward the Acropolis after your stroll through Ermou Street and enter the first little tavern you find. If you chance on a working man's tavern you will be amazed at the prices. The portions of food will cost no more than twenty-five cents. Order unresinated wine (aretsinoto krasi) or beer (they understand the word), then go into the kitchen and point out what catches your eye. I highly recommend fish soup (psaro-soupa) in all working class taverns, or baked macaroni with white sauce called pastitsio. In the kitchen you will see a variety of veal stews with okra, or string beans or onions. They are all cooked in a rich tomato sauce. If you prefer something less rich ask for plain roast veal (moskari psito).

After lunch, go back to your hotel and either sleep or read the section on Greek history and art to help you enjoy your afternoon visit to the National Archaeological Museum.

First Afternoon

From March 1 to September 30 the National Archaeological Museum is open from 8 A.M. to 2 P.M. and from 3 to 6 P.M. The rest of the year it is open from 9 A.M. to 4 P.M. except on Sundays, when it opens an hour later. It is closed every Monday and if that is the only day you will spend in Athens, go instead to the Benaki Museum which is described on page 71.

The National Archaeological Museum has many more rooms than one suspects. In particular, Room I contains Mycenaean jewelry, masks and arms that fit the descriptions in Homer. In Room XII is the magnificent bronze, a replica of which can be seen at the United Nations—a bearded man, left arm extended, the right obviously gripping a shaft. It is either Zeus about to hurl a thunderbolt, or Poseidon ready to throw his trident. Room XIV has the superb marble athlete of Polycletus, a young man crowning himself with a victory wreath. Don't miss the little jockey of Artemision in Room XVI. The Ephebos of Antikithera is in Room XXIII, so is the superb bronze Ephebos of Marathon.

These are my favorites among the big pieces. There are innumerable others. The miniatures in the showcases run the whole gamut from bawdy to heroic. One floor up from Room

XVI are the exhibits of Greek ceramic art, possibly the most complete collection in the world and not to be missed. The museum also has one of the best Greek coin collections anywhere.

On Mondays, when the National Archaeological Museum is closed, visit the Benaki Museum instead, a very short walk from Constitution Square along Queen Sophia Street. It was donated to the nation by Antoine Benaki, a Greek millionaire art lover. It has superb Byzantine icons, two El Grecos and other paintings that show the links between Byzantine and Renaissance art. There are also magnificent examples of Arab, Persian, Coptic and Chinese decorative art, some of the world's richest embroideries and dazzling displays of jeweled, chased swords, daggers and richly ornamented firearms. The lithographs and watercolors should not be missed, nor the fine carpets from Asia Minor, Isfahan, Caucasus, Turkestan and Samarkand. In the basement is a unique collection of rich Greek national costumes and jewelry.

The Benaki Museum is open every day except Tuesday and Sunday from 9:30 A.M. to 1:30 P.M. and 4:30 to 7:30 P.M. between March 1 and December 31. The rest of the year it is open from 9:30 A.M. to 2 P.M.

After the museum closes you can do some shopping before going out to dinner. Most of the shops are near Constitution Square.

For handicraft you may try the small shop opposite the Grande Bretagne hotel on the north corner of Constitution Square and Venizelou Avenue. They have fine rugs and scarfs as well as other handmade items. There are many other excellent handicraft shops in that area. Rhodes pottery is a good buy, so is silver peasant jewelry, as are old copper village utensils. Continuing along Venizelou Avenue, away from the square, in the next block there is a fine fur shop, Sistovaris, with women's accessories, and a Jean Dessès salon, featuring the famous couturier's wares.

At Jan Smuts Street (or Voukourestiou Street) directly behind the Grande Bretagne, in the arcade, are some good modern jewelry shops. Along Venizelou Avenue and its parallel street, Stadiou (or Churchill) Street, you will find good shoe-shops and custom shirtmakers for men.

Greek tavernas and restaurants begin filling for dinner at about 10 P.M. but you can eat earlier. I suggest this first night that you take a taxi to Tourkolimano (your hotel will give bus routes if you prefer). This is a small yacht harbor, dominated by the Royal Hellenic Yacht Club and ringed with outdoor seaside restaurants. They are more or less equal in quality and the seafood is superb. Try the broiled red mullet (barbouni sti skara), any of the lobsters, or kalamarakia tiganita, a delicious species of baby squid. If you do not want resinated wine, order white Pallini Alpha, Santa Elena, or Minos Rose.

You may rent one of the little boats moored nearby and take the trip around the harbor, past the breakwater, to the next cove and back. You will see the lights of the Attic coast and their shimmering reflection. Greeks stay up nearly all night; I think, however, that by now you should be ready for sleep.

LOCAL TOURS

Tours are available around Athens either by private car or bus group. These tours, in some cases, are more expensive propositions than a do-it-yourself expedition, but they provide a guide who will probably turn out to be charming, informed and even a great deal of fun.

BUS TOURS

A four-hour bus tour with guide covering the National Archaeological Museum (the Benaki Museum on Mondays), a tour of the city, the Stadium, the temple of Olympian Zeus, the small church of St. Eleftherios, Athens Cathedral, the Acropolis and its museum, costs $3.70 per person.

The "Athens by Night" guided bus tour, starts at 8:30 P.M. and ends at 1 A.M., includes dinner at a taverna, folk dances, night club with floor show, and costs only $7 per person. A shorter tour, without the night club, but including dinner at a taverna, costs $5 per person. The same tour, without the dinner, is a mere $2 per person.

PRIVATE CAR TOURS

Itinerary	Party of one, $ per person	Party of two, $ per person	Party of three, $ per person	Party of four, $ per person	Party of five, $ per person
Acropolis, its museum, Areopagus, Pnyx, Theseion, the Agora, the Stoa of Attalus, 3 hours	12.50	7.00	5.50	5.00	4.50
A drive through the main streets and then a visit to the National Archaeological Museum, 3 hours	12.50	7.00	5.50	5.00	4.50
Condensed tour of the Acropolis, the National Archaeological Museum and other monuments, 4 hours	18.00	12.00	7.50	6.50	6.00
Athens by Night, drive through the tavern and restaurant district. Dinner at a first-rate taverna. Greek songs and folk dancing. Price includes meal. Starts at 9 P.M., ends at will	32.00	19.00	15.00	13.00	12.00

You may book through your travel agent or your hotel in Athens, but your hotel may need a few days' advance warning if the demand is heavy. Prices above are approximate. Each person in a party of five would pay $4.50 for a three-hour guided tour of the Acropolis and its surrounding monuments by large limousine, but for one person such a tour would cost $12.50.

Morning, Second Day

Go swimming. (For those who do not wish to swim, alternatives are suggested on page 75.) Take a taxi to the beach or ask your hotel where to board the very frequent buses that are crowded generally only on weekends. There are several beaches with showers, changing facilities and lockers. The price of admission to these is, at most, 15 drachmas or 50 cents and more usually 15 cents. You may tip the locker-room attendant, if you wish, 2 drachmas or 6 cents.

South of Athens, starting with those nearest the city there are beaches with changing facilities at Old Phaliron, Kalamaki, Alimos, Ellinikon, Glyfada, and Vouliagmeni. Farther out the beaches do not have huts or showers.

The best, in my opinion, are the Astir beaches at Vouliagmeni and Glyfada (admission 50 cents). The first is $5.25 by taxi from Athens, the second $3.50. For these and the taxi rides to the other beaches which are all outside city limits you pay for the trip both ways, whether you return by taxi or not. Ask your hotel to help you arrange for the driver to come back or to wait for you. This will cost you less than hiring two separate taxis. Bus tickets to Vouliagmeni and Glyfada respectively are thirty-five and twenty cents each way. Transportation costs to other beaches are as follows:

Beach	Taxi	Bus
Palaion Phaliron	$1.80	10 cents
Kalamaki	$2.00	13 "
Alimos	$2.40	15 "
Ellinikon (Agios Kosmas)	$2.50	16 "
Voula	$4.00	26 "
Varkiza	$6.10	40 "
Lagonissi	$8.00	52 "

For $28.50 one person can hire a car with guide for half a day to drive along the coast and swim where he wishes. (The cost for each person is $15 for a party of two; $11 each for three; $9 each for four; $7.50 each for a party of five.) Such an arrangement is convenient but more expensive than striking out on your own.

Near all the beaches mentioned above are small restaurants which serve fresh fish, lamb chops, eggs, chips, a variety of Greek dishes, wine and beer, and a meal should not cost more than $1 to $2 per person, depending on the class of restaurant. Some beaches have their own restaurants and cafeterias, the beaches at Glyfada, Vouliagmeni and Lagonissi for instance.

For those who do not want to swim, I would suggest a drive along the lovely coastline to Cape Sounion, at the very tip of Attica, where perch the remains of a magnificent temple to Poseidon. The promontory, yellow, rocky, sparsely speckled with dark green bushes, looks over a small fishermen's bay, a haven where caiques keep company with pleasure boats anchored in the blue water. Though there isn't much left of the great temple to Poseidon it is remarkably beautiful; just the base and two rows of columns rising from the bare, baked earth. You can hire a taxi, rent a private car for the prices mentioned above, or take a bus. A taxi should take you to Sounion and back, wait a couple of hours while you eat, for about $15 to $18, depending on waiting time. Fix the price in advance. The bus fare is 85 cents each way.

Other alternatives are a drive to the top of Mount Parnes (about $15 by taxi with two hours wait; 50 cents by bus). The Mont Parnes Hotel will give you an excellent meal.

If you are tired of the uncompromising and lambent ocher of the Athens plain, drive to Lake Marathon. Within half an hour you are driving through a green landscape on the way to the white marble dam that holds the blue lake which quenches Athens' thirst. The little valley is beautifully landscaped, ablaze with oleanders and bougainvillaea. The tourist pavilion overlooks the lake and will give you a fairly decent meal. ($13 by taxi including a two-hour wait. 40 cents by bus.)

LOCAL TOUR TO SOUNION

Bus tours to Sounion with dinner included cost $5 per person and start at 4 P.M. Inquire of your hotel or travel agent for bookings. If there are enough of you, a tour can be arranged for the morning on request.

Second Afternoon

Take a short rest after lunch.

There is a variety of things you can do. If on your first day in Athens you missed the National Archaeological Museum, you should go there. You may want to visit the Benaki Museum if you missed that.

Alternatives include the Agora, the marketplace and commercial and intellectual heart of ancient Athens. The American Archaeological School has done remarkable work in restoring the Stoa of Attalus, a second century B.C. colonnaded arcade once bustling with lawyers, businessmen, magistrates and teachers taking shelter from the sun and rain. The museum at the Agora is open from 9 A.M to 4 P.M. except on Sundays and holidays when visitors are admitted between 10

A.M. and 2 P.M. only. If you manage to snare an American archaeologist for this visit, you will have a particularly rewarding time.

You may have had your fill, temporarily, of ancient Greece and prefer to explore more of the Byzantine civilization. If so, visit Daphni, a magnificent eleventh century church belonging to a former monastery, and used for centuries by the monks for worship. Some of the world's best mosaics are to be seen here and the dome has a splendid stern Christ, an austere Messiah, a figure of dread inspired more by the Old than New Testament. Here the Saviour is represented as a demanding God of discipline.

The Monastery Park in September is open till 11 P.M. to accommodate a wine festival. For an entrance fee of less than a dollar you can sample as much as you wish of any wine exhibited, plus snacks. Greeks, who know a good bargain when they see one, thoroughly enjoy this festival and add the proper atmosphere. Folk dances and singing are thrown in for good measure. The taxi ride costs $2 return, plus extra for waiting. The bus costs 15 cents each way. Your hotel will direct you to the bus stop.

Between June and October the Athens Symphony Orchestra plays every Monday night in the Odeion of Herodes Atticus below the Acropolis. From late July till early September, during the Festival of Athens, great foreign orchestras and conductors play there, or classical plays are performed. The program varies each year so either consult your travel agent, if you wish to book seats, or one of the Greek Tourist Offices whose addresses are given at the back of the book.

Instead of the theater, you may prefer folk dancing by Dora Stratou's troupe, or ballet by Ralou Manou's company, which often interprets the works of modern Greek composers. This group may not offer superb ballet, but it usually performs outdoors in a lovely setting where you can also eat. Your hotel, or any of the travel agencies will give you directions on how to locate these troupes.

NIGHT CLUBS

There are plenty of night clubs, of course, with floor shows and dancing. Floor shows start late, often not before midnight —Greeks are night people—but you can dance beforehand. Below is a selection compiled from the list issued by the National Tourist Organization of Greece:

Acropole, Patission Street, on the roof of the Acropole Palace Hotel. Orchestra, dancing, floor show.

Akrotiri, at Agios Kosmas, on the coast, 20 minutes from Athens, orchestra, dancing. Telephone 981124. Taxi ride each way $2.50. You can arrange to have the same taxi pick you up for the return journey at a reduced price.

Asteria at Glyfada, 25 minutes from Athens, orchestra, vocalists, floor shows, dancing, excellent food. Telephone 046461. Taxi ride each way $3.50, less if you arrange to have the driver bring you back later.

Athinea, 6 Venizelou Avenue. Orchestra, vocalists, dancing. Telephone 620677.

Auberge at Varybopi, 35 minutes from Athens in the foothills, orchestra, dancing. Telephone 019636. Taxi, $4 each way, less if the driver brings you back later.

Dzaki, 11 Mourouzi Street, orchestra, dancing. Telephone 711185.

Hilton Hotel night clubs, the Galaxias roof garden and the Athenee. Both these feature Athenian night life tailored to the taste of the affluent American night-club patron. Telephone 720201.

Kokylia at Lagonissi, 45 minutes from Athens along the coast. Closed on Mondays. Orchestra, dancing. Telephone

048511. Taxi $8.00 each way, less if you arrange for the driver to bring you back.

Maxim, 6 Othonos Street on Constitution Square. Orchestra, floor show, dancing. Telephone 225155.

Racetrack night club at the Hippodromos, 15 minutes from Athens. Ask your hotel. Smart Athenians go there to eat and dance at night. Taxi $1 each way.

TAVERNAS

If you want to visit a taverna and listen to the bouzouki and guitar, here are some you should enjoy (compiled from the National Tourist Organization list):

Adam, 8 Makriyanni Street. Telephone 910795.

Andonatos, Eratosthenous Street, near the Stadium. Cephalonian specialties, including a great meat pie full of calories and taste, worthy of those Walter Scott describes in *Quentin Durward*. Telephone 719149.

Epta Adelphia, 39 Yperidou Street. Telephone 237800.

Erotokritos, 1 Lyssiou Street. Telephone 222252.

Palia Athina, 4 Flessa Street. Telephone 236571.

Spiti Tou Aria, in Plaka. 29 Mnisikleous Street. Excellent food, guitars and bouzoukia, fine wines. Approximately $3 a head for a good evening. Telephone 237555.

Thraka, 22 Fokionis Negri Street. Telephone 810486.

Vakchos, 2 Vakchou Street. One of my favorites. The host is indefatigably attentive, the guitarists charming and will play softly in your lady's ear for a $3 tip. The place is decorated with the castaways of everybody's attic, a whimsical commentary on what our tastes look like a generation or two later. Alas, the excellent chef was fired.

Vassilenas, Piraeus. You don't choose your food. You are served a succession of small dishes, seventeen or more—most of them great delicacies. This custom was started by the original owner, a grocer by day, an innkeeper by night and a fanatical amateur artist of the kitchen range. Telephone 462457. Taxi $2.00 each way, less if you arrange for the driver to bring you back.

DELPHI

HOW TO GET THERE

Take the bus from Athens to Delphi (4 hours).

Prepackaged tours to Delphi are available and are listed in Section I.

Buses run three times a day from Athens to Delphi, and cost $2.28 one way, $3.63 round trip.

Private transportation. Taxis and cars, with or without chauffeurs, can be hired. For rates see Section I.

DELPHI HOTELS

Prices without meals: Category A, $6.66 single, $10.20 double; Category B, $3.00 single, $4.40 double; Category C, $1.95 single, $2.90 double.

Category	Name
A ** (R)	Amalia
A ** (R)	Delphi (or Xenia)
A ** (R)	Vouzas
B *	Castalia
B ** (R)	Oracle
B ** (R)	Xenia (at the port of Itea)
C	Apollon
C	Pythia

Village rooms are available. For bookings see page 16.

SIGHTS ON THE WAY

Eleusis, which you pass on the way from Athens to Delphi, is simultaneously a budding industrial center and a small country town, although the rural features are fast disappearing and in the not too distant future Eleusis will simply be another segment of the huge Athens urban area.

Eleusis, in ancient times, was the center of the Eleusinian mysteries, a cult involving secret initiation ceremonies dedicated to the gods of the religion that preceded the worship of the Olympian gods. The ritual dealt mainly with the myth of Persephone, daughter of the goddess Demeter, patroness of agriculture. It is alleged that one day as Persephone was gathering flowers in a meadow with her companions near Eleusis, Pluto, god of the underworld, suddenly appeared in his chariot drawn by four black horses and seized her. As she struggled to escape, the earth opened and the chariot disappeared into the chasm. Demeter was sick with grief and, in fury, withdrew her gifts of fertility from the earth. Zeus, fearful that mankind would die, sent Hermes to the underworld with orders to retrieve Persephone on condition that she had eaten nothing while with Pluto. Since Persephone had eaten some pomegranate seeds, she was made to spend part of each year as Pluto's wife in his kingdom. This she did living with Pluto in his palace, and exercised great powers.

The myth was symbolic of the seed that is planted in the earth and flowers in spring. The religion built around the myth entailed belief in resurrection and an afterlife. There is a fine museum in Eleusis that is worth a visit if you have time.

The next landmark on your way is Thebes, where Oedipus slew his father and in error married his mother, suffering the torments depicted by Sophocles in his play. The museum isn't much here. The area around Thebes is called Boeotia, a rich plain by Greek standards. When you enter Boeotia, you pass from the world of seamen to that of the landsman.

In ancient Greece the word Boeotian was a synonym for clodhopper, and the plain is flat—about as flat as you can get in Greece—though the mountains you will cross to Delphi are clearly visible. Tobacco and wheat are grown here. You will pass through Thebes, which though old in history is now a small, run-down country town, and you may see gypsies returning from the fields in their gay carts.

The Boeotian villages stand on high ground, as they stood in antiquity, to catch the breeze and for defense. And you can see both horse-drawn carts bearing iron plows and harvest combines, which are quite numerous but look incongruous, for Greece is just entering the mechanized age in agriculture. The norm still is the horse and the man, followed by his womenfolk.

Once you start climbing, the air becomes fragrant with wild herbs and pine. A few kilometers before reaching Delphi, high up on the mountain you will pass Arachova, a true mountain village, where the Greeks trapped the Turkish army in their fight for independence during the last century. The Greek seeks the company of his fellows at the café, public square, or along the main street, which in Arachova is lined with curio shops offering the handwoven bags that originally were made for shepherds to carry their lunch.

The people of Arachova are quite proud of an old brigand called Karathanasis, a fabulous shot who could bring down swallows with a six-shooter. He once took part in an assassination attempt on the leader of the opposition. His fellow would-be assassin was the Chief of Police. The brigand was given a pardon after betraying his comrades. He eventually became a fairly respected shipowner.

WHAT TO DO

It is a seven-minute walk from the little town of Delphi past the museum and on to the temple of Apollo. This housed the famous Delphic oracle, which was consulted by the entire known world of the ancients. On the way, you get the full benefit of the magnificent view that makes Delphi one of the most beautiful places on earth. The ancient Greeks so admired it and thought it so special that they believed it to be the very center of the earth.

Delphi stands on a ledge 1700 feet above the sea and is cool at night even in the hot summer. Over the shrine towers an enormous rocky cliff and below lies a valley of shimmering olive trees ending in the light blue bay of Itea. The whole area is cradled by the massive peaks of the Parnassus and the Helicon to the north; to the south, beyond the bay of Itea, one sees the shores and mountain ranges of the Peloponnesus, across the Gulf of Corinth. Sunsets are superb. As the sun sinks lower and shadows grow longer, the Parnassus and the Helicon grow violet; the leaves of the olive trees down in the valley no longer gleam silver, and the bay beyond shines here and there with the winking lights of boats.

Before you reach the temple of Apollo, which dominates the entire site, you will pass the treasury of the Athenians— the various Greek states built such treasuries in Delphi; there are others, besides the Athenian, all clearly marked. There is also a fine amphitheater and a large stadium near the main precinct of the shrine. Past the sacred spring, Kastalia, and below the motor road, there is the Tholos, a circular temple to Athena Pronaia, and the Gymnasium. Signs direct you along the short walks to all these locations.

Apollo's temple is the dominant structure and the largest. Under the floor of the temple, in a rock chamber, the priestess Pythia sat on a bronze tripod to make her prophecies. There was not just one Pythia; three maidens held the title simultaneously and relieved one another on the tripod, chewing narcotic herbs, breathing the sulfur fumes that emanated from the earth under the temple. Thus drugged, Pythia uttered incoherent cries which the priests "interpreted" into the famous ambiguous prophecies. For instance, when King Croesus asked whether he should attack the Persians he was told that if he did so, he would destroy a mighty kingdom. He attacked, only to have his own kingdom destroyed.

An even more famous oracle was that given to the Athenians as the Persian army advanced on their city. They consulted the oracle which told them to entrust themselves to wooden walls. The Acropolis at the time had wooden walls. Some Athenians maintained that the oracle clearly meant they should stand and fight on the Acropolis. Themistocles, the Athenian statesman and admiral, contended however that by wooden walls the oracle obviously meant the ships of the fleet and it was his counsel that won the day. At least that is what Herodotus, father of history, reported, and since he was in Athens at the time, or shortly thereafter, one would assume that he knew. However, recent archaeological findings seem to suggest that Themistocles had convinced the Athenians to fight at sea long before the last-minute intervention of the oracle. Herodotus never could resist a good story.

Then, it is not impossible that wily Themistocles, having decided how to fight the Persians, bribed the oracle to give him a prophecy to strengthen his hand. Bribing the oracle, or rather the priests, was not an unknown practice. An earlier

Athenian, Clisthenes, the man who made Athens into the world's first democracy, acquired great influence in Delphi by rebuilding a temple destroyed by earthquake. Thus having become a benefactor, he managed, says Herodotus, to dictate interpretations to the priests on political questions. Then, when the Spartans, who had conquered Athens, went to Delphi for counsel, they were told to free the captive city, which allowed Clisthenes to become ruler of Athens.

Despite such lapses, and despite its ambiguity, the oracle had immense prestige not only among Greeks, but also among the Persians, Egyptians, Etruscans, Lydians and Phoenicians. One reason for the oracle's authority was its extreme antiquity.

Delphi was a source of prophecies from remote ages. Because the site was subject to violent earthquakes and landslides, the earliest oracle was dedicated to the gods who hold sway beneath the earth. The legend holds that Poseidon, god of the sea, also known as the "earth shaker," then became the patron of Delphi. Apollo, the god of light and enlightenment, arrived much later in the form of a dolphin, swimming behind a Cretan ship bound for Itea. The Greek word for dolphin is *delphini*, hence the name of the location.

At Itea, Apollo manifested himself to the Cretans and commanded them to become the priests of a shrine which he would establish on the high ledge they could see above. The Cretan sailors protested that no one would come to worship at so remote a spot, but Apollo promised there would be so many offerings that their sacrificial axes would never be idle. Having reassured them, he went up to Delphi and slew the dragon that guarded the oracle. The dragon's name was Pytho or Python—hence the name of the priestess, Pythia.

At first the priestess was available for consultation only once a year, on Apollo's birthday. Later she prophesied once a month and sometimes every day if the omens were favorable. Those who sought advice from the oracle came as supplicants, wearing wreaths of laurel. They purified themselves, sacrificed an animal and then posed their question.

The priests made a point of being well informed and became, in fact, a political brain trust that could be of genuine help to a statesman.

Their influence declined gradually, through a series of invasions and lootings—by the Gauls in 279 B.C., Nero in A.D. 66, and Constantine the Great who in the fourth century carried to his city hundreds of statues. Since he had made Christianity the official religion of the Roman Empire he would not allow so important a center of the old religion to survive. Julian the Apostate later tried to turn back the clock and resurrect the oracle, but in vain. Delphi became a simple mountain village. What her conquerors spared was buried in a succession of landslides brought on by earth tremors.

Thus ended the historic role of this shrine which, from its earliest history, had been more than an oracle. Delphi had also acted as a sort of central bank, lending money from its treasuries to various states. And it was the seat of the best-known Amphictyonic League in Greece, a sort of embryonic United Nations whose members met twice a year to settle disputes peacefully. Every four years, the Pythian games were held at Delphi, during which all fighting stopped. Athletes came from far and wide to compete and it is to one of them that we are indebted for that superb bronze statue The Charioteer, which almost seems to breathe. Now housed in the Delphi Museum, The Charioteer almost was destroyed by a landslide, but by some miracle the falling rocks formed an arch over the treasure. The Charioteer used to stand in a chariot drawn by bronze horses and some pieces of the horses can be seen in the museum.

The statue was commissioned in 478 B.C. by the brother of
Gelon, tyrant of Syracuse in Italy. Gelon had entered a chariot in the Pythian games and won. His brother honored the
victory by commissioning this beautiful group, depicting the
very moment when the young driver is standing listening to
the cheers of the crowd.

His only rival in grace at the Delphi Museum is the marble
"quarter-miler," a svelte boy, poignant with the beauty of
youth.

Outside, dainty Ionian columns stand amid the wild holly-
hocks along the sacred way. The air is full of bird songs, the
swish of tall shapely cypresses in the breeze and the darting
noise of bright green lizards.

You should take a full day to see the ruins and the museum.
You could profitably spend two whole days visiting them.
There are lovely walks that you can take. There is even a night
club in Delphi and various restaurants. Across the street from
the Hotel Vouzas, and at the corner of the Apollo Hotel, is a
small taverna where you can get typical Greek mountain
dishes, such as lamb on the spit, or kokoretsi, various innards
from the lamb wrapped round the spit.

I would recommend a walk away from the shopping and
main street of Delphi, which is full of the usual souvenir
shops, and along the little cobblestone paths that skirt the
homes of the local inhabitants. There are many charming little houses with enclosed courtyards neatly whitewashed—
tourists have made the people of Delphi prosperous.

If you decide to stay on in Delphi you might take a bus
down to the seaport of Itea. It is a charming little town where
you can catch the ferry to cross over to the Peloponnesus, a
passage of 22 nautical miles. Itea itself is only 20 kilometers
from Delphi. It has a class B hotel called Xenia, and a motel
plus two class C hotels, the Plage and the Parnassos. It is full

of taverns along the beach and the swimming is fine. The taxi down to Itea and back would cost about $4.00 plus whatever the driver and you agree upon for waiting time. Should you want to stay in Delphi a fair amount of time and begin to long for a cinema, Itea is the place to go.

THE SARONIC GULF

HOW TO GET THERE

Prepackaged cruises are available to one or more of these islands and are listed in Section I.

Ships sail several times a day from Piraeus and neighboring small ports. All these little ships are like waterborne buses. In Athens phone 631965 for information on the hydrofoils or 472700 for the slower boats.

A steamer sails four times a day to *Aegina* (70 minutes) and costs $1 first class, 66 cents tourist, each way.

A hydrofoil sails to *Poros* (50 minutes) and costs $3.35 return.

Slower steamers take 2½ hours and cost from $1.40 first class to 90 cents tourist.

A hydrofoil sails daily to *Hydra* (70 minutes) and costs $3.70 return.

The daily hydrofoil to *Spetses* (90 minutes) costs $4.70 return. There are cheaper but much slower steamers to Hydra and Spetses.

SARONIC ISLANDS HOTELS

Prices without meals: Category A hotels $4.00 single, $5.85 double; Category B hotels $2.20 single, $3.00 double; Category C hotels $1.70 single, $2.50 double.

Address	Category	Name
Aegina	A ** (R)	Miranda
"	B *	Nausica
"	C *	Brown
"	C	Galini
Hydra	A ** (R)	Xenia
"	C	Hydra
"	C	Miranda
Poros	A ** (R)	Xenia
"	B * (R)	Chryssi Avgi
"	C	Aigli
"	C	Manessi
Spetses	A ** (R)	Xenia
"	B ** (R)	Star

WHAT TO DO

The Saronic Gulf lies between Athens and the Argolis. It is dotted with islands, the most important of which are Aegina, Poros, Hydra and Spetses. If your stay in Greece is limited, a visit to one or more of these little islands will give you, even in one day, some idea of what island life is like—essential to an understanding of Greece. Nearly everyone sooner or later falls in love with some island, and there is no reason why you should deny yourself the pleasure. If you wish to see two or more islands in one day, take a prepackaged tour.

AEGINA

Aegina has long been a favorite of the Athenians, who can see this island from their city; a conical but gentle mountain rising from the sea. Less arid than some other Greek islands, it nurtures rows of pistachio trees in the fertile folds of its rocky ridges, and considering its size there is a considerable amount of flat land. The harbor is round, with a tiny white church at the end of the jetty. It has a small port, ringed by small houses two or three stories high, with shops on the ground floor selling the island's famous sponges and potteries, or patisseries specializing in sugared pistachio nuts, or gay tavernas, and groceries, ship chandlers, boat suppliers. There seem to be painters everywhere, trying to capture on canvas the island's special shining, multicolored image.

You must visit the temple Aphaea, a 15-cent, 13-kilometer ride by bus from the main harbor. The temple rises on a hill over a small fishing village called Agia Marina, where you can get a meal and swim on an excellent beach. The goddess Aphaea, later confused with Athene, was a Cretan goddess, worshiped in prehistoric times on Aegina. The best of the temple friezes are now in the museum at Munich, the rest can be seen in the National Archaeological Museum in Athens. The temple itself, Doric in style, stands on high ground above the blue sea, and is well worth seeing.

Aegina once rivaled Athens in power and its coinage and measures were used throughout the Mediterranean as a standard. She outdid the Athenians in bravery at the naval battle of Salamis against the Persians, and was awarded the prize for valor—one reason probably for the hatred the ancient Athenians felt toward Aegina, which Pericles called the "eyesore of Piraeus" before he turned it into a dependent state.

If you decide to stay, there are two night clubs that function during the summer near the main town. You should not fail to sample the katsoula, a sort of small delicate red sole, which can be found nowhere else. The islanders eat it fried in butter, but you can also have it broiled over charcoal with lemon.

There are many small boats for rent, of all sizes, shapes and prices, but these are items for which you must bargain. Grab a sympathetic-looking Greek to help you.

If you are interested in fishing ask the tourist police or your

[1] The Parthenon, Athens

[2] The Parthenon, Athens

[3] Archaic horses, Acropolis Museum, Athens

[4] Jockey of Artemiseum, National Archaeological
Museum, Athens

[5] Cycladic head, National Archaeological Museum, Athens

[6] Warrior's head, National Archaeological Museum, Athens

[7] Silver libation vessel from the royal tombs, National Archaeological Museum, Athens

[8] The Minotaur, National Archaeological Museum, Athens

[9] Antinoüs, Delphi Museum

[10] Vatopedion Monastery, Mount Athos

[11] Village wedding, Thebes

[12] Battle between Zeus and centaurs, temple of Zeus, Olympia Museum

[13] Bronze horse, Olympia Museum

[14] Fresco, Naupactus. Virgin Mary helping the Christian fleet at the Battle of Lepanto

[15] Dance at Tourkolimano

[16] Peasant of Crete

[17] Ruins at Delos

[18] Minoan ruins, Malia, Crete

[19] Byzantine icon, Samos

[20] Island transport, Corfu

[21] Cyclades architecture

[22] Island of Syros, Cyclades

[23] Windmill, island of Mykonos

[24] Annunciation, island of Skopelos

[25] Island of Skyros

[26] Street scene in Skyros

[27] Monastery of the Prophet Elias, island of Santorini

[28] Island of Skiathos

hotel to put you in touch with a good fisherman. Fishing is allowed anywhere in Greece all year round. This no doubt is why Greek waters have been overfished; their surviving denizens, having learned the various tricks employed by fishermen, are suspicious and hard to catch.

POROS

This little island is lush with pine, orange, lemon and olive trees. The mainland, which is so close you feel you could touch it, is covered at this point with a lemon forest which fills the air with fragrance in springtime. Poros was originally associated with the cult of Apollo. Later it became a shrine to Poseidon, the god of the sea, whose ascendancy was marked by the construction of a temple where official representatives of neighboring states came to worship in ancient times. There are very few ruins of this temple, nor are there any traces of the tomb of Demosthenes, the famous Athenian orator and general who vainly fought against the Macedonians and fled to Poros; there they defeated him and he committed suicide. An hour's walk from the town of Poros takes you to the temple of Poseidon.

If you want to swim, you can go to the Convent of the Virgin (the Moni tis Panaghias) by bus and motorboat for less than 15 cents. There is excellent spring water, and also plane trees, pines, and a beautiful sandy beach. Several little tavernas serve freshly caught fish, fried or broiled, and the usual lamb chops, or lamb on the spit.

If you are staying in Poros, it is worth crossing over to the mainland for a walk among the lemon tree forest, a five-minute trip by motorboat, costing less than 6 cents. There you can catch one of the very frequent buses for the trip to nearby ancient Troezen, the birthplace of Theseus, which has interesting ancient ruins as well as medieval churches.

HYDRA

The town is the principal attraction of this island. Its houses snake along the steep cobble paths of the hillside, which overlooks a little blue harbor. Bright colors, strong shadows and dazzling reflections of the light from the white-washed walls force the eye, for relief, to the water with its variety of gay yachts, whose owners come to be seen as well as to see. The rest of the island is mainly rock, gray-yellow, gorse-strewn, thistled, and humming with cicadas. There are a few olive trees and cypresses that are higher than the spires of the small churches punctuating the tortuous paths winding up hill after hill from the steep rocky coast, which is bathed by one of the clearest waters of the Mediterranean. In the town is a plain slab of stone marking the tomb of Admiral Coundouriotis who defeated a superior Turkish fleet in 1913.

Skin diving is exciting in this sea that is translucent and passes from turquoise to light blue, revealing the speckled fins and delicate lines of fish that were used as models for vase decorations by the ancient Mycenaeans.

Hydra, an arid speck of rock approximately twelve miles by three on which very little grows, always had to make its living by the sea. Its enterprising sailors, by the time the Greek war of independence started in 1821, had put together a large merchant fleet with which they bore the major burden of the war's naval operations. The great shipowning families emptied their coffers of gold sovereigns and doubloons to arm their merchantmen. But the war exhausted Hydra; it never regained its wealth or prominence.

To swim, walk 15 minutes to Kamini, or to Mandraki which is 30 minutes away on foot. They do not have sand. You dive in off the rocks. You can rent one of the island motorboats to take you swimming or you can simply swim off the jetty outside the harbor.

There are many souvenir shops in which to browse, especially one run by the local tourist committee. The harbor abounds in little restaurants that serve excellent inexpensive seafood which you eat at sidewalk tables watching the girls go by.

On June 12, with much dancing, singing and drinking in the streets, the island celebrates the memory of Miaoulis, another admiral, hero of the independence struggle. There are even greater celebrations on August 15, the feast of the Dormition of the Virgin Mary.

SPETSES

Spetses is the smallest island of this group, only a mile and a half off the coast of the Peloponnesus. It is covered with pine trees, olive trees, almonds, fig trees. It also produces some good wine and excellent honey. This agricultural activity is rather surprising considering there is no spring or well on the island. Each house, however, has an underground reservoir to collect rain water. Water is also brought by ship from Piraeus and Poros.

Though no ancient text mentions Spetses in classical times, relics keep turning up which indicate that the island was in fact inhabited and must have flourished. It followed the historical pattern of its neighboring islands—Byzantine rule, Venetian and later Turkish domination.

To live, the people of Spetses turned naturally to the sea, using timber from their forests to build a considerable fleet. In the Napoleonic wars, her shipowners became very rich stepping into the shoes of the merchantmen of the big powers embroiled in war.

But the Greek war of independence exhausted Spetses as it

did Hydra. Spetses now is chiefly a resort for Athenians, a charming haven, with some grand houses that belong to the old families.

This is an excellent place for relaxing in the sun on one of the many beaches that you can reach, either by walking about half an hour, or in a little horse-drawn carriage. There are beaches all round the island and some just across the strait on the mainland which you reach by motorboat. Tavernas are plentiful and their specialty is psari à la Spetsiota, fish baked with oil, tomatoes, onions and herbs. They also serve stifado, a meat and onion stew famed throughout Greece. The island boasts two night clubs, Blueberry Hill and Bongo.

Island cloth and sandals are good buys.

THE ARGOLIS PENINSULA

HOW TO GET THERE

Take the bus from Athens to Nauplion (3½ hours). You should use Nauplion as your base of operations and treat the whole region as one site.

Prepackaged tours are available and are listed in Section I.

Buses run ten times a day from Athens to Nauplion and cost $2.03 one way, $3.50 return. On the way you can stop at Corinth to visit the ruins, and continue on a later bus to Nauplion. From Nauplion there are several buses a day to Epidaurus (40 minutes, 33 cents) and to Mycenae via Argos (30 minutes, 31 cents).

Private transportation in Argolis. Taxis are available, or cars, with or without drivers, can be hired. (For rates see Section I.)

ARGOLIS HOTELS

Prices without meals: Category A hotels $4.90 single, $6.60 double; Category B hotels $3.90 single, $5.70 double; Category C hotels $1.70 single, $2.90 double.

Location	Category	Name
Corinth	A ** (R)	Tourist Pavillion
Nauplion	A ** (R)	Amphitrion
"	A **	Bourtzi
"	B ** (R)	Xenia
"	C	Amymoni
"	C	Poseidon
"	C	Hotel des Roses

Location	Category		Name
Nauplion (*cont'd*)	C		Megali Vretania
"	C		Semiramis
"	D	(R)	Chryssi Akti
Epidaurus	A **	(R)	"Xenia One"
"	D	(R)	"Xenia Two"
			(hostel with dormitories)

SIGHTS ON THE WAY

On the road from Athens, you will pass Eleusis, site of the famous mysteries, the religious rites dedicated to the gods of the soil and the agricultural cycle of withering and rebirth (for more on these see page 82). You will then drive along the isthmus which joins the Peloponnesus to mainland Greece, on a winding road cut out of a precipice. Here, according to legend, Theseus fought various brigands on his way to find his father in Athens. Here, too, Malikertis, son of Ino, fell from the precipice into the sea below and was saved by a dolphin, a legend celebrated in numerous statues and frescoes both ancient and modern.

If you wish to pause, do so at Kineta, 53 kilometers from Athens, a lovely beach shaded by pines. Then you reach the bridge over the Corinth canal. The Corinthians in ancient times built a slipway over which they would tow their ships from one side of the isthmus to the other. If hard pressed in battle, the Corinthian navy would simply pull itself across from one sea to the next, leaving a frustrated enemy, unable to give chase. (You can see the remains of this slipway if you turn off the main road after crossing the canal and drive to Isthmia 6 kilometers away.)

The idea of cutting a canal at this point was thought of by Periander, a sixth century B.C. tyrant of Corinth, but the task proved much too difficult at the time. Later Nero, the Roman emperor, gave his backing to the idea, inaugurating the event by taking a golden chisel to the rocks. He assigned thousands of workers to the task, but when he was overthrown in Rome the plans were abandoned. The slipway over the isthmus continued in use until the tenth century A.D. Finally in 1882 a French company began work on the present canal which was completed in 1893.

After the canal you pass through new Corinth and branch off to old Corinth about 4 kilometers from the new town.

CORINTH

The old city was fabulously rich, a tremendous trading center full of wholesalers and brokers, attracting artists, artisans and skilled craftsmen who made the city renowned for its pots and ceramics. It was the place where the ancients went to sin. The priestesses at the Temple of Aphrodite gave their favors in return for offerings to the goddess.

Corinth, which helped Sparta defeat the Athenians, her commercial rivals, later fell to the Macedonians, the Romans and to every conqueror who swept through Greece.

Old Corinth is dominated by its Acropolis called the Akrokorinthos, a fortress from earliest times. If you climb to the top you will see the ruins of an ancient temple, a quaint little Christian church, a square tower built by the Crusaders, a Turkish minaret and the remains of the famous temple to Aphrodite, the goddess of love, whose priestesses were such a tourist attraction. There is also a large cistern which the ancients used to collect rain water to supplement the spring that every acropolis had—a primary consideration for the choice of one hill over another for fortification was the availability of drinking water.

Many invaders besieged the Akrokorinthos—the Goths, the Slavs, the Normans. In 1208 the Byzantine commander of the

Akrokorinthos jumped to his death from the ramparts rather than be captured by the Franks who were conquering the Peloponnesus at that time.

Near the foot of the Akrokorinthos is a tremendous engineering feat of ancient times—the harbor, an enormous hole literally dug out of the shore and then connected to the sea by a channel. On the northwest side of this harbor is an early Christian basilica, the largest of its kind in Greece. Nearby is the agora with its tribune from which St. Paul addressed the Corinthians. Take note of the temple of Apollo, near the agora. The pillars—of which seven remain standing—were each carved out of single pieces of stone.

The museum is well arranged and has an excellent collection of Corinthian ceramics and small handicrafts, in their proper historical order, which enables you to see the development of art throughout the city's history.

If you have branched off to old Corinth, you will now retrace your steps and proceed through a mountain pass, then the Argive plain, dotted with crenelated rocks, covered with aromatic shrubs and orchards, until you reach Nauplion, your base of operations for the Argolis.

WHAT TO DO

First Day

Take a walk around Nauplion, a charming town with a charming legend to explain its founding in prehistoric times. Amymoni, the daughter of King Danaos, was walking along what is now the Nauplion waterfront, when a small deer ran before her. She shot at it with her bow, but missed and hit a sleeping satyr who woke with a roar of pain. When he saw the beautiful girl, he threw himself at her. Poseidon, god of the sea, heard her cries and rushed ashore. He rescued her and she rewarded him with her favors. Soon enough a son was born—Nauplios, who was to take part in the expedition for the Golden Fleece.

When Nauplios returned to his birthplace from that adventure, he was told of a spring called the spring of Amymoni and on the site he built the city of Nauplion. This spring, incidentally, is the one in which Hera (also known as Juno), wife of Zeus, used to bathe, regaining her maidenhood after each dip.

In modern history Nauplion has been ruled by the Franks, the Venetians, and the Turks. It was, from 1823 to 1834, the first capital of modern Greece, until the government was established in Athens.

Dominating the town is the Venetian castle, the Palamidi. To see it, you can drive part of the way up well-paved roads, but you must walk 999 steps to the top, where there is a small but necessary bar. The Palamidi is a remarkable example of defensive fortification. During their war for independence the Greeks took it in November 1822. The Turks were never able to retake the fortress and it became a symbol of Greek independence. There is a satisfyingly gloomy descent into the dungeons where prisoners were tortured and put to death. All is properly somber.

In the middle of the harbor is another little fortress called the Bourtzi which has been made into a delightful hotel.

The finest beach for swimming is called Tolo, 11 kilometers from the town. There are delightful little tavernas near the shore at Tolo where you can order fresh fish, broiled or fried to your taste. Sample the excellent tomatoes and fresh fruit of the region. Just off shore in the limpid waters are two tiny islands full of partridges.

In town you can eat at the restaurant Megali Vretania or at one of the taverns right on the waterfront. At night you eat by a sequined sea, the islands pale in the silver blue light, while guitar and bouzoukia players stroll from table to table. On the way back to your hotel, you will pass the fortress which at night looks like a surplice on the bosom of the cliff and you will wake in the morning to a flaming sunrise over the blue Aegean, ready for the ride to Mycenae, which is your first order of business on your second day in Argolis.

Second Day

Mycenae. This was the heart of the Mycenaean civilization, which according to some archaeologists stretched as far north as central Greece and touched most of the Aegean islands. The harsh, uncompromising landscape surrounding the site seems to fit the history, myths and savagery of the rulers of the city.

According to legend the city was established by Perseus, who slew the Medusa, the woman whose hair was coiling snakes and at whom one could not look without turning to stone. Perseus, instead, looked at her reflection in his polished shield and slew the monster with a backward thrust. Perseus is also alleged to have brought the one-eyed giant Cyclops from Asia to build the great city walls of Mycenae, which you enter through the Gate of the Lions. Inside you pass, on the right, six tombs of the dynasty of Perseus. Beyond is his palace, which was once burned, and the ruins of various homes. Inside the walls is the legendary tomb of Agamemnon who led the Greeks against Troy and returned to be slaughtered by his wife, Clytemnestra and her lover Aegisthus; their tombs are also said to be there.

To visit Mycenae is to visit the remains of a remarkable civilization of 3500 years ago, a civilization which created luxurious homes with plumbing and the unbelievable architectural achievement of the city walls.

The most beautiful discoveries from the tombs are in the National Archaeological Museum in Athens—golden masks, vases, weapons, ornaments and everyday utensils, buried with the kings, their bloody queens and murderous progeny to help them along in the afterlife.

Historically, Mycenae reached the peak of its glory at the time of the fall of Troy, about the year 1183 B.C. The city then dominated the neighboring states of Tiryns and Argos, as well as most of the Peloponnesus and the neighboring islands. The murder of Agamemnon provides material for some of the most dramatic pages of Greek tragedy. After an interval in which Mycenae was ruled by Clytemnestra and her lover Aegisthus, Orestes, son of Agamemnon, slew Clytemnestra, his mother, and ascended the throne. In the next generation the Dorians from the north invaded the Peloponnesus and destroyed Mycenae. The city, which had been the peer of Egypt and Babylon, was never to achieve such glory again. We next hear of the Mycenaeans at the battle of Thermopylae, when eighty of them went to the aid of Leonidas, king of Sparta, who with only three hundred men held off the Persian army at the pass. The Mycenaeans fought in yet another battle against the Persians, but they boasted of their victory so much that their neighbors of Argos in jealous fury destroyed Mycenae once more. Thereafter, only a village remained on the site. The second century A.D. Greek traveler and writer Pausanias described parts of the old walls and the Gate of the Lions and claimed to have seen the graves of Agamemnon and Clytemnestra. Then Mycenae slept until the nineteenth century when travelers rediscovered the city and began to carry off various objects of art.

The first major excavation was made in 1876 by the German archaeologist Heinrich Schliemann who uncovered the royal shaft graves where the kings were buried in sealed tombs dug out of the rock. He unearthed tremendous treasures, as did the Archaeological Society of Athens and the British Archaeological Society later on.

You could spend a whole day at Mycenae but if you are pressed for time you should go to Epidaurus for the afternoon and evening, especially in June and July when the famous Greek tragedies and comedies are performed on weekends.

EPIDAURUS

You drive inland up the escarpments of the hills, serpentining through the bluffs, plunging down again beyond the coastal range into a valley of silvery green olives rooted in light brown earth, and on into the formal avenues of birch and pine that lead to the sacred grove of Epidaurus. Signposts guide you to the shrine of Asclepius, god of medicine, son of Apollo and Aegli, a maiden who was reared on Mount Myrtion and suckled by a goat. This fourth century B.C. temple built by Theodotos was adorned with sculptures by Timotheos, some of which, representing a battle of the Amazons, remain.

Near the temple, and just to the north, is the Avaton where the sick, who had come to be healed, spent the night hoping to dream prophetically of a cure. (All structures are adequately marked.)

Here were galleries and steam baths as well as chambers where people would be given analysis, something close to today's version, by priests who probed the very soul of the patient, till he fell exhausted and, after a long sleep, awoke relieved of his anxieties.

Do not miss the Tholos, a small circular building near the temple of Asclepius.

The museum at the site houses the famous carved prescriptions attributed to Asclepius. Many were written by Hippocrates, a mortal not a god, but the greatest physician of ancient times. Which herbs to use and how to use them, diets, medication—the things that kept the ancients healthy—they are all listed. There would undoubtedly be many more treasures in the museum if Epidaurus had not been sacked and totally looted in 86 B.C. by the Roman general Sulla, who carried away all the treasures donated to the shrine by those who had been cured.

But the marvel of Epidaurus, its amphitheater, survives and each year on the weekends of June and July the great old tragedies are re-enacted there.

In most of the plays the actors wear masks and have no microphones, yet the voice carries through the entire amphitheater, a triumph not only for the actor, but for the designer of the amphitheater, whose acoustics remain a model never since equaled. Polycletus the younger gave it a rare harmony of line and an airiness that seems surprising in an arena that can accommodate fourteen thousand people to this day. And the acoustics were no accident. There are anxient texts on how to achieve such perfect sound.

You could return to Athens arriving after midnight, or return now to Nauplion.

MYKONOS AND DELOS

HOW TO GET THERE

Take the ship from Piraeus to Mykonos (6 to 8 hours). From Mykonos take the little motorboat that serves Delos (30 minutes).

Prepackaged tours are available and some are listed in Section I.

Ships sail six times a week from Piraeus to Mykonos and cost from $5.25 first class to $1.86 deck, each way. (Nomikos, Foustanos, Lagas, New Epirotiki shipping lines.)

Motorboats from Mykonos to Delos run frequently and cost $1.30 or less.

MYKONOS HOTELS

Prices without meals: Category A, $4.70 single, $7.65 double; Category B, $4.00 single, $5.40 double; Category C, $2.60 single, $3.60 double; Category D, $1.00 single, $1.50 double.

Category	Name
A ** (R)	Lito
B * (R)	Xenia
C * (R)	Delos
D	Apollon

Youth Hostel, also rooms in private homes, from $0.60 to $0.82 a night.

MYKONOS

Mykonos is the most famous Aegean island, one frequented by film stars and millionaires. You may well anchor next door to the superb three-master of Niarchos, the shipowner, and for all you know you may be eating at the table next to him ashore. Mykonos has a compulsion for beauty, with its white houses, contoured soft as if of adobe yet cubist in design. Balconies edge over the cobbled streets and outside staircases spill geraniums, gardenias, jasmine, basil and morning glories from biscuit tins, colored pots and painted oil drums—a perpetual flower show with each householder striving to surpass his neighbors.

The much-photographed windmills, sails reefed, spin in the lazy breeze and church bells herald either evening or morning services. There are enchanting squares around each turn of the cobbled paths, perhaps a fountain here and there where tots fill miniature buckets, intent upon grownup chores because their mothers are busy either weaving or selling the wonderful cloth of the island to visitors.

You will undoubtedly meet Peter the Pelican, waddling around, trailing his clipped wings. And wherever you go you will hear the persistent clicking of looms, as you roam the streets past the houses of those members of the international set who make Mykonos their home in the summer—living in village houses elaborately restored outside and transformed inside into palaces. They collect driftwood, daub at canvases, move about barefoot in bleached jeans, leading an affluent, bohemian life. The stunning girls dressed in peasant clothes are usually not from Mykonos, but are rich visitors.

But it is all marvelous, picturesque, enticing and unforgettable. It is effortlessly full of character from the architecture of a superb Byzantine church like the Paraportiani to the street vendors like the "Admiral" who is festooned from his neck to his belly with dozens of bells, which he sells as ornaments.

You will be overwhelmed by the endless opportunities for great photographs and probably will overwork the camera. And when you get tired there are cafés, tavernas and restaurants by the waterfront, where you can have superb suckling pig or seafood. You will most probably become involved, as the night goes on, in a party at which you, other patrons of your particular taverna and the islanders join together in drinking, singing and dancing. Young fishermen earn their ration of ouzo by dancing for the visitors. The men somersault, spinning through the air slowly as if to defy gravity, and give their unsmiling all to the dance, for the Greek dance is serious business, it is a paean to manhood. To cap the performance they lift, between their teeth, a table laid for four and holding it steady, so that the wine will not spill, they dance on for what seems an eternity. As the music dies the dancer will set the table down, his stoop becoming a brief bow. For reward he will drink the four glasses of wine whose contents he managed so well.

By that time, particularly if the mood is ripe, you will feel compelled to stroll through the streets once more, simply enjoying yourself.

DELOS

Next morning you should visit Delos, a major archaeological treasure house. You get there from Mykonos by motorboat in half an hour. When you arrive you will be dazzled by the wealth of the ruins and wonder how an islet, no more than four miles by less than a mile, could have supported

such a civilization, or why it was ever chosen to become a
center of the Apollonian cult, a Pan-Hellenic shrine equal in
importance to Delphi, Olympia and Epidaurus.

The story of the rocks and ruins shows that history started
in Delos about 3000 B.C. By 1600 B.C. the island had reached
its first peak of glory and various finds have revealed that at

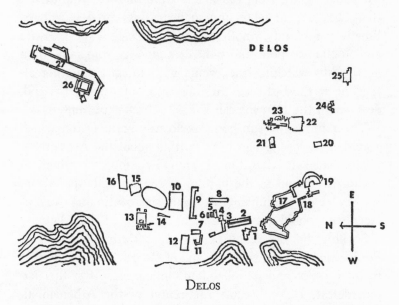

DELOS

1. Agora of the Competalists; 2. Portico of Philip; 3. Propylaea,
monument of the Hexagons, house of the Naxians; 4. Great temple of Apollo; 5. Athenian temple of Apollo; 6. archaic temple of
Apollo; 7. Shrine of Artemis; 8. Shrine of the Bulls; 9. Portico of
Antigone, Minoa fountain; 10. Agora of the Italians; 11. Agora
of Theophrastos; 12. Stoa of Poseidon; 13. Establishment of the
Poseidoniastai; 14. Archaic marble lions; 15, 16. Two palaestras;
17. House of Dionysus; 18. House of the Trident; 19. Theater;
20. House of the Dolphins; 21. House of Inopos; 22, 23. Shrines
of the Eastern gods; 24. Lair of the Dragon; 25. Temple of Cynthian Zeus and Athena; 26. Gymnasium; 27. Stadium.

that time Delos was very much under the influence of the Mycenaean civilization.

At what time precisely the cult of Apollo began is not accurately known. The god is supposed to have been born on this island where his mother Leto, yet another of the many mistresses of Zeus, fled to avoid the ire of Hera, Zeus's wife. To punish Leto, Hera did not tell the midwife of the gods that Leto was in labor and so her pains lasted nine days. Finally out of pity, another goddess, Iris, told the midwife and Apollo was born under the eyes of Zeus, who stood on a nearby hill watching the events with interest. Another attendant at the birth was Artemis, sister of Apollo, the goddess whom the Romans call Diana, patroness of hunters.

The minute the sun god Apollo was born, Delos, which according to legend had been drifting about the Aegean sea, finally ended its navigation. Diamond columns were built to anchor the island to the bottom of the sea and Apollo's favor protected its inhabitants from the continuing fury of Hera, who would not forgive them for having helped Leto.

So holy did the island become that Darius, Emperor of Persia, who attacked the mainland of Greece, ordered his fleet to leave Delos and its inhabitants unharmed. After the Persian defeat, Delos became the center of the Athenian alliance which united most of the islands of the Aegean. The treasury of the alliance was at Delos, in charge of special chancellors known as Ellinotamiae, who would lend money from the treasury to members of the alliance in need of financial assistance.

By then there were no real Delians. The belief had developed that neither death nor birth should occur here since these two events were polluting and no pollution could be allowed on an island which was a center of spiritual cleansing for the ancient Greeks, who went at regular intervals to worship at the shrines of the sun god Apollo. Those who emigrated to the island had to leave before they died, but meanwhile they prospered from the great flow of pilgrims, especially in the winter months when Apollo left the rigors of Delphi's mountains for the better climate of Delos.

Eventually the Delians, or at least those Greeks who considered themselves to be of Delian descent, returned to the island, living first as subjects of Athens, then setting up their own independent government, which became allied with Rome. This alliance brought about their downfall, for in 88 B.C., Mithridatis, a barbarian king from the Black Sea, in fighting Rome, attacked its ally Delos, slaughtered twenty thousand inhabitants in one day and looted the treasury.

Delos never recovered. By the time Christianity was established, the old Apollonian cult had already died and slowly all the inhabitants went away, leaving the shrine to the elements. It was undiscovered through the centuries and is now one of the most imposing cities of antiquity, rivaling Pompeii in its riches.

Near the jetty is the agora of the Competalists (1) and immediately to the north the portico of Philip (2) dedicated to Apollo by Philip of Macedonia in the fifth century B.C. From there along a wide road bordered by ruined colonnades you walk north to the shrine of Delian Apollo, which you enter through the Propylaea (3). There are in fact three temples to Apollo, the Great temple (4), a large Doric edifice completed toward the end of the fourth century B.C.; the Athenian temple to Apollo (5) built at the end of the fifth century B.C.; the Archaic temple (6), dating from the sixth century B.C. Nearby is the shrine of Artemis (7) where many statues of the goddess were found.

East of the temples to Apollo is the shrine of the Bulls (8); just north, the portico of Antigone (9), which is nearly 140 yards long; to the north of that is the Agora of the Italians (10), built in the second century B.C. and the largest building in Delos, richly decorated with mosaics and statues. Another agora, that of Theophrastos (11), is adjacent to the temple of Artemis. Nearby is the Stoa of Poseidon (12). From there you walk along the row of sacred lions (14) to the hall of the Poseidoniastai of Beirut (13), where there are various chapels and a cistern. A number of interesting statues, mosaic floors, courtyards with colonnades round them, were found here. Immediately to the east there used to be a sacred lake from which flowed the waters of the River Inopos, long since dried up leaving no trace. And to the north of the lake are ruins of two palaestras (15 and 16) where wrestling matches took place. You continue uphill and to the northeast, to the gymnasium (26) and stadium (27).

If you haven't brought food with you, you can get a meal at the tourist pavilion or you may wish to return to Mykonos and come back another time to visit the rest of the ruins. But if you feel fairly energetic you can retrace your steps to the harbor and then move in the opposite direction from that followed earlier. You will be entering the so-called theater quarter.

Walk along the paved road to the theater and past a series of houses with colonnaded courtyards, cisterns, wells, workshops, all very reminiscent of Pompeii. There are remarkable mosaics in the house of Dionysus (17) and the house of the Trident (18). You will finally reach the theater (19), a late fourth century B.C. edifice. Climb to the highest seat so that you can enjoy the view, then walk uphill to the house of the Dolphins (20) where there are more mosaics, and to the house of Inopos (21) near a reservoir. Next are the shrines of Eastern gods (22 and 23), the gods of the Egyptians and Syrians, then the lair of the Dragon (24) and finally the temple of Cynthian Zeus and Athena. To explore farther, walk toward the shore from the theater through the commercial quarter with its ruins of offices, shops and warehouses, some showing marks of a fire.

There is a museum (ask the guides on the island to direct you to it) containing sculptures from the archaic period, seventh and sixth centuries B.C., a few fine classical pieces and a rich collection of tombstones called the funerary steles. There are, too, exhibits of votive offerings, household objects, prizes and inscriptions.

If you stay on Mykonos longer, there is wonderful swimming at one of the many beaches, such as Tourlos, 20 minutes on foot or 10 minutes by boat; Megali Ammos, about half an hour's walk or 5 minutes by bus; Ornos, 40 minutes on foot or half an hour by the little bus that serves the beach. These beaches have waterfront tavernas where you can eat and drink. There is yet another beach at Plati Gialos, and if you are a collector of Cycladic churches, there are 360 dotted along the little paths that meander around the rocky rim of the island.

RHODES

HOW TO GET THERE

Either fly from Athens to Rhodes (80 minutes) or take a ship (14 to 18 hours).

Prepackaged tours and cruises are available to Rhodes and some are listed in Section I.

Planes fly twice a day from Athens to Rhodes and cost $17.50 one way, $31.50 round trip. (Olympic Airways.)

Ships sail from Piraeus to Rhodes six times a week and cost from $11.50 first class to $3.40 deck, each way. (Nomikos, Lagas, Typaldos, Cavounidis, New Epirotiki shipping lines.)

Private transportation in Rhodes. Taxis are available. Cars, with or without drivers, may be hired. (For rates see Section I.)

Local tours in Rhodes. There are half-day bus tours (CHAT) to the principal sites. Fares cost from $2 to $2.50.

RHODES HOTELS

Prices without meals: Category AA, $11.00 single, $16.00 double; Category A, $5.30 single, $7.40 double; Category B, $4.30 single, $5.70 double; Category C, $3.00 single, $3.90 double; Category D, $1.00 single, $1.80 double; Category E, $0.60 single, $1.00 double.

Category	Name
AA	Grand Hotel
AA	Hotel des Roses
AA	Miramare
A ** (R)	Belvedere
A * (R)	Cairo Palace
A *	Elafina
A ** (R)	Ibiscus
A ** (R)	Mediterranean
A ** (R)	Park
B ** (R)	Delfini
B ** (R)	Oceanis
B ** (R)	Palm Hotel
B ** (R)	Poseidon
B * (R)	Soleil
B * (R)	Spartalis
B * (R)	Thermai
C * (R)	Achilleion
C * (R)	Africa
C * (R)	Aphrodite
C * (R)	Atlantis
C * (R)	Chateau Fleuri
C * (R)	Hermes
C * (R)	Laokoon
C * (R)	Royal
C * (R)	Tilos
D	Crystal
D	Ialysos
D	Nea Agora
E	Athenaion
E	Carpathos

There is a students' hostel. For bookings see page 16.

WHAT TO DO

The island of Rhodes is a garden. The principal town has sparklingly clean streets, splendid avenues lined with trees, beautiful parks and a fine plan which preserves the city's distinctive air.

Wherever you are, there is something to admire. The public buildings are imposing, though a little pompous since many were built by the Italians under Mussolini. The Roman Catholic Church of St. Francis is but one of many interesting Christian edifices on this island, which was one of the homes of the Hospitalers or Knights of St. John of Jerusalem. But the considerable medieval Christian culture lives side by side with the earlier glories of Rhodes.

The story of the island began in mythology. When Zeus was parceling out land to the gods after the great flood, he gave this island to Apollo or Helius, the sun god who found Poseidon's daughter, Rhode, already there, fell in love with her and named the island after her. Thus the island became known as Rhodes, Bride of the Sun.

Cadmus, son of the King of Phoenicia, passed through Rhodes while searching for his sister Europa, who had been abducted by Zeus. While there, he founded a temple to Poseidon in fulfillment of a vow he had made during a storm at sea and he dedicated a bronze cauldron inscribed with Phoenician letters, which, according to legend, is how the Phoenician alphabet was brought to Greece. Rhodes always was a link with Asia.

In prehistoric times Rhodes was colonized by the Phoenicians, the Cretans and later by the Dorians. At the beginning of the sixth century B.C. the island was taken by Persia, but after the Persian defeat, at the hands of the Greeks, it joined the first Athenian Confederacy in 478 B.C. against which it revolted at the end of that century. In 480 B.C. the three main cities on the island—Lindos, Ialysus and Camirus—decided to found a new city which they called Rhodes. It replaced Lindos as capital and rapidly grew into a flourishing commercial, religious and political center.

The city later came under the influence of Sparta whose

yoke it threw off in 394 B.C. In 378 B.C. it entered the second Athenian Confederacy but a few decades later withdrew once more. Alexander the Great imposed a garrison here because the island allied itself with Persia against the Macedonian, but on Alexander's death the Rhodians allied themselves with Egypt and successfully withstood a year's siege by the Macedonian heirs of the great commander.

Next Rhodes entered into an alliance with Rome and it was during this period that it reached its height of importance and influence, trading throughout the Mediterranean world. The code of maritime law developed on the island was so good that three hundred years later Emperor Augustus of Rome adopted it throughout his empire.

The city became an outstanding artistic and literary center with a distinct school of sculpture and a renowned school of rhetoric attended by Cato, Cicero, Caesar, Brutus and other famous Romans.

Chariot races, athletic and musical contests were held annually in the summer at a festival dedicated to the sun god Apollo, and four horses were hurled into the sea as a sacrifice to this god, whose colossal bronze statue, the Colossus, one hundred feet tall and one of the seven wonders of the ancient world, stood on the breakwater which protected the old harbor of the city of Rhodes. The statue survived until 224 B.C. when it tumbled down during an earthquake.

St. Paul first brought Christianity to Rhodes, but the old way of life did not really change until Christianity was proclaimed the island's official religion in the fourth century A.D.

As an outpost of the Byzantine Empire, Rhodes was subjected to many attacks: by the Persians in A.D. 620, the Saracens in A.D. 653 and by Haroun al Rashid, the famous caliph of Baghdad.

In 1097 Rhodes was conquered by the Crusaders and became an apple of discord for the Venetians, the Genoese and the rulers of Pisa. Rhodes also became a regular stopover for the leaders of the Crusades, including King Philip of France and Richard the Lion-Hearted.

In 1310 Rhodes was taken by the religious and military order of the Knights of St. John of Jerusalem who held it until 1522 when they lost it to Turkey. In 1912 the Italians took the island and held it until the end of World War II when they returned it to Greece.

Traces of all these eras can be seen on the island.

The old harbor of Rhodes with its three windmills from the Byzantine period no longer has a Colossus, but at its entrance are two columns adorned with statues of the lovely gazelles of the island. You can sit and gaze at this harbor the whole day, but it is most beautiful in the evening as it catches the colors of the dying sun.

The tall, imposing medieval walls of the city are considered unique and a particularly fine example of medieval architecture. The gates that lead to the old city are very fine, especially the gate called Amboise which is flanked by towers and faces the famous fortress of the Knights, a fourteenth century edifice fairly faithfully restored by the Italians. It is a massive three-floor structure with turrets, crenelations, ancient mosaics brought by the Knights from other islands, medieval furniture and fine old pottery.

Inside the walls is the old city, a fairyland from the Middle Ages come to life. The houses have quiet courtyards behind vast gates, the cobbled streets are lit by wrought-iron lamps, and at night when the moon plays on the stonework of these courtly mansions it is easy to forget the twentieth century.

In the old city are shops, an old bazaar, potters, and some charming inexpensive umbrellas that have become, for some reason, a specialty of the island. While in the old city you should visit the museum, established in the former hospital of the Knights, a lovely fifteenth century building which now displays coins, pottery, some examples of the work of Rhodian sculptors, and of course the famous statue of Aphrodite.

From the old city, walk the 2½ kilometers to the Acropolis with its temples to Zeus, Athena, and Apollo, and the old stadium and the theater. You get a magnificent view of Rhodes. The Acropolis drops sheer to the Aegean Sea below.

If you are so inclined, ask for directions to the aquarium with its fascinating collection both live and preserved.

If you have done all this during the course of a morning, and I don't advise you to hurry, you should spend part of the afternoon either resting or swimming at one of the lovely beaches nearby.

The evening is yours. Your hotel will tell you about the bars and night clubs, of which there are quite a few, and you can dance till dawn, tasting some of the island's seafood and wine.

Alternatively, you might take a taxi or bus to Rodini, 10 kilometers away, an enchanting spot full of brooks, ponds, beautiful flowers and well equipped with restaurants where you can also dance away a good part of the night. If you have overindulged, there is a medicinal spring nearby, called Kallithea, whose water is supposed to cure any digestive ailment.

The next day visit Lindos, 56 kilometers down the east coast of the island. The drive is lovely. Lindos has a splendid Acropolis with the famous temple to Athena Lindia, built in the fourth century B.C., a most elegant religious edifice. The Makra Stoa or colonnade was 270 feet long; the twenty columns that have been restored give an idea of how this structure looked when it was part of the ceremonial entrance to the temple of Athena. There is also a medieval castle on a hill against the blue sky with the sea far below.

The little town of Lindos has many fifteenth century houses, a thirteenth century church to the Virgin Mary with interesting mosaics and murals, as well as a lovely beach where you can cool off after your visit to the temple. Nestling in the shadow of a rock just below the Acropolis is the picturesque cove where the Apostle Paul landed on his visit to Rhodes.

Only 15 kilometers from Rhodes on the west coast is Ialysus with a fine acropolis on the summit of Mount Filerimos. Here are ruins of temples to Athena and Zeus, a Doric fountain from the fourth century B.C. and a medieval monastery to the Holy Virgin, with a subterranean chapel containing beautiful frescoes.

Ten kilometers down the west coast from Ialysus is the Valley of the Butterflies or Petaloudes, where thousands of red butterflies hover in the air as you walk through their sanctuary. Eleven kilometers on is the old city of Camirus, shaped like an amphitheater with an agora, temples, shops, thermal baths and many ancient houses.

These are but a few of the sights in Rhodes, but the whole island is a scenic delight. What else you should visit depends on the time of year and what local festival is taking place. There is always something doing; your hotel or the tourist police will tell you where you can see a village wedding, a wine festival or country dances.

CORFU

HOW TO GET THERE

Either fly from Athens to Corfu (1¾ hours) or take the bus through Corinth, Rion and Igoumenitsa, where it boards a ferry (15 to 18 hours).

Prepackaged tours are available and are listed in Section I.

Planes fly daily from Athens to Corfu and cost $16.20 one way, $29.10 return. (Olympic Airways.)

Buses run once a day from Athens to Corfu and cost $5.85 one way, $10.50 return.

Private transportation in Corfu. Cars, with or without drivers, can be hired. Taxis are available. (See Section I for rates.)

Local tours in Corfu. Some tours are available within Corfu. For information on these ask at your hotel or your travel agent on the island.

CORFU HOTELS

Prices without meals: Category AA, $8.00 single, $11.65 double; Category B, $4.33 single, $7.43 double; Category C, $3.00 single, $3.90 double.

Category	Name
AA	Corfu Palace
AA	Miramare
A *	Castello
B * (R)	Astir
B ** (R)	Corfu

Category	Name
B ** (R)	Xenia
C * (R)	Ionion
C * (R)	Calypso
C	Splendid

Village rooms can be rented. For bookings see page 16.

WHAT TO DO

You do not visit Corfu to look at ruins but to live well, to indulge in an affair with an island and to see the difference between the rest of Greece and the Ionian. Corfu was never run by the Turks. Instead she felt the benefit of the Renaissance while under the Venetians, of the enlightenment while under the French, and finally the influence of the British when they were at their peak during the Napoleonic wars. It is what these Europeans have left in Corfu, blended with the basic Greek spirit of the island, that you see.

Not that Corfu does not have a splendid ancient history beginning suitably with a mythical love affair, this time between Poseidon and Corcyra, daughter of the river god Asopus. Poseidon seduced her and brought her to the island which was then named for her (the modern name for Corfu in Greek is Kerkyra). The son she bore to Poseidon was Phaeax, ancestor of the Phaeacians, who according to Homer inhabited the island when Odysseus made his last stop there on his journey home after the Trojan wars.

Corfu was colonized by Corinth in 734 B.C. It prospered, acquired a large fleet and dominated the seas around, establishing daughter cities on the mainland. The people of Corfu stood on the sidelines during the Greco-Persian wars and later they quarreled with their mother city, Corinth, and sought the help of Athens. The Athenians agreed to help and this was one of the prime reasons for the Peloponnesian war which pitted Athens against Sparta and led to the downfall of Athens.

The Romans took the island in 229 B.C. and it later became part of the Byzantine Empire. As that empire weakened, a series of conquerors passed through Corfu—the Goths, the Normans, the Genoese, the Venetians; later the French held the island, then the Russians and finally the British who governed Corfu from 1814 to 1864, when they returned it, together with its neighboring islands, to Greece.

The most profound influence was exercised by the Venetians, who held the island for four centuries and allowed a large measure of autonomy. Music and poetry flourished and to this day Corfu is perhaps the most musical part of Greece, an enticing blend of the basic Greek character, Italian liveliness, French verve and British humor. Nowhere is the mixture more apparent than in the architecture of the city. It is mostly Italianate with some very fine Georgian buildings lining the narrow streets, which boast arcades, colonnades and charming little squares with churches, fountains and statues. The main square, called Spianada, is lined with trees, flower beds and a pavilion where two local bands play on balmy evenings—the people of Corfu could not live without music.

The distances in the city are very small and I advise that you walk. A surprisingly large number of people understand English and will give directions. You will see but may not visit the two Venetian castles, now a military school, about a hundred yards from the main square on a promontory that was separated from the mainland by a moat, dug probably in Byzantine times. The moat has become a harbor for yachts and pleasure boats. The royal yachts are moored in a little cove of the fortress itself.

The next major point of interest in the city is the very fine

Georgian building erected by the British for their governors. Here sentries are posted by the kilted Royal Guard whenever the royal family is in residence on the island during the summer. The king does not live here, but at Mon Repos, one of the former summer residences of the British governor general, a villa set in a large park in the traditional style of colonial governors.

There are beaches everywhere, but the best are on the west coast, half an hour to an hour from the city by private car or bus. There are even better beaches that you can reach by motorboat which your hotel can help you hire. If you want to gamble, there is the Casino Achilleion; there are many restaurants where you can dance.

Two outings I recommend are to Kanoni and Paliokastritsa. Kanoni is only 4 kilometers (2½ miles) from the town. It is the site of an old French battery overlooking a small bay with two enchanting islands, one bearing the shrine of the Virgin of Vlachernai and connected by jetty to the mainland. From here a small boat will take you to the other, Pontikonisi or Mouse Island, which has a delightful Byzantine church. The same boat will then take you across the bay to Perama where there are several very pleasant restaurants with fine seafood and tables set in gardens that stretch down to the sea.

Paliokastritsa is 26 kilometers from the town, a magnificent little bay where you can eat marvelous fresh lobster. It has an interesting twelfth century Byzantine monastery dedicated to the Virgin Mary. The water of the bay is a medley of blues because of the multicolored rocks on the bottom and skin diving here is particularly good. The best fishing is off the north coast, which you reach either by car or by motorboat.

If you are interested in religious festivals Corfu has several. Each year, with full participation by the bishops in their regalia, the peasantry comes dressed in local costume for Palm

Sunday's solemn ceremony celebrating the anniversary of the island's salvation from cholera in 1629. Another festival is the day before Christmas, when the island celebrates one more narrow escape, this time from starvation. It is said that St. Spyridon, patron saint of the island, appeared in the dreams of several sea captains, making them divert their wheat-carrying ships to Corfu, where the crop had failed and people were dying in the streets.

On August 11, yet another miraculous intervention by St. Spyridon is celebrated, commemorating the night when a ghostly monk, brandishing a cross in one hand and a lighted torch in the other, chased away the Turks who were laying siege to the island. And on the first Sunday in November the whole island turns out to give thanks to St. Spyridon yet again, for saving Corfu from a cholera epidemic in 1673. This feast was established by special decree of the Venetian governor who, though a Roman Catholic, was convinced that the miracle had occurred. The bona fide body of the saint is paraded around the streets of the town while the bishop and clergy sing hymns of thanks. Corfiotes, incidentally, believe that the shoes of the mummified saint have to be changed every forty days because he wears them out walking the streets at night protecting his people from evil.

Every summer there is Cricket Week—a habit acquired under the British—and British teams, usually from the Mediterranean fleet, are invited to play against the island's eleven. The date of this occasion can never be fixed far in advance for it depends on the availability of a British team. But it is a nostalgic occasion. Naval detachments salute one another, guns go bang, the girls wear their best, and in the evening there is much brave playing by the island bands, which practice the whole year for this great event.

CRETE

HOW TO GET THERE

Either fly from Athens to Crete (1 hour) or take the ship or ferry (12 hours).

Prepackaged tours and cruises are available and some are listed in Section I, beginning on p. 44.

Planes fly from Athens to Heraklion daily and cost $12.66 one way, $22.80 round trip. They also fly from Athens to Canea daily and cost $10.75 one way, $19.35 round trip. (Olympic Airways.)

Ships sail six times a week from Piraeus to Canea and Heraklion and cost from $8.30 first class to $2.60 deck. (Typaldos, Cavounidis, Nomikos, New Epirotiki shipping lines.)

Ferry boats run daily from Piraeus to Canea and cost from $11 first class to $3 third. (Crete's Ferry Boats Co.)

Private transportation in Crete. Cars, with or without drivers, and taxis can be hired in Crete. (For rates see Section I.)

Local tours in Crete. There are bus tours within Crete to the various archaeological sites, organized by CHAT or CRETA TOURS. These range from $2 for a 2½-hour tour of Knossos to $10.70 for a one-day tour, including lunch.

CRETE HOTELS

Prices without meals: Category A, $5.28 single, $7.34 double; Category B, $3.80 single, $4.60 double; Category C, $2.24 single, $3.20 double.

Category		Name
A *	(R)	Astir (Heraklion)
A *		Minoa (Canea)
A **	(R)	Minos Beach (Agios Nikolaos)
A **	(R)	Xenia (Heraklion)
B *	(R)	Ariane (Heraklion)
B *	(R)	Candia (Heraklion)
B *	(R)	Cosmopolite (Heraklion)
B **	(R)	Xenia (Rethimnon)
C *	(R)	Acropole
C *		Crystal (Sitia)
C *		Kreta (Ierapetra)
C *		Lato (Agios Nikolaos)
C *		Park Hotel (Heraklion)

Some monasteries offer rooms. For bookings see Section I.

WHAT TO DO

Crete is a mood, an experience, yours for the taking if you give yourself time to soak in the atmosphere. There are not many places so small where you can say that you have seen a distinct world; there are not many places so small which have contributed so much to civilization and deserve to be called great.

The Greeks call Crete the Megalonisos, meaning the "great island." The forces that have clashed here, crushing one another through the centuries, have left vivid traces on the stark face of the island which was the cradle of the first European civilization, the Minoan, the tremendous sea power whose tentacles reached as far west as Gibraltar and as far north as the Black Sea. The roots of this civilization are lost in the murky depths of mythology. Men, gods and heroes wrestled to dominate the earth—Minos himself, the traditional king of Crete; Radamanthis, the great judge and lawgiver; the Minotaur, the monster with the body of a man and the head of a bull; Theseus, who slew the Minotaur. These are all symbols of this tremendous ancient struggle. There always was a struggle in Crete—the island is dotted with the fortresses of the Venetian, the Genoese and the Turk. Wherever you go in Crete there are the wraiths of ancient heroes.

Shadows of artistic giants lurk everywhere. Great artists painted the walls and fashioned vessels for the Minoan palaces. Later came Domenikos Theotokopoulos, known as El Greco, the unknown poets of great popular epics of the Christian era which still await translation into English and French, and Nikos Kazantzakis, the writer of *Zorba the Greek, Freedom or Death*, etc., one of the great literary figures of our century. You see prototypes of Kazantzakis' characters everywhere in Crete—untamed, sarcastic, full of life, fluid, possessed, dancing and fighting.

Also from Crete came Eleutherios Venizelos, the great statesman of modern Greece.

Crete divides the Greek seas from the African seas. It has nearly half a million people who live along the tremendous spine of mountains which stretch west to east, first the White Mountains, then the Psiloritis and Dikti. There are no great plains, just a few flat stretches at the foot of the mountains, some valleys and some plateaus. Up among the peaks there are wild gorges and caves, in one of which Zeus is said to have been born.

There are fine harbors near Canea, a NATO base, Rethimnon and Heraklion, as well as gulfs, bays, anchorages and beautiful beaches.

And there are of course the vestiges of the fantastic Minoan civilization, which flourished between 4000 and 1200 B.C. when Crete had one hundred cities and was a sea power, fabulously rich from trade, piracy and tribute.

Legend holds that Minos himself built the palace of Knossos. And Theseus, son of the king of Athens, was sent there as part of the human tribute Athens paid each year to the king of Crete. Theseus killed the Minotaur, the monster that fed on human sacrifice, and left the island with Ariadne, daughter of Minos.

The palace of Knossos is an astonishing structure and the most imposing ruin of ancient Knossos, though some of the smaller structures that have been unearthed should be visited. The king of Knossos was not only the chief executive and head priest, but also the foremost trader of the city. His palace, therefore, contained special spaces for worship, trading, and for artisans, as well as the chambers in which the king and queen lived.

The palace was first built in the year 2000 B.C. It was destroyed in 1750 B.C. and immediately rebuilt, so it is obvious the destruction was not caused by conquest and defeat. There is a great deal of writing to be found from that period; the earliest does not depict whole words, only syllables. The palace was again destroyed in 1550 B.C. and rebuilt without any changes. Some alterations were made between 1450 and 1400 B.C. It was at that time that the throne room was built and writing—known as Linear B—began to appear, and it would seem it was used only in palaces, both in Crete and on mainland Greece at Mycenae, Pylus and elsewhere. This script which puzzled archaeologists for generations was finally deciphered by an amateur, the late English architect Michael Ventris.

The palace consists of two wings, conglomerations of buildings on either side of the central courtyard. The throne room is to the west of the central courtyard. It has an antechamber and the throne room, itself, with the throne of Minos flanked by two murals depicting griffons. There are seats all round, most probably for the elders, and facing the throne is the holy font, used for ritual cleansing, to which one descends by a staircase. The Minoans worshiped gods of the earth, if we are to judge by the painted symbols—the double axe and snake, which are characteristic of such deities.

The west wing also contained the treasury, a grand staircase, the long corridor of storerooms. To the west of the storerooms was the trading courtyard. A road led from the trading courtyard all the way to the harbor.

The east wing contained both living quarters and various chambers used chiefly by artisans—goldsmiths, potters, painters, etc. There is a grand staircase in the east wing too. The building here must have been three stories high. The apartments of the queen are large and airy and festively decorated with murals of dolphins, ladies of fashion, and dancers.

Notice the hall of the double axes, the baths, the hall of the goddess of the doves. The workshops of the artisans began at the courtyard of the stone spout and stretched to the north, away from the queen's quarters.

The bullfighting or bulldancing was held at the northeast corner of the palace. From there visit the hall of columns.

Be sure not to miss the vestiges of the amazing plumbing system developed by the Minoans. There are pipes for water and pipes for sewage which you can inspect just beyond the trading courtyard. Northwest from the palace, where they have unearthed part of the city of Knossos—a very large city indeed—there are also traces of water and sewage systems, indicating that such luxuries were not reserved only for kings.

South of the palace is another building which archaeologist Sir Arthur Evans, the discoverer of Knossos, called caravanserai. This may be the earliest known example of an apartment house.

The final destruction of Knossos came in 1400 B.C. and it seems fairly certain the city was then ruled by people from mainland Greece. But the Minoan civilization continued in other parts of the island till the Dorians, another group of mainlanders, invaded Crete in the thirteenth century B.C. You don't hear of the Cretans again until the time of Alexander the Great, when Cretan ships were part of the fleet of Nearchos, Alexander's famous admiral who explored the coast of Africa.

It is amazing that so much survived these successive invasions and those that followed. The Romans conquered the island in the second century B.C.; Crete became a province of the Greek Byzantine Empire until the ninth century; the Saracens, Arabs from Spain, landed, slaughtered the archbishop, sold the men they captured into slavery and turned the great island into a nest of pirates.

In A.D. 961 the Byzantine emperor, Nikiforos, with 3300 ships took the Arab capital, situated on the site of modern Heraklion, tore down the walls of the Arab fortresses, turned the mosques into churches and re-Hellenized the island.

In A.D. 1204 the Franks of the Fourth Crusade conquered Crete, to be followed two years later by the Genoese and the Venetians who proceeded to divide Crete into feudal fiefdoms constantly at war with one another. They threw out Greek Orthodox bishops, installed Roman Catholics and turned the inhabitants into serfs.

The Venetians held the island for 450 years, despite twenty-five revolutions. The Turks conquered Crete in 1669 and tried to subdue its rebellious citizens by slaughtering the men, enslaving the women and abducting young boys for service in the Sultan's guard. But the Cretans fled to the mountains and for two centuries the island was never fully enslaved because up on the high peaks and in the inaccessible gorges, Cretans lived as outlaws, gun in hand.

There were epic risings about every eleven years and to put

down the last, in 1898, the Turks launched a massacre of such proportion that the civilized world took note, and forced Turkey to grant autonomy to Crete under the son of the king of Greece. In 1913 the island at last rejoined Greece, after Venizelos, a Cretan, had become prime minister of Greece, fought the Ottoman Empire and defeated it.

One wonders how any art treasures survived so much violence, and we must assume that what has been found is but a fraction of what the ancient Cretans wrought. The best pieces are in the museum at Heraklion, which you should visit after your trip to Knossos when you will better be able to appreciate the exhibits, having seen the setting from which they came.

The exhibits are arranged chronologically and are very adequately labeled. You will see pottery dating from before 4000 B.C., stone implements, axes, hammers, clubs, etc., smaller tools of bone which were obviously used to decorate the pottery.

And so you proceed from showcase to showcase, from the first painted European vases to some of the most lovely stone pottery. There are many seals, urns, vases and little statuettes of marble or alabaster. Then come the axes and daggers, and a fine display of gold ornaments and jewelry.

There is also a vase showing an acrobat somersaulting over the horns of a bull, one of the scenes most commonly associated with the customs of the Minoans.

A delightful exhibit is the model of a Minoan town actually made by the Minoans themselves, which contains buildings resembling some of the small apartment blocks of today.

Upstairs, the great Minoan frescoes have been housed. The decorations of walls are either in relief or flat painting, which was one of the most developed arts of the period.

In the evening, drive to the little mountain village of

Arkanai, 16 kilometers from Heraklion. There are buses at Heraklion and the journey costs 8 cents each way, but the last bus leaves the village for the return journey at 7 P.M. which is much too early. If you are a good bargainer you could get a taxi for five people to take you there, wait while you have dinner, and return for $6. There are two tavernas in Arkanai, one called Myriofyton and the other called Rodakinies which features a cabaret where local artists perform the traditional Cretan dances.

After dinner, and before you retire, you may wish to visit the tomb of Kazantzakis overlooking the harbor of Heraklion, which he loved so much.

If you stay longer and want to swim, there is a local beach. The hotel will tell you where to catch the bus, or you can rent a taxi. There usually are taxis waiting to carry you back. Or take the marvelous, scenic drive from Heraklion to Sitia.

If you have time, you should visit Phaestos, the site of another Minoan palace, 55 kilometers from Heraklion. On the drive you pass the ruins of Gortyna (capital of Crete under the Romans) where there is an ancient quarry with so many passages that some archaeologists believe it to be the famous labyrinth of the Minotaur.

At Phaestos is an enormous platform, the foundations of the palace, standing on high ground above a fertile plain, a patchwork of greens and yellows with copses of trees, and as a backdrop the majestic mountain range which rises gently at first and then turns stark and somber as if hacked by some protean chisel. At dawn and dusk the light turns violet.

The people of Phaestos considered themselves great humorists and are said to have rehearsed the technique of joke-telling from an early age. The palace was smaller than that at Knossos but richer. The grand staircase, forty feet wide, is particularly impressive.

OLYMPIA

HOW TO GET THERE

Either take the bus from Athens to Olympia (8 hours) or take the fast train (5½ hours).

Prepackaged tours are available and some are listed in Section I.

Buses from Athens to Olympia leave once a day and cost $4.30 one way, $7.70 return. There are many more buses to Olympia from Patras or Pyrgus.

Trains run from Athens to Olympia once a day and cost $6.65 each way.

Private transportation from Argolis. If you are in the Argolis and want to take the trip to Olympia, a taxi will cost no more than $50, so from there you could team up with another three or four people and share the bill.

OLYMPIA HOTELS

Prices without meals: Category A, $5.20 single, $7.20 double; Category B, $4.30 single, $5.40 double; Category C, $2.00 single, $2.60 double; Category D, $1.00 single, $1.50 double.

Category	Name
A ** (R)	Spap
B ** (R)	Nea Olympia
B * (R)	Xenia
C **	Apollon
C	Iraion
D	Kronion

SIGHTS ON THE WAY

The drive is from Athens to Corinth (see page 98 for description) then along the north coast of the Peloponnesus past several delightful beaches, notably Xilokastron which is recommended if you like to watch nordic maidens in bikinis —they have a camping site there. The scenery is beautiful all the way to Patras, the third largest town in Greece, and beyond to Pyrgus, a small provincial town with interesting churches. There you turn inland toward Olympia.

WHAT TO DO

I strongly advise an overnight stay at Olympia as you need at least ten hours sightseeing for even a cursory visit to its treasures. Keep in mind that in spite of the lush vegetation the sun burns fiercely here in the summer, so plan your tour for before 10 A.M. and after 5 P.M. You can rest and visit the museum between these hours.

The setting for Olympia is an enchanting valley between the rivers Kadeos and Alpheios. Nature here has surpassed any landscape architect, creating a location of rare beauty and serenity. Protecting the valley from the north is the green and holy hill called Kronion, after Kronos, father of Zeus. There are innumerable bronze statuettes in the museum attesting to the veneration felt for Kronos before the cult of Zeus was firmly established.

This location had a tremendous fascination for the ancient Greeks, who flocked here from every corner of the land to worship, making the valley a Panhellenic shrine, an eternal symbol of Hellenism, a center of classical beauty and an embodiment of the ancient Greek ideal of a healthy mind in a healthy body. Olympia was the first and most important of

man's experiments toward universal peace. During the qua-
drennial Olympic games a truce was called in the wars between various cities or states, and young men shed their
armor, to compete for the simple crown of leaves, while their
elders tried to settle differences that had led to war.

In the ninth century B.C. neighboring kingdoms decided
that Olympia was holy ground which should never see battle,
and no wars were ever fought there between Greeks. The first
Olympic games were held in 776 B.C. and from that year on
the Olympiads were faithfully recorded. The year 776 B.C. has
always been considered the date when Greek prehistory ended
and true history begins.

The original competition was in running, and the games
lasted only one day. The pentathlon, wrestling, horse races,
chariot races and pangration (a combination of boxing and
wrestling) came later. The athletes did not compete to establish records then, but merely to win with honor the wreath of
leaves cut with a golden knife from an ancient wild olive tree,
said to have belonged to Zeus. Any man who won in three
successive games had the right to erect his statue in Olympia.
The games continued until A.D. 393 when they were abolished
by the Byzantine emperor Theodosius.

In A.D 522 and 521 a terrible series of earthquakes brought
down the temples, and tons of earth from the holy hill
Kronion buried the ruins. But the catastrophe was a blessing,
for the earth hid the treasures from the depredations of invaders and the Hermes of Praxiteles was saved for Greece and
the world. Later the River Alpheios changed course, deposit-
ing a protective layer of silt as a further shield against dese-
crators and Olympia lay buried until 1829 when a team of
French scholars started the first dig at the site of the great
temple of Zeus (removing some pieces of the sculpted friezes

which are now in the Louvre). But only in 1875 did systematic digs start.

What you see today cannot be separated from the landscape. The ancient Greek choice of location for any shrine was always connected with the personality of the god to be worshiped there. In Olympia the god was Zeus, master of heaven and earth, ruler of gods and men. And at sunset you can see why Olympia was favored by Zeus as his shrine.

Legend has it that the vale of Olympia was the home of a beautiful nymph called Arethousa. An ardent young man, Alpheios, son of Poseidon, fell in love with her and was so impetuous in pressing his suit that Arethousa fled to Sicily. Disconsolate, Alpheios begged his father to help him reach his beloved. Poseidon, god of the sea, transformed Alpheios into a river flowing so swiftly that its current could cross the sea to reach and embrace Sicily, so that Alpheios could imagine he was embracing his love. Arethousa is beautifully depicted on Sicilian coins.

THE ALTIS

(Note: Figures in parentheses refer to the plan on page 138.)

You enter the Altis, the holy precinct, by the Prytaneion (24), a square building where the holy flame burned eternally. This was carried throughout Greece to announce the beginning of the Olympic games, as it is now carried throughout the world. In the Prytaneion, a feast was held for winners on the last day of the games. Next is the Heraeon, temple of Hera or Juno (21). This is the oldest known temple in Greece and the holiest place in the Altis. Built in the seventh century B.C., it originally had wooden columns. Each time one of them wore away, it was replaced with a column of stone in the style of the era during which the particular column was

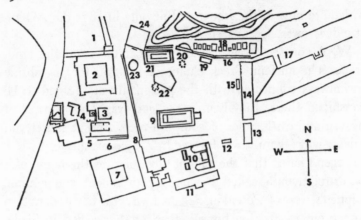

OLYMPIA

1. Gymnasium; 2. Palaestra; 3. Theokoleon; 4. Heroon; 5. Fifth century Christian basilica, foundations of an ancient palace, possibly Phidias' workshop; 6. Dependency of Phidias' workshop, or house of the Phaedryntes; 7. Leonidaion; 8. Official gate of the sanctuary; 9. Temple of Zeus; 10. Vouleftirion; 11. South Stoa; 12. Roman gate, possibly of Nero; 13. Southeast Stoa (Nero's house); 14. Stoa of Echo or Poekile; 15. Altar of Zeus; 16. Bases (Zanes); 17. Stadium; 18. Treasuries; 19. Metroon; 20. Exedra of Herodes Atticus; 21. Heraeon (temple of Hera); 22. Pelopeion; 23. Philippeion; 24. Prytaneion.

erected. Thus the Heraeon records the development of the Greek column.

Beyond the Heraeon is a circular pavilion, the Philippeion (23) surrounded by a gallery with Ionic columns. Here were housed five statues in ivory and gold, works of the sculptor Leocharis, representing the Macedonian royal family. The building was begun by Philip, king of Macedonia, and completed by his son Alexander the Great. There is an enclosure around a small mound, the Pelopeion (22), dedicated to Pelops, the mythical hero who gave his name to the Peloponnesus. Next is the Metroon (19), dedicated to the goddess

Rhea, mother of Zeus, and to Kyveli or Cybele, an oriental goddess of fertility who came to be identified by the Greeks with Rhea. Kyveli was regarded as the mother of the arts and special protectress of cities. Her priests, called Corybantes, were emasculated to commemorate the emasculation of Atys (beloved of Kyveli) and were dressed like women to achieve unity with the goddess. Her festivals were celebrated with wild dances and orgiastic excesses, accompanied by the resounding music of drums and cymbals.

Nearby is the Exedra (20), the platform of Herodes Atticus, which was in effect the waterworks of Olympia, a semi-circular edifice with a rectangle inside, the whole ornamented by numerous marble statues. Above was a marble ball (now in the museum) inscribed with the date these waterworks were built.

Next to the waterworks are the treasuries (18), temple-like buildings of various epochs, mostly Doric in style, which contained donations from various states.

Then you come to the Stadium (17), which could seat 45,000 people. Its sides were mere inclines of earth. The judges had stone seats on the south side. Facing them to the north was the seat for the priestess of Demeter, goddess of agriculture, the only woman allowed to watch the games. The field itself is 192 meters long instead of the usual 186 meters, because according to legend Hercules measured out the length with his feet, which were naturally larger than those of the average man. The stadium is outside the holy precinct.

You should now turn back toward the precinct to visit the Echo gallery, also known as the Poekile Stoa (14), which is said to have thrown back the voice seven times. At its entrance by the altar (15) look across the piazza to the temple of Zeus (9), the main shrine of Olympia, built around the middle of the fifth century B.C. It is of local stone in Doric style and once housed Phidias' ivory and gold statue of Zeus, considered to be one of the seven wonders of the ancient world. The friezes of Parian marble are still magnificent, despite the mutilations they have suffered, and can be seen in the museum.

Directly south of the temple of Zeus is the Vouleftirion (10) where the athletes took the oath to compete with honor and the elders met to settle differences.

To the east was the most famous "hotel" of classical Greece, the Leonidaion (7), a square structure surrounded by 138 Ionic columns. It was used to house statesmen visiting Olympia for the games.

To the north of this structure is a Byzantine church (5) built in 426 by Theodosios the Second on top of an earlier Greek structure which, according to descriptions of the traveler Pausanias, was the workshop of Phidias. Archaeologists have unearthed many instruments for working gold and ivory, as well as molds for fashioning the gold plates. But one of the most touching finds is surely the small vase marked "I belong to Phidias."

Then there are a wrestling arena (2) and a gymnasium (1) where athletes practiced for the games.

By now you may need a rest before visiting the museum, which is open Sundays and holidays from 10 A.M. to 1 P.M. and 2 P.M. to 6 P.M.; Mondays from 12 noon to 1 P.M. and 3 to 7 P.M.; other days 8 A.M. to 1 P.M. and 3 to 7 P.M.

At the museum you should pay particular attention to the Victory of Paionios, the Hermes of Praxiteles, the magnificent collection of bronze artifacts and the statues from the east frieze of the temple of Zeus, depicting preparations for the chariot race between Oenomaus and Pelops. Pelops, an ancestor of Hercules, had to race Oenomaus for the hand of Oenomaus' daughter, Hippodamia. Pelops bribed a servant to tinker with the wheels of Oenomaus' chariot, as a result of which Oenomaus died. When the servant tried to collect his bribe, he was hurled into the sea by Pelops. As he fell, the servant uttered a curse which brought disaster to many of the descendants of Pelops. Pelops succeeded to the throne of Oenomaus, conquered the whole of the Peloponnesus and became the richest and most powerful of the princes of Greece. Agamemnon was one of his descendants on whom the curse certainly worked.

The statues of the western frieze depict the battle between the centaurs and the Lapiths, overseen by the imposing figure of Apollo. You will notice a difference in style between the eastern and western portions. Those of the east pediment, where a race between Pelops and Oenomaus is being prepared, are serene and hardly move. Those of the west are characterized by great movement and obvious tension.

The Victory of Paionios was commissioned by the Messinians and donated to Olympia after their victory over Sparta during the Peloponnesian wars.

The Hermes of Praxiteles holds on his left arm the baby Dionysus, son of Zeus and Semeli. The statue depicts the occasion when Hermes carried the child to the nymphs to protect it from the wrath and jealousy of Hera, wife of Zeus. This statue represents the peak of technical perfection in ancient Greek sculpture. It was once painted and some traces of the coloring can still be seen in the hair. It was unearthed in pieces from the temple of Hera, which is where Pausanias wrote that he saw it.

The collection of bronze artifacts can be seen in the west wing of the museum. There are numerous seals, helmets, breastplates and other pieces which indicate that the ancient Greek warrior was covered from head to toe in armor.

For philatelists there is a display of stamps connected with the modern Olympics.

There is no night life in Olympia. You eat at your hotel and may wish to visit some of the curio shops there; better perhaps simply to gaze on Olympia and ponder the civilization that could produce such a city, so many centuries ago.

SPARTA AND MYSTRAS

HOW TO GET THERE

Either take the bus from Athens to Sparta (6 hours), or fly to Kalamai (55 minutes) then take a bus to Sparta (1½ hours).

Prepackaged tours are available and are listed in Section I.

Planes from Athens to Kalamai fly Mondays, Wednesdays and Saturdays and cost $8.25 one way, $15 return. (Olympic Airways.)

Buses run four times a day from Athens to Sparta and cost $3.50 one way, $5.70 return. From Kalamai to Sparta there are two buses a day, costing 77 cents each way.

Private transportation in Sparta. You can hire taxis in Sparta (see Section I for rates).

SPARTA HOTELS

Prices without meals: Category B, $3.60 single, $5.00 double; Category C, $2.60 single, $3.82 double.

Location	Category		Name
Mystras	B *		Byzantine Palace
Sparta	B **	(R)	Xenia
"	C **	(R)	Dioskouroi
"	C *		Menelaion

SIGHTS ON THE WAY

For a description of what you will see along the way from Athens to Argos, see the section on the Argolis.

Five kilometers from Argos you reach Kefalari, a beautiful spot with little restaurants and a brook which is the source of the Erasinos River. The view is lovely and the air usually cool. Five kilometers farther on you come to Myloi, a small town near Lerna where the American Archaeological School is doing a dig. Here, it is alleged, the Lernaean Hydra, the many-headed monster, lived until it was slain by Hercules. There used to be a lake here, said to be bottomless, which the Emperor Nero tried to plumb and failed.

Then the road begins winding up the mountain, affording lovely views at every turn. Don't worry about the way the driver takes the turns. He knows them well and will take care not to endanger himself or his passengers.

Tripolis is a neat little city in the middle of a small plateau with some nice churches and much civic pride. It was the first important location taken by the Greeks in 1821, during the war of independence. Just outside Tripolis you will pass the site of ancient Tegea which has some interesting classical ruins and a Byzantine church with excellent mosaics.

From here on, it is view after enchanting view, first of Lake Taka, then of the wild Taïyetos Mountains, which form the peninsula called Mani whose people claim descent from the Spartans, are great fighters, and until recently practiced the vendetta. You start climbing down toward the valley of the Eurotas, ancient Laconia, home of the Lacedaemonians, and so you reach Sparta.

WHAT TO DO

Walk around the town in the morning or the evening when it is cooler, if you visit it in summer.

Sparta is a pretty little town built by King Otho (first king of modern Greece) in 1834 on the ruins of one of its ancient suburbs. It has lovely avenues and squares, a spacious cathedral and a fine old church, St. Nikon. You can see a third century B.C. mosaic depicting the kidnaping of Europa by Zeus, another of his extramarital affairs. There is an air of peace as if the old, old city of Sparta were resting from its exertions and its former glories, which began when the Dorians came down into Greece at about 1100 B.C. The Dorians established a powerful state in this valley and insisted that they keep the race pure, which created many difficulties for them later as they lost so many men during their wars.

What springs to the mind of most who hear the word Sparta is the antithesis between its customs and those of democratic Athens. Sparta was dominated by an aristocracy which elected the Efores—the world's first commissars, in fact—who were the real rulers, while the hereditary kings only led the army in battle or performed at ceremonials. Deformed children were thrown down a precipice. The young were taken from their mothers and brought up in camps, sleeping on reeds from the age of seven, whipped for the slightest infraction and fed a mixture of ox-blood and vinegar, called the black broth.

The male Spartan was in constant military service, and frequently away in distant wars. Conjugal morals suffered as a result; Spartan women were known for their promiscuity and the pure Spartan blood was liberally mixed with that of the male slaves, the helots, on whom the economy depended. The whole society from the helots to the Efores was divided into rigid castes with strictly prescribed duties, enforced by the death penalty. The strict discipline was at first the strength of Sparta, which had the best troops in Greece. Occasionally they even brought forth a commander who was not only brave, but also a military genius, and they managed to defeat Athens in her own element, winning a series of naval battles over the Athenian fleet. Thus Sparta, a small town, provincial in every sense, rose to supremacy in Greece.

But the racist Spartans turned everyone they conquered into slaves, treating them as inferior, in need of Spartan domination, and made them work for the greater glory of Sparta. Naturally their subjects hated them and rebelled, causing the Spartans to become even more harsh, and so in a vicious circle of hatred, rebellion and repression, Sparta was finally and conclusively defeated by the Thebans in 371 B.C.

Some generations later, in the third century B.C., two enlightened Spartan kings tried to reform the caste system, realizing that the state was weakened by the hatred and suspicion which surrounded the dwindling band of "pure" Spartans. But the Efores drowned the reform in blood.

From then on it was all decline; defeat at the hands of the Macedonians, conquest by Rome, destruction by Alarich and his Visigoths in A.D. 396 and by the Slavs in the ninth century. It was then that the last of the Spartans finally abandoned their city and took to the mountains. Other conquerors passed through, the Franks, the Venetians, and the Turks, who came, were thrown out, and came again finally to take the town in 1715.

All these invaders destroyed what buildings they found, and there had never been many. When one thinks of the wealth of monuments in Athens, one is tempted to agree with Thucydides who said that if someday Sparta lost its power and there remained only its temples and the foundations of its public buildings, future generations would doubt she ever had the strength to deserve her reputation.

Compared with the great artistic centers of Greece, Sparta has to be deemed inferior. Even so, in any other part of the world, some of the archaeological finds at Sparta would be considered treasures.

In the archaic period Spartan pots were fine and so were the bronzes. In the city you can see the remains of a small temple incorrectly called the tomb of Leonidas, the king who led the three hundred against the Persians at Thermopylae. There was an agora, of which some vestiges remain next to the ruins of an old theater near the town.

Seven hundred yards or so south of the Eurotas River, archaeologists have unearthed the ruins of a temple to the goddess Artemis, where famous contests of fortitude were held—young men were whipped till they bled and those who neither cried out nor winced won a prize.

In the museum near the main square you will see the incomparable Spartan bronze miniatures, some archaic stone statues which are strikingly contemporary in technique, as well as the magnificent pots of Sparta.

MYSTRAS

The main reason, however, for a visit to Sparta is Mystras. It is only 4½ kilometers away (and there are very frequent buses to and fro). You drive west toward the rugged Taïyetos Mountains, through a gorge, to the slope on which Mystras is built, a vast cemetery of buildings, rich and poor with palaces, arches over narrow streets, churches, all built at different periods and showing therefore a panorama of the architecture of Byzantium and of the Frankish conquerors who founded the city in 1249 and whose castle dominates the scene. The Franks were thrown out ten years after they established the city and Mystras became a center of Byzantine power. One of its local rulers, Constantine Palaeologus, became the last emperor of Byzantium, only to die when the Turks sacked Constantinople in 1453.

The Metropolis of St. Demetrius, which also houses the museum, started out as a basilica and was changed subtly by other architectural accretions. There are remarkably well-preserved murals in this church, as well as sculptures of such different styles that they obviously were imported. Outside the Metropolis, on the road, is an iron fence protecting a stone stained by the blood of the bishops massacred by the Turks in 1760.

Nearby is the small church of Evangelistria which has some excellent samples of decorative sculptures.

A little farther on is the Church of the Saints Theodoros, the oldest church in Mystras, built in the octagonal style characteristic of inland Greece. Unfortunately its murals are in poor condition.

Next is the cloister of the Guiding Virgin, also called the Afendiko, a fascinating building combining the basilica style with the cruciform, the five-domed standard Greek Ortho-dox pattern. Murals and sculptures are particularly well pre-served and some are very fine.

A must is the convent of Pantanassa, the only inhabited place in Mystras. The nuns, who specialize in restoring icons and murals, will offer you cool spring water and sweetmeats. Despite their otherworldliness they do have a telephone and a little handicraft shop where you can buy knitwear, hand-loomed cloth, carvings, all in traditional Byzantine style. A nun will act as your guide through the monastery, which is built on a very steep mountain slope and has a magnificent view of the valley. Note the fine steeple and chapel, which also is a combination of the basilica and cruciform styles. This is the best preserved monument in Mystras and has beautiful murals. Its sculpted decorations are admirably varied.

There isn't much to do in Sparta at night except to have a good meal, either at the Xenia Hotel or the Diethnes Restaurant or at Troungakou. If you are returning to Argolis, it will take 3½ hours by car.

METEORA

HOW TO GET THERE

Either fly from Athens to Larissa (70 minutes) then take the bus to Trikala (1½ hours) which connects with buses to Meteora (45 minutes); or go direct to Trikala from Athens by bus (7 hours) to pick up the bus to Meteora (45 minutes).

Prepackaged tours are available via Delphi. (See Section I.)

Planes fly from Athens to Larissa on Mondays, Tuesdays, Thursdays and Saturdays and cost $9.60 one way, $17.25 return. (Olympic Airways.)

Buses run five times a day from Athens to Trikala and cost $3.35 one way, $6 round trip. There are eleven buses a day from Trikala to Meteora that cost 40 cents one way, 75 cents round trip.

Private transportation. Taxis can be hired either in Larissa or Trikala for the trip to Meteora. (See Section I for rates.)

METEORA HOTELS (at Kalabaka)

Prices without meals: $4.20 single, $5.30 double.

Category	Name
A ** (R)	Divani (swimming pool)
A ** (R)	Xenia

SIGHTS ON THE WAY

Delphi is one of the usual, principal sites from which to continue on to Meteora. From Delphi, retrace your steps to

Levadia and from there go to Lamia by way of Thermopylae, where Mount Kallidromion, in ancient times, came down to the sea to form the pass defended by three hundred Spartans against the Persian army. River silt has since widened this passage, which could no longer be held by so few men. The drive is beautiful to Lamia, from where you proceed for about 36 kilometers north to Domokos, the ancient city of Thaumakoi, that affords a marvelous view of the plain of Thessaly into which the road descends.

Once on the plain, you can go to Larissa through this agricultural heartland of Greece, and from Larissa west to Trikala, or you can drive direct from Domokos to Trikala along a road that skirts the plain of Thessaly to the west.

Trikala is built on the site of a temple to Asclepius and from this region came the most renowned ancient horsemen who developed that breed of horses depicted on friezes of the Parthenon. From Trikala the road is very straight and lined with trees until Kalabaka (or Kalambaka, depending on the map you have), a small town at the foot of the Meteora, which stand out at a great distance—stark crags like coarse pillars raised by a race of giants.

WHAT TO DO AND SEE

The setting is extraordinary, dominated by the gray, granite rocks themselves, among the most forbidding works of nature in the world. Nothing grows on them. Human beings, seeking refuge from the vanity of the world, and communion with God, brought life to these pillars. Hermits began inhabiting the caves in the eleventh century and by the fourteenth century monks living in monasteries at the foot of these gaunt rocks started to build on the summits to avoid the destruction that every passing marauder brought.

The most famous of these monks, St. Athanasius, built the Monastery of the Metamorphosis (Transfiguration) and the Monastery of the Panaghia on the crag called Platys Lithos, or "broad rock," which he renamed Meteoron. Meteor is the same word, but these crags were no visitors from outer space; they acquired their shape at the bottom of a prehistoric sea in the distant millennia, before the dinosaurs.

Since the monks sought shelter against incursion, they never built paths to the top of the crags. They themselves and all the material for their extensive buildings were laboriously hauled in baskets up the cliffs.

Eventually twenty-four monasteries flourished on these natural pillars, forming a privileged autonomous, monastic town, and owning a great deal of property in the plain below. As the number of monks grew, religious vocation diminished and internecine feuds began. About A.D. 1550 following several Turkish attacks, the monasteries began to decline, monks steadily left their retreat and the Meteora lost their luster. By the eighteenth century the Meteora had become a sort of religious penal colony to which priests and monks were banished by the church hierarchy.

Only five monasteries still function. Principal among these is the Monastery of the Transfiguration, over 1800 feet above sea level. This is inhabited and its feast day is April 20. Its church, an important Byzantine relic, has a twelve-sided dome, excellent murals and some fine portraits of St. Athanasius. There are extensive remains of the old monstery, especially the refectory with its round abbot's dining table, and the library is particularly rich.

On another crag is the Monastery of Varlaam. Fine murals adorn the main church of All Saints and the little chapel of the Three Hierarchs. Perched on another crag are the Monastery of St. Stephen, which has good murals, and the three-domed Church of St. Charalambos with its marvelous altar carvings, bishop's throne and psalter stands. A great deal of mother-of-pearl is used for decoration.

The Monastery of the Holy Trinity stands on a crag which can be reached by a winding staircase (140 steps). Part way up is the Chapel of St. John the Baptist which contains fine icons by Nikodemos, one of the more celebrated artists of the Greek medieval church. On yet another crag stands the Convent of Rasani, with a church that boasts some excellent murals.

The view from each of the crags is superb on a clear day, with the broad plain stretching from the sparkling sea to the cloud cover of Mount Olympus. To the west, the mountains that form the spine of Greece cradle close to the Meteora, brooding, cut with gorges, pierced with caves, stretching layer after layer and turning darker with the distance.

It would be much too tiring to attempt the return journey the same day. The small town of Kalabaka at the foot of the Meteora has perfectly adequate hotels and you might enjoy a stroll through its little streets.

MOUNT ATHOS

HOW TO GET THERE

Take the bus from Salonica to Ierissos (5 hours) then a boat to Daphni, the port for Karyes, capital of Mount Athos (2 hours). In this case I would recommend *prepackaged tours* as the simplest way to visit the holy mountain. See Section I.

Buses run three times a day from Salonica to Ierissos and cost $1.60 each way.

Boats run twice a day from Ierissos to Daphni and cost $1 or less each way.

Private transportation. A taxi from Salonica to Ierissos and back, with a considerable wait, costs about $29. Cars with or without drivers can be hired in Salonica for the trip. At Ierissos you can hire a motorboat to take you around Mount Athos for $9 per day. You will have to sleep ashore in monasteries and provide your own food.

MOUNT ATHOS HOTELS (at Ierissos)

Prices without meals: $0.65 single, $1.00 double.

Category	Name
E	Acanthos
E	Acrogiali
E	Athos

MOUNT ATHOS HOTELS (at Ouranoupolis)

Prices without meals: $4.22 single, $5.50 double.

B ** (R)	Xenia

FORMALITIES FOR ENTERING

For a permit to visit the monasteries of Mount Athos, apply either to the Ministry of Foreign Affairs, Church Department, Athens; the Ministry for Northern Greece, Church Department, Salonica, or to offices of the National Tourist Organization Offices of Greece (see page 340) which will arrange your permit. If you land by yacht at Ouranoupolis, the manager of the Xenia Hotel there will undertake to get you a permit. If you want to stay at any of the monasteries, apply to the Holy Community at Karyes, the capital of Mount Athos. They will give you a Diamonitirion—a letter of recommendation—your pass for four days' hospitality at the monasteries of the holy mountain. Women may not enter the peninsula, and while their husbands are doing so the wives may sun themselves on the beaches or pass the time at one of the hotels.

SIGHTS ON THE WAY

You drive from Salonica through Stagira, the birthplace of Aristotle. The ruins are not particularly impressive but you might wish to stop.

At Ierissos, before entering Mount Athos, you will have to show the papers you have obtained permitting you to visit the peninsula. I would then get to the monasteries by motorboat rather than on foot or by mule. The sea trip along the coast is enchanting and the gay blue water will serve to remind you as you pass through the stern monastic institutions that Greece can laugh as well as worship.

WHAT TO DO AND SEE

This whole thin peninsula, stretching out into the blue Aegean and ending in the tall conical peak called Athos, is of the stuff that legends are made. The ancients believed that the giant Atho threw an enormous stone at Poseidon, the sea god, in a brawl, and the stone became Mount Athos. Later, in trying to round this promontory, the Persian fleet was destroyed during an enormous storm. When Xerxes reassembled his fleet for a second assault on Greece he cut a canal at the narrowest part of the Athos peninsula, near Ierissos, to avoid having to navigate the point.

The Christian history of Athos also begins with a legend. After the crucifixion, Mary, Mother of Jesus, set sail for Cyprus with St. John, but a tempest carried them off course all the way to Athos, where they anchored close to an ancient shrine dedicated to the god Apollo. When Mary stepped ashore, Apollo's statue shattered into pieces. The Holy Virgin rested awhile and before re-embarking, blessed the mountain and made it holy, declaring it her own garden and forbidden to all other women, which is why no females are allowed there to this day.

Athos became a great refuge for hermits, until in the tenth century the tremendous first monasteries were built. By the sixteenth century there were forty monasteries and nearly forty thousand monks from all nations of the Greek Orthodox faith—Serbs, Bulgarians, Russians, Greeks of Asia Minor, etc.

The monasteries flourished between the sixteenth and nineteenth centuries and during that period the harshness of their life eased; certain monasteries began to allow meat at table, while the monks' cells became a little more comfortable than before.

The Turks left Mount Athos alone and it became the intellectual center of the Orthodox world, with many schools, art workshops and extensive libraries. The Greek army took Mount Athos in 1912 and from 1920 it has been the only monastic state in Europe, a self-governing theocratic democracy, protected by Greece and governed by the Holy Community, a council with twenty members. Greece is represented by a governor whose seat is at Karyes where the Holy Community meets.

The monasteries have now lost the properties they once owned outside the peninsula. Nevertheless, the magnificence of their setting remains. The three thousand or so monks still on Mount Athos maintain this considerable relic of the past with its twenty important monasteries that are veritable museums, treasure houses of murals, manuscripts, holy vessels and vestments of surpassing artistic value and beauty. Entering Mount Athos is like stepping back into medieval Byzantium.

You must begin your visit at Karyes, the capital of Athos. It has some old cook-houses, some dark and mysterious workshops, narrow cobble paths between the buildings, all very old except for the government building. Don't miss the fine old Church of Protato, which means the Church of the First, built in the tenth century as a basilica without a dome. It has beautiful murals painted by Panselinos, the leading artist of the Macedonian School. You can see some of his works in the "Lead Church" about thirty minutes on foot from Karyes, a little chapel with a lead roof standing in a tiny valley surrounded by wooded hills.

If you want to spend the night in Mount Athos you should try to stay at the Monastery of Koutloumousiou, which is near Karyes. This is as comfortable as you can get on Athos;

standards are very low on the holy mountain, with no plumbing—a deterrent to some.

Unless you plan to spend a considerable amount of time studying the incomparable treasures of this holy mountain, go to Daphni, the little port near Karyes, and complete the tour of the mountain by boat. There are some monasteries you must not miss. The oldest and richest is Lavra, at the southeast tip of the peninsula. Founded in A.D. 963 by a monk who enjoyed the protection of Emperor Nikiforos Fokas of Byzantium it was the most powerful of all the monasteries.

There are some splendid murals by the Cretan monk Theophanis whose painting is not traditional Byzantine—his coloring is brighter and his ornamentation extremely rich. The Chapel of St. Nicholas has some of the most beautiful murals of the post-Byzantine era, painted by Catelanos, a very fine artist. The refectory is a wonderful room in the shape of a crucifix and has twenty-four marble tables. The walls are covered with some of Theophanis' best compositions. The Lavra library is the richest of all those on Mount Athos, containing many very rare books and scrolls. There is also a fine collection of holy vessels.

From Lavra you will proceed up the east coast to the Monastery of Iviron. This too was founded in the tenth century and was once very rich, acting in the eighteenth century as a banker, lending money to other monasteries. It burned in 1865 and was rebuilt immediately with enormous walls that make it look like a colossal castle. It has some marvelous painting by Theophanis and its main chapel is the most beautiful on Mount Athos, a gem of Byzantine art with a lead roof, four domes and a multicolored marble floor with a fine Byzantine mosaic centerpiece. It has a magnificent library containing fifteen thousand rare books.

Finally, you should visit the Monastery of Vatopedion, a sort of medieval village of every style from Byzantine to Renaissance, with turrets and domes and steeples—all surrounded by high walls. Its principal church is astonishingly rich.

SECTION III

LESS WELL-KNOWN
PARTS OF GREECE

Places to discover

INTRODUCTION

There are just so many superlatives with which to describe the delights of Greece. Sir Compton MacKenzie, in his latest book, *Greece in My Life*, says that most places in Greece are so very beautiful they defy description. Nearly everywhere the sea is bluer, clearer, gentler, than anywhere else; the mountains, range after range, change color with the sun hourly; each region, each village, each little valley is a distinct world, with people whose charming local differences are a constant source of stimulation.

In this section I describe those places which do not come under the general heading of The Classical Landscape. These are neither the best known, nor the richest in archaeological or Byzantine interest, nor often well endowed with hotels, restaurants and other establishments that the traveler looks for. Nevertheless, they are worth visiting. They will most reward those who are prepared to put up with some shortcomings in order to sample the charms of less frequented places.

I will not go into long descriptions of these places, nor will I give you very much history, since it is connected with the history of Greece as a whole. Instead you will get the essentials: How to get there; hotels; plus a little on what to see and do. Most of the locations in this section I would classify as retreats where you are bound to discover something you might make your own.

IONIAN ISLANDS

HOW TO GET THERE

Cephalonia and Ithaca. Take the bus from Athens to Patras (5 hours). The bus boards a ferry to Cephalonia (3 to 4 hours) and continues to Ithaca (another 1½ hours). There are two buses daily from Athens, costing $4.75 one way, $7.80 round trip.

Zakinthos. Take the bus from Athens through Patras to Kyllini (6 hours). The bus boards the ferry to Zakinthos (2 hours). There are two buses daily from Athens, costing $5.30 each way.

IONIAN ISLANDS HOTELS

Prices without meals: Category B, $3.00 single, $4.35 double; Category C, $2.48 single, $3.22 double.

Address	Category		Name
Cephalonia	B *	(R)	Xenia
"	C	(R)	Aigli
"	C *		Ainos
"	C	(R)	Armonia
"	C *	(R)	Tourist
Zakinthos	B *	(R)	Xenia
"	C		Phoenix

Rooms are available in private houses. For bookings, see page 16.

CEPHALONIA

The ferry boat from Patras puts into the harbor of Sami on the east coast of the island, in the strait between Cephalonia and Odysseus' other island, Ithaca. This strait safe from all weather was the source of Odysseus' fortune, for small merchantmen wishing to use this passage had to pay tribute or be despoiled. Homer called Odysseus' followers Cephalonians, not Ithacans, and Cephalonia claims Odysseus as a native son.

Cephalonia furnished Venice with stately firs for her war galleys and firs still crown the principal mountain of the island. From Sami you drive over a mountain pass toward Argostoli, the capital, on the southwestern corner. The road twines between strawberry trees and thyme, whose perfume is supposed to be stronger here than anywhere else on earth. Stop at the pass to view the plain of Argostoli and its fjord, dark blue in the shade of the peaks. On the drive you will see that Cephalonians do not plant trees lightly. First they climb the hillock to survey the land, then they consult others at the café. Where would a new tree best enhance the view? And baby trees are not planted only for the pleasure they give, but to add to the dowry of the farmer's daughters.

There isn't much to see in the way of ruins, one or two minor pre-Mycenaean ruins only. Most of the fine churches were destroyed in the 1953 earthquake that shook the Ionian islands (except Corfu). However, those churches that have been rebuilt display splendid icons salvaged from the quake. In particular you should visit the village of Kaligata whose altar screen with its fine paintings is the pride of the island.

Cephalonia is a place where you mainly swim, skin dive, do a little fishing and roam the tavernas to have the lovely local wines and excellent seafood. There is an excellent wine called Robola, the ancestor of sherry, and Mavrodaphni, which is sold at the Tavern of Demosthenes near the main square of Argostoli and is a rich red wine resembling the best Pommard. Unfortunately less than an acre is now devoted to the grape which produces Mavrodaphni, so this may be your last chance to taste a wine that once was celebrated thoughout Europe and immortalized by Stendhal in *The Red and the Black*.

In the evenings go to the main square where you will find the rest of Argostoli sitting at café tables or strolling around, unless it is Sunday night when the local band plays.

This island was once magnificent with a high degree of civic pride and civilization, but now Cephalonia, which boasts a number of rich shipowners, is chiefly an island that exports talent to the rest of Greece.

ITHACA

This is the legendary island of Odysseus, just off Cephalonia, and is really two mountains connected by a narrow neck about seven hundred yards wide. The coast is indented by gulfs and little fjords and there are any number of tiny uninhabited islets all around. This is a marvelous place for relaxing, swimming, fishing and shooting in the proper season. The municipal museum, though small, contains a fairly interesting collection of Mycenaean vases.

You can visit an old acropolis about 5 kilometers from the town on the site of old Alalkomenae, dating from the seventh century B.C.

ZAKINTHOS

The Venetians called this island the Flower of the Levant, and it is indeed most beautiful, evoking praise from all who ever visited it, including Edgar Allan Poe. Like Corfu and the other Ionian islands, it passed through the usual hands—from Saracen to Byzantine rule to Venetian domination to French, then British rule until finally in 1864 these islands were returned to Greece by the British government.

An island for relaxation, swimming and sailing. There are few ruins here.

NAUPACTUS

HOW TO GET THERE

Take the daily bus from Athens. This is a six-hour trip, via the Rion ferry, and costs $3.10 one way, $5.10 return.

NAUPACTUS HOTELS

Prices without meals: Category C, $1.72 single, $2.60 double. Category D, $1.00 single, $1.70 double.

Category	Name
C	Rex
D	Nea Hellas

WHAT TO SEE

In the Gulf of Corinth, opposite Patras, is Naupactus, known in the Middle Ages as Lepanto. This historic city was given by Athens to the Messenians, the vassals of Sparta, who revolted against their masters and fought so long and so well that they escaped the usual slaughter visited upon rebels by the Spartans. Naupactus was a stronghold of Athenian power during the Peloponnesian war between 431 and 404 B.C. and was used as a base of operations against Sparta.

In the waters off this picturesque little town, Cervantes, author of *Don Quixote*, lost his arm in 1571 in the famed sea battle which broke the Turkish drive toward Europe.

The harbor is enchanting, flanked by fortresses on either

side of its entrance. A fine castle dominates the town, photo-genic medieval narrow streets wind around walled gardens that are a riot of blooms. Nearby there are fine beaches, lovely brooks, majestic plane trees and well preserved homes of several great families who shed their blood for Greece's independence in the last century.

PYLUS

HOW TO GET THERE

Fly from Athens to Kalamai (55 minutes) and then take the bus to Pylus (80 minutes).

Planes fly from Athens to Kalamai on Mondays, Wednesdays and Saturdays, and cost $8.25 one way, $14.85 return.

Buses run from Kalamai to Pylus six times a day and cost 67 cents one way, $1.20 return.

PYLUS HOTELS

Prices without meals: Category B, $3.22 single, $4.03 double; Category D, $1.00 single, $1.50 double.

Category	Name
B * (R)	Xenia
D	Navarinon
D	Trion Navarchon

WHAT TO SEE

This charming little town on the shores of Navarino Bay was built by the French after the combined fleets of France, Russia and Britain destroyed the Turkish navy in the bay in 1828 and thus secured Greece's independence. A small museum contains some mementoes of this battle. There is also a pleasant little Byzantine church nearby. But the principal reason for visiting Pylus is to take the 10 kilometer journey by bus or car to old Pylus, the legendary home of Nestor, the sage of the Greeks during the Trojan wars.

In ancient times it was a place of considerable importance and Nestor's palace was as fine and wealthy as Agamemnon's at Mycenae. This was established during excavations in 1939 led by Professor Carl W. Blegen of the University of Cincinnati.

The palace is a huge rectangle, divided like the Minoan palace at Knossos in Crete into endless pantries, rooms, halls and corridors. It also has queen's apartments, bathrooms with intricate drainage systems and tubs, and grand staircases to the upper floors. The great hall or throne room was surrounded by a sort of minstrel's gallery where the ladies sat. A large circular, decorated hearth was found in the throne room, where presumably slices of bulls' thighs wrapped in fat were roasted when Nestor gave one of his huge parties—in one pantry alone over 2800 drinking cups were found! Fragments of terracotta chimney pots to carry off the smoke have also been discovered.

One of the most important finds during the digs was an archive room. In this were over a thousand clay tablets, fragments inscribed with the famous script known as Linear B. These were the first to be found on the Greek mainland and prove that the Greeks had a written language as early as 1300 B.C. The script was deciphered in 1952 and the tablets were shown to list inventories of stores, wheat, olive oil, fish, etc., as well as accounts of work to be done and goods to be supplied to the palace. The palace was eventually destroyed by fire and the site was never again occupied so that the outline of the original structure has not been confused by remains of later buildings as at Mycenae and Tiryns.

In the neighborhood of the palace, many tombs were discovered and some excavated. They contained swords with ivory handles, fragments of gold leaf, small objects of art and other funerary offerings. Skulls have been found that could be those of Homer's heroes.

MONEMVASIA

HOW TO GET THERE

Buses run once a day from Sparta, take 2½ hours, and cost $1.30 one way, $2.30 return. Inquire locally in Sparta.

HOTELS

There are no hotels at Monemvasia, but village rooms can be rented.

WHAT TO DO

Monemvasia was known as Malmsey to Shakespeare, who wrote that Richard III of England drowned one of his brothers in a butt of Malmsey wine.

Monemvasia is a wild rock sprouting from the sea just off the southeastern tip of the Peloponnesus. King Minos of Crete had a naval base there and Monemvasia was used as a stronghold throughout history, especially by the Byzantines who gave it some very fine fortifications and the magnificent Church of St. Sophia, built by the Emperor Andronicus II.

The little town itself is more or less as it was in Byzantine days—the only inhabited Byzantine settlement in Greece, in fact. By the shore are tavernas that serve red mullet cooked local style with onions and Malmsey wine. For a dollar you can rent a boat for a whole morning of fine fishing.

CRETE

See page 126, Section II, on how to get there and hotels.

Section II described Heraklion and the neighboring Minoan palaces of Knossos and Phaestos. But these sites by no means exhaust the charms of one of the most remarkable islands in the world.

To visit the western part of Crete, you either go direct to Canea from Athens or drive there from Heraklion along a fine road with marvelous scenery along the towering Mount Ida, on whose slopes is the famous monastery of Arkadi, founded by the Emperor Heraclius in the seventh century. It is today one of the most sacred shrines of Crete, a monument to the island's heroism. It played a major part in successive risings against the Turks and finally on November 7, 1866, when the Turkish army was on the point of taking it, the abbot ordered the monastery blown up, killing both the defenders and three thousand of the enemy. This date is celebrated as the national holiday of Crete.

From Arkadi drive back down toward the coast to the little town of Rethimnon, which is dominated by a ruined fort. Its waterfront is among the most picturesque in Greece and its beach one of the best in the whole Mediterranean. There are minarets, charming narrow medieval streets, some lovely Venetian mansions with fine carved woodwork and grand staircases displaying coats of arms with Latin inscriptions. The paved courtyards are full of flowers, and artisans bent over their workbenches in these old streets remind one of medieval paintings. In what used to be the club of the Venetians, the Loggia, there is now a museum with a respectable collection of statues, inscriptions, mosaics, pots and a particularly fine exhibit of coins.

Carnival week, beginning fifty-six days before Greek Easter, is a particularly spectacular party in Rethimnon and so is the wine festival during the last week of July. Even if people don't get precisely drunk, they become happy enough to dance till dawn.

From Rethimnon continue westward to Canea, the administrative capital of Crete and possibly its most beautiful city, built on the ruins of rich, ancient Cydonia. The city flourished under the Romans who took it in 69 B.C., was totally destroyed in the seventh century A.D. and was rebuilt in 1210 by the Venetians who used to call it the Venice of the East. In 1645 it was taken by the Turks, who improved its fortifications and held it until 1913 when Crete returned to Greece.

The old city is marvelously preserved, an old Venetian world with its castle, splendid medieval streets and fine walled gardens. It has restaurants where you can dance, gay tavernas set on the foothills and along the coast where you will see some good local dancing as the raki begins to warm the Cretan blood.

From Canea, strike south toward the White Mountains and the land of Sfakia, formerly a place of prodigious and famed vendettas. Its people are supposed to be the purest descendants of the old Dorian invaders of 1000 B.C. Many of them are tall and blond and wear national costume which consists of breeches, high boots, embroidered waistcoats and cummerbunds, and, around their heads, black kerchiefs. This wild country was never really conquered by any of the foreigners who took Crete.

Visitors are honored guests and are likely to find themselves inveigled into a feast. The Sfakianoi are polite and will not openly show the contempt they feel if you refuse to drink as hard as they do.

During World War II thousands of British, Australian and New Zealand troops were evacuated from Sfakia village on the south coast of Crete and the Germans never managed to take the region.

East of Heraklion there is more enchanting scenery and there are more ruins from the Minoan period, at Mallia for instance. Then you come to the marvelously exciting plateau of Lasithi and the large nearby cave where Zeus was born. (There is another cave in Crete said to be Zeus's birthplace but no other part of Greece dares claim Zeus, king of the gods, as a native born.)

Eventually you will reach Agios Nikolaos, a charming little port on the truly stupendous Gulf of Merabela. This port was established by the people of Sfakia and should be used as your base of operation while visiting the surrounding countryside. There are some excellent category A beach bungalows near the town. You can drive 18 kilometers to Gournia, a complete Minoan agricultural town, a sort of Pompeii with its small houses, courtyards and tiny streets sufficiently intact to give the visitor an idea of life at the time of the Minotaur. It has a provincial palace, of which very few vestiges remain, but the most interesting sight is the town itself with its homes of various styles, clustered in neighborhoods, amid remains of oil presses and carpentry shops.

Beyond Agios Nikolaos you can visit Sitia on the north coast (from here the roads are poor) and Ierapetra on the south coast. If you are hardy enough, push on to the east coast and the village of Kato Zakro with its astonishing, newly excavated Minoan palace of 150 rooms, ranking in archaeological importance with Knossos and Phaestos. The excavation, under the supervision of the Director of the Athens Acropolis, is being financed by the American benefactors Mr. and Mrs. Leon Pomerance of Great Neck, Long Island. This palace site has no surrounding cultivable valleys; obviously its rulers made their living by straddling the international trading route from Greece to the Middle East. The great bronze saws, the largest yet found on Crete, may be evidence that the settlement exported wood. Elephant tusks imported from Syria have been unearthed, as well as great Cypriot copper ingots.

The central courtyard is 40 by 100 feet. Two of its sides were colonnaded and the main entrance had a façade of finely cut stone. The only objects found on Crete with gold still adhering to them were unearthed here. Sir Arthur Evans, who reconstructed the palace at Knossos, found gold foil and correctly surmised that this was used to cover works of art. Now archaeologists have produced proof for his theory.

DODECANESE ISLANDS (listed alphabetically)

HOW TO GET THERE

A plane goes Mondays and Thursdays to Cos. For the other islands take one of the ships that serve this group, from Piraeus or Rhodes. Schedules vary, so check with the shipping lines indicated after each island. Schooners make interisland trips, but these are not scheduled.

Prepackaged cruises are available to some of these islands. (See Section I.)

Carpathus. Ships leave from Rhodes twice a week, take 6 to 7 hours, and cost $1.67. Inquire locally in Rhodes.

Castellorizo. A ship leaves Rhodes twice a week, takes 6 to 8 hours, and costs $1.50. Inquire locally in Rhodes.

Cos. Ships leave Piraeus daily, except Sundays, take 16 hours, and cost $8.67 to $3.15. (Lagas, Nomikos, Cavounidis, Foustanos, New Epirotiki lines.) The plane leaves Athens on Mondays and Thursdays, takes 85 minutes, and costs $14.17 one way, $25.50 return. (Olympic Airways.)

Kalimnos. Ships leave Piraeus daily, except Tuesday, take 14 hours, and cost from $8.60 to $2.55. (Lagas, Nomikos, Cavounidis, Foustanos, New Epirotiki lines.)

Leros. Ships leave Piraeus three times a week, take 11 to 12 hours, and cost from $8.63 to $3.87. (Lagas, Nomikos, Cavounidis lines.)

Patmos. Ships leave Piraeus three times a week, take 11 to 12 hours, and cost from $8 to $4.25. (Lagas, Nomikos, Cavounidis lines.)

Symi. Ships leave Rhodes Mondays, Wednesdays, Fridays, take 2 hours, and cost 67 cents. Inquire locally in Rhodes.

DODECANESE ISLANDS HOTELS

Prices without meals: Category B, $3.20 single, $4.75 double; Category C, $1.50 single, $2.30 double; Category D, $1.00 single, $1.50 double.

Address	Category	Name
Cos	B * (R)	Xenia
"	C	Zephyros
"	D	Aktaion
"	D	Avra
Kalimnos	C	Myrties
"	C	Thermai
Leros	D	Diethnes
"	D	Siza
Patmos	B *	Dimotikos Xenon

Village rooms can be rented on all islands. For bookings see page 16.

CARPATHUS

Despite its spartan accommodation, Carpathus will reward the visitor. The island is very wooded, full of velvety beaches and picturesque bays. It has many springs with water that tastes as water should: fresh, cold, sparkling and untainted with chlorine. It is inhabited by people who retain the customs of old—their festivals are unspoiled examples of Greek folklore.

Weddings in Carpathus always take place on Sunday and the preceding week is given over to the preparations. On Monday, specialists cut the wood ceremoniously for the bridal feasting and this is followed by a supper that can go on all night. Wednesday is "baking day" after which there is another feast that goes on almost till dawn. On Friday the sheets that form part of the bride's dowry are put on show by girls who must be first-born and not orphans. Saturday is the day of the "slaughterers"—relatives of the lucky couple who kill the live-stock and poultry for the wedding feast. At night a special group called "The Inviters" roams the village streets with guitars and lyres to issue invitations to guests.

On Sunday, music is heard early at the houses of both bride and bridegroom and both families raise flags of multicolored silk to proclaim the start of the ceremonies. Young men sing songs in praise of the bride, composing as they go along.

The church ceremony is followed by an enormous meal and a dance called the Foumistos, really a contest to try the skill and stamina of relatives of the bride and groom, and this lasts till only one person is left standing.

On Monday there is a parody of the wedding with the best man playing the lead and this is followed by more drinking and dancing.

The following Sunday the newlyweds go to church to be blessed and there is one last feast for close relatives. All these operations take place in colorful local costumes.

CASTELLORIZO

This is the southernmost island in Greece and takes its name from its medieval castle built of red stone near the harbor. Almost nothing grows on the arid rock; rain water is thriftily collected in cisterns by each householder. Castellorizo's main income comes from fishing and sponge diving at which the islanders are traditionally successful. There are some rather lovely little churches to visit, but the principal attraction is a fantastic blue grotto, 45 minutes by motorboat from the main harbor, a fairyland of blue stalactites. This is considered the most beautiful grotto in the whole Mediterranean, superior by far to that on Capri. This is yet another of the many Greek islands which you visit to enjoy the seascape, to swim and sunbathe, and to watch people who have retained, unspoiled, their ancient customs.

COS

After Rhodes, Cos is the most developed Dodecanese island for tourists and a considerable fishing center that sends large quantities of seafood to Athens, Piraeus and Salonica. There is a museum whose proudest exhibit is a fine fourth century B.C. statue of Hippocrates, the father of modern medicine and a native son of Cos.

One part of the main city is surrounded by well-preserved medieval walls built during the Crusades. You can visit an excellent palace of the Hospitalers or Knights of the Order of St. John and an early Christian basilica built on the site of an ancient gymnasium where a marvelous mosaic has been unearthed, depicting either gladiators or two people dueling—the experts have not yet decided which. In the city they will show you a plane tree which Hippocrates himself is said to have planted. Four kilometers from the city of Cos are the ruins of a temple to Asclepius, god of medicine. It is similar to that at Epidaurus and was in fact a hospital, an ancient version of a medical research center.

To swim, you walk twenty minutes to Faro, north of the city. This is a superb golden beach with some little restaurants where you can dance at night. There are many beaches around the island, most of them more secluded, but no problem to get to, if you hire a local motorboat.

KALIMNOS

This is the world capital of sponge diving and one of the most picturesque and beautiful islands anywhere. The whole island is house-proud and civic-minded. The buildings are always freshly painted in vivid colors and town and village bristle with church steeples. The people are interested and interesting, speak many languages and are of many and varied educational backgrounds.

There is a characteristic architecture of Kalimnos, almost cubist in design when viewed from the hilltops above; squares and oblongs harmoniously succeed one another, and fit the contours of the landscape. On their homes the islanders use a lot of white and blue. These are the Greek national colors, once vainly forbidden by the Italians who held the island. In the harbor are the decorative Greek boats—Greek fishermen have a compulsion for color. Their boats, pointed at both ends, may have a light blue gunwale, pastel green hull, bright red keel, a vermilion deck and yellow oars—an impossible mixture anywhere but under the bright Greek sun.

You can visit a pleasant, small archaeological museum with statues, statuettes, jewelry, pots and coins. Also the boatyards are particularly interesting; they turn out schooners of up to 200 tons. Swimming, boating and fishing are a delight here.

LEROS

Leros was the naval stronghold of the Italians in World War II. It is a beautiful island with a very good, dry, cool climate. The island suffered extensive damage in World War II but was rebuilt thanks to donations from its emigrant sons in America and Egypt. Fortunately this reconstruction has not changed the characteristic architecture. Carnival is particularly picturesque and involves a great deal of mutual teasing in verse, a custom which prevailed in ancient Athens. The island has lovely beaches and good fishing.

PATMOS

Though charming and full of delightful little beaches, Patmos has a forbidding Biblical landscape, which is very fitting, for here St. John the Divine wrote the Apocalypse. This was the most significant event in the island's history. It became a Christian center with pilgrims coming from far and near to worship at the cave where St. John wrote his inspired text. The most considerable structure on the island is the medieval Monastery of St. John, built like a castle with crenelations. The central shrine is beautifully decorated with a fine carved altar screen and murals, one of which depicts the vision of the Apocalypse. The monastery shelters a golden cross donated by Catherine of Russia, the diamond-studded miter of Patriarch Neofytos VI, many golden holy vessels and priceless ninth century embroideries. The library is a veritable treasure trove of medieval manuscripts, including 325 rare books written on parchment. The rarest of them all, a codex, was stolen by an Englishman in 1803 and is now in Oxford University.

Here again there are marvelous beaches and good fishing. This is another island whose delights await discovery.

SYMI

A tiny island, Symi is blessed by a fine cool climate, and though it lives principally off the sea by sponge diving and fishing, it also has orchards of orange, lemon and olive trees. The proud people of Symi, out of their scanty means, have built many fine homes and delightful churches, especially in Yalos, the main harbor. Here, too, you can see on the government building an inscription which marks the spot where the Axis powers surrendered the Dodecanese to General Gigantes (then Colonel), the commanding officer of the heroic Greek Sacred Regiment, which liberated this island group in the Second World War. If you love boats, don't miss the little boatyard.

EASTERN AEGEAN ISLANDS

(listed alphabetically)

HOW TO GET THERE

Either take the plane to Lemnos, Lesbos, and Samos, or take one of the little ships that serve this island group from Piraeus. Schedules vary, so check with the shipping lines indicated after each island. Schooners make interisland trips, but these are not scheduled.

A *prepackaged tour* goes to Lesbos. See Section I.

Chios. Ships leave Piraeus daily except Sundays, take 12 hours, and cost from $7.80 to $2.20. (Typaldos, Nomikos lines.)

Lemnos. Ships leave Piraeus twice a week, take 24 hours, and cost from $8.35 to $3.17. (Nomikos, Typaldos lines.) A plane flies from Athens daily, takes 70 minutes and costs $11.40 one way, $20.55 return. (Olympic Airways.)

Lesbos. Ships leave Piraeus daily, take 16 hours, and cost from $9 to $3. (Typaldos, Nomikos lines.) A plane flies from Athens daily, takes 80 minutes and costs $12.80 one way, $23 return. (Olympic Airways.)

Samos. Ships leave Piraeus daily, except Sunday, take 15 to 16 hours, and cost $8.60 to $2.65. (Foustanos, Lakoniki Nomikos lines.) A plane flies from Athens on Mondays, Wednesdays and Fridays, takes 80 minutes and costs $12.85 one way, $23.10 return. (Olympic Airways.)

Eastern Aegean Islands Hotels

Prices without meals: Category A, $4.50 single, $6.00 double; Category B, $3.45 single, $4.30 double; Category C, $1.73 single, $2.75 double; Category D, $1.00 single, $1.50 double.

Address	Category			Name
Chios	B	*	(R)	Xenia
"	C			Aktaion
Lemnos	A	**	(R)	Akti Myrinis
"	C			Lemnos
Lesbos	B	*	(R)	Lesvion
Lesbos (Mithymna)	B	*	(R)	Delfinia I
Lesbos (Sigri)	B	*	(R)	Delfinia III
Lesbos (Eressos)	C		(R)	Delfinia II
Lesbos	C	*	(R)	Sappho
Samos	B	*	(R)	Xenia

Village rooms can be rented on all islands. For bookings see page 16.

CHIOS

Chios, an island just off the Turkish coast, is another of the places which I would recommend as a retreat for swimming, fishing and sailing. The new capital city is built on the site of an ancient town but no vestiges have yet been unearthed.

The word *chios* is Phoenician and means masticha—a chewing gum from the local masticha trees. Chiots, who were great merchants, bartered masticha for goods from Phoenicia. Their age of glory came during the sixth century B.C. when they produced the historian Theopompos, the poet Ion, and two Stoic philosophers, Theocritus and Ariston. From Chios also came Glaucus, the first sculptor to model successfully in metal. His work was famous throughout the ancient world and adorned temples in Delos, Athens and Delphi.

During the war of independence a Turkish expeditionary force killed all but 30,000 of the island's 100,000 inhabitants. Lord Byron and Victor Hugo wrote about this massacre and the French painter Delacroix commemorated it in a famous painting.

Today you can visit a Byzantine and a Genoese castle. Eight kilometers from the main city is the principal Byzantine structure on the island, a monastery built by Emperor Constantine Monomachos in the eleventh century. The church has mosaics of a superb quality.

You will notice a slight Eastern flavor underlying most of the popular art and folklore of the island.

LEMNOS

According to legend the Argonauts, on their epic journey to fetch the Golden Fleece, stayed here three years, increasing the island's population by many offspring. So fond did the Argonauts become of the beautiful Lemnos girls that Hercules—who alone remained on board ship throughout the lengthy stopover—was anxious lest they forget their mission completely. Here, too, Hephaistos (whom the Romans called Vulcan), the divine blacksmith-husband of Aphrodite and patron saint of artisans, was supposed to have his forge.

Another island legend is that the women of Lemnos once ceased their worship of Aphrodite who in punishment afflicted them with a frightful smell. Their husbands, in disgust, turned to slave girls from Thrace. The island's women became so incensed at this that, one bloody night, they slaughtered every man on the island.

In historical times Lemnos was always an ally of Athens, so Sparta destroyed the island. There followed the historical pattern of most other Greek islands—Roman conquest, Byzantine rule, a takeover by the Crusaders, Turkish domination and finally, in 1912, reunion with independent Greece.

The island is delightful, with some interesting ruins on the north and east coasts, excellent beaches within easy reach of the capital, Mirini, and some medicinal springs said to be good for rheumatism, stomach ailments, and gynecological troubles—quite a range.

The enormous bay of Moudros, an important allied naval base in World War I, is marvelous for quiet sailing.

LESBOS

Also known as Mytilene, this is a mountainous, fertile island in the north Aegean, just off the Asia Minor coast. According to the legend, the severed head of Orpheus floated here after it had been tossed into the Hebrus River by the Maenads. His lyre also was washed ashore, but at the request of Apollo and the Muses it was transferred to the heavens where it formed the constellation Lyra.

Lesbos was a member of the Confederacy of Delos under the Athenians but revolted in 428 B.C. The Athenians, who subdued the rebellion, voted in their assembly to put the entire island's adult male population to death and sell the women and children into slavery, and a ship bearing this order was dispatched to the island. The day after the vote was taken, however, a reaction set in, the vote was rescinded and a second ship—which was promised a large reward if it overtook the first—set sail from Athens to countermand the terrible order.

The second ship arrived at the island at the same time as the first. Only the revolutionary ringleaders were executed. The Athenians then took over the Lesbian fleet, pulled down the city walls, but spared the population. Eventually the

Romans came, followed by the Byzantines, the Crusaders, the Byzantines again and finally the Turks.

The poet Sappho came from Lesbos, and love between women has been called "lesbian" since she wrote about it. The musician Terpander, the poets Lesches and Arion, and the philosophers Theophrastus and Cratippus were from the same island.

Today it is known for its excellent olive oil and fine soaps. It boasts a petrified forest and some medicinal springs. There are few ruins, although systematic archaeological digs have yet to begin here.

Principally, Lesbos is a place for long, lazy days on the marvelous beaches, one of which, 54 kilometers from the main city, at a place called Vatera, is 8 kilometers long. Also the island has delightful folklore, lovely costumes, gay dances, indigenous popular music and some fine local painters. Here and there you will see some of the talented primitives of the late Theophilos, a fey gentleman who wore an ancient Greek helmet, a kilt and carried a large curved sword as he wandered from village to village painting murals in tavernas in exchange for food.

SAMOS

Famous for its wine, this is a lovely island with a marvelous climate—mild in winter and cool in summer. It has imposing, forested mountains which extend right down to the shore and it produces oranges and fine grapes. Whole hillsides are planted with beautiful almond trees and when they blossom in spring the island is like a garden.

From Samos came Pythagoras, the famous philosopher and mathematician, and Aristarchus, another great mathematician. Its most famous ruler was Polycrates, patron of the arts who sheltered Anacreon, the poet, in his court. Polycrates turned Samos into a great naval power, trading throughout the Mediterranean. The fleet was not above piracy and plunder and it made Samos enormously wealthy. The Athenians could not tolerate a possible challenge to their supremacy and under Pericles they conquered Samos.

Thereafter, little was heard about this island, even in the Middle Ages. But it had its moments of glory during the Greek war of independence. It has few remnants of its past, but its villages, little towns, tavernas and beaches are delightful and its people are among the most hospitable and pleasant in Greece. You will drink the local wine in quantity, with no regrets the next morning.

ALEXANDROUPOLIS AND SAMOTHRACE

HOW TO GET THERE

Fly from Athens to Alexandroupolis (1¾ hours), then take a schooner to Samothrace (3 hours). A ship leaves Athens for Samothrace every Monday and returns on Tuesday.

Prepackaged tours are available and are listed in Section I.

Planes leave daily from Athens to Alexandroupolis and cost $16.33 one way, $29.33 return. (Olympic Airways.)

Schooner passage costs less than a dollar.

Ships from Piraeus to Samothrace cost $14.90 first class, $4.25 deck. (Typaldos Lines.)

ALEXANDROUPOLIS-SAMOTHRACE HOTELS

Prices without meals: Category A, $4.00 single, $5.25 double; Category C, $1.90 single, $2.69 double.

Address	Category	Name
Alexandroupolis	A ** (R)	Astir
"	C ** (R)	Olympion
"	C	Tourist Hotel
Samothrace	C	Xenia

Village rooms can be rented on Samothrace. For bookings see page 16.

ALEXANDROUPOLIS AND THE ISLAND OF SAMOTHRACE

If you decide to spend some time in Alexandroupolis, it will prove one of the least expensive places you have ever visited. It has a lovely beach, offers a fine local caviar, very good cloth and carpets. The waters round about are particularly rewarding for underwater exploration. But above all, Alexandroupolis is the place from which to visit Samothrace, 22 nautical miles away.

Samothrace has long been considered one of the most beautiful, peaceful places on earth and was favored by the ancients as a honeymoon retreat. It was also famed in ancient times for its excellent food, particularly its cheeses, some of which can be sampled to this day.

Homer says that Poseidon climbed the highest peak in Samothrace (1600 meters) to observe the battle between the Greeks and Trojans. Later, the island was the home of the mysteries of Cabiri, mysteries that eventually rivaled those of Eleusis. It was on Samothrace that Philip of Macedonia met Olympias, whom he married and who bore him Alexander the Great.

Perseus, the last king of the Macedonian line, fled to Samothrace after his defeat by the Romans. He sought refuge in the sanctuary where he was trapped and taken prisoner.

On the island, which was still held by Turkey in 1863, the French found and carried off that superb statue, the Victory of Samothrace, which now dominates the grand staircase of the Louvre in Paris. The island has ruins of a sixth century B.C. temple, traces of a later temple, a few rows of seats from an ancient theater, and traces of the central area of the sanctuary uncovered in 1939 by a New York University archaeological expedition headed by Carl Lehman.

KAVALLA AND THASOS

HOW TO GET THERE

Fly from Athens to Kavalla (95 minutes) then take a small boat or ferry to Thasos (45 minutes).

Prepackaged tours are available and are listed in Section I.

Planes leave Athens daily for Kavalla and cost $14.25 one way, $25.65 return. (Olympic Airways.)

Ships. There are several small ships or ferries daily from Kavalla that cost fifty cents per person. Inquire at the harbor master's office in Kavalla.

KAVALLA AND THASOS HOTELS

Prices without meals: Category B, $4.68 single, $6.50 double; Category C, $1.88 single, $3.38 double; Category D, $1.38 single, $2.02 double.

Location	Category	Name
Kavalla	B ** (R)	Astir
Thasos		
(Makryammos)	B ** (R)	Xenia
Thasos	B * (R)	Xenia
(Limin)		
"	C	Palladion
"	C	Theano
Thasos		
(Limenaria)	D	Panellinion

Village rooms can be rented on Thasos. For bookings see page 16.

KAVALLA AND THE ISLAND OF THASOS

Kavalla, built on the site of old Neapolis, is the port of ancient Philippi, where Octavian and Marc Antony defeated Brutus and Cassius. St. Paul founded a church here and it was to Philippian converts that he addressed one of his Epistles. Today Kavalla, with its large harbor, is an important center for Greece's tobacco industry, and it is a good place from which to visit Thasos, just 16 nautical miles away.

Thasos is a beautiful island, unusually green for Greece with trees that grow almost on the beaches and branches that edge over the water. It has many small coves for swimming and secluded little valleys to explore. It has, moreover, an entire ancient city with substantial fortifications that stand to this day. Here you can see a fine theater of the Hellenistic period, the foundations of a fifth century B.C. temple to Apollo, the remains of two altars at the ruins of a shrine to Poseidon, a huge altar to Hera, wife of Zeus, and the remains of a shrine to Dionysus and Hercules.

The museum on Thasos contains numerous statues, including that of a smiling youth (*kouros*) carrying a ram; a fine girl's head dating from 530 B.C.; part of a statue of Pegasus and a magnificent model of the head of a horse.

The restaurants offer very good seafood. The specialty, if you care to try it, is baked octopus.

SALONICA

HOW TO GET THERE

You can go from Athens to Salonica by bus (7 hours), by train (8 hours), or by plane (65 minutes).

Buses run five times a day from Athens, cost $6.63 one way, $11.83 return.

Trains run several times a day from Athens, cost $10.87 first class, $7.25 third class.

Planes fly daily from Athens and cost $12.85 one way, $23.10 return. (Olympic Airways.)

PELLA: HOW TO GET THERE

Buses run hourly from Salonica, take one hour, and cost 52 cents one way, 93 cents return.

Local tours in and around Salonica are available. Inquire locally in Salonica.

SALONICA HOTELS

Prices without meals: Category AA, $6.95 single, $10.00 double; Category B, $3.65 double; Category C, $2.00 single, $3.00 double.

Category	Name	Address
AA ** (R)	Mediterranean Palace	11 King Constantine Ave.
B ** (R)	Elissavet Motel	171 Monastiriou Street
B * (R)	Pella	65 Dragoumi Street
C	Ariston	5 Lloyd George Street
C	Excelsior	10 Kominon Street
C	Louxemvourgon	8 Kominon Street
C	Minerva	12 Syngrou Street
C * (R)	Rex	9 Monastiriou Street
C	Tourist	15 Mitropoleos Street

WHAT TO SEE

For more Byzantine treasures, after those of the Meteora and Mount Athos, you should visit Salonica (called Thessaloniki by Greeks), the capital of Macedonia in northern Greece, built near the site of Pella, the ancient capital of Philip of Macedonia and his son Alexander the Great, who conquered almost the entire known world in the fourth century B.C. Salonica was founded in 316 B.C. by Cassander, brother-in-law of Alexander the Great. Later, under the Romans, it became the region's hub of military power and a flourishing commercial center. Cicero was exiled here in 58 B.C., and Pompey briefly took refuge in the city after his defeat at the hands of Caesar in 49 B.C. Under Constantine the Great (A.D. 306 to 337) Salonica became a metropolis, that is, the seat of an archbishop, and evolved into the second capital of the Byzantine Empire.

It then suffered the same fate as the rest of Greece—it was attacked and looted by Saracens, Venetians, Slavs, the Crusaders and finally by the Turks, from whom the city was retaken in 1912.

It is most remarkable for its churches which show a clear connection between the Byzantines and the ancient Greeks both in architecture and decoration. Prominent among the churches you should visit are:

(1) The Church of St. George, also known as the Rotunda, a Roman building erected around A.D. 390 and converted into a Christian church in the fifth century. Its mosaics are the oldest in Salonica and show strong influence from the Hellenistic period.

(2) The Church of St. Demetrius, a large basilica with five naves. It is said to mark the site of the martyrdom of St. Demetrius, the patron saint of the city. Next to the apse is the small chapel of St. Euthemios, built in A.D. 1303 with a crypt and baptistery. Under the church are Roman baths.

(3) The eighth century Church of St. Sophia is one of the most superb monuments of the city and of all Byzantium. Architecturally it is a transitional building, from the period when churches were evolving from the basilica with dome to the cruciform shape with dome. Built during the reign of Emperor Leo II, it took over forty years to complete. Its ceiling mosaic is remarkably beautiful and, alone, worth a visit to Salonica.

(4) The Church of the Virgin, known as Panaghia Ton Chalkeon, is one of the most elegant and charming Byzantine structures in Salonica. It is cruciform with domes and was founded by St. Christophorus, who is buried in the wall of the church.

These are but a sprinkling of the city's fine Byzantine monuments.

The old city of Salonica has a distinctive Eastern flavor, with narrow winding, cobbled alleys and small patisseries featuring Anatolian specialties. Here, too, you can sample marvelous Oriental dishes. Salonica boasts some fine carpet stores and very good primitive copper work. Salonica's university town is lively and a flourishing seat of learning.

Pella, the capital of Alexander the Great, is 40 kilometers from Salonica and archaeologists are only now digging there in earnest. Already they have revealed that not only was this city powerful, but it was as beautiful as the Latin scholar Titus Livius described. You can see some very fine mosaics and the palace where Alexander was born. This fantastic general was one of the world's great strategic and tactical innovators. The renowned philosopher Aristotle was his tutor and instilled in Alexander great humanitarian principles. He was one of the few conquerors who thought as much of those he conquered as of his own people, and he carried Greek civilization not only to the edge of India, but also throughout Egypt and along the north African coast, penetrating as far south as the desertlands. Wherever he went he left fine cities, nearly all of them named after him.

About 12 kilometers from Salonica there is a delightful little resort area called Panorama, set on pine-covered slopes with pleasant little open-air restaurants. The beaches are good, and here and there along the gulf are fishing villages where you can order excellent broiled seafood.

KASTORIA

HOW TO GET THERE

Either fly to Kozani (1¾ hours) and then take the bus to Kastoria (2¼ hours), or take the bus to Kastoria direct (12 hours).

Planes fly from Athens to Kozani on Tuesdays and Thursdays, cost $13.30 one way, $24 return. (Olympic Airways.)

Buses from Kozani to Kastoria run four times a day, cost $1.17 one way, $2.10 return. Buses from Athens direct to Kastoria run once a day and cost $7.24 one way, $13.33 return.

KASTORIA HOTELS

Prices without meals: Category A, $4.00 single, $5.00 double; Category C, $2.20 single, $3.45 double.

Category	Name
A ** (R)	Hotel Xenia du Lac
C	Akropolis
C * (R)	Keletron
C * (R)	Orestion

WHAT TO SEE

This beautiful city, cradled by imposing mountains, and set on the clear Kastorias Lake in northern Greece is rich in relics of Byzantine glory. The emperors of Constantinople made it a practice to exile potential rivals to Kastoria and these men left not only fine residences, but also churches generously endowed with murals, carvings and vessels of exceptional wealth. The Turks too left their architectural mark, so that you may see, side by side, fine Byzantine and Turkish residences. These houses, large by Greek standards, are medieval in influence with three floors, the first having no windows, and large rooms ranging in style from Arab to Baroque, yet somehow in a harmonious blend.

Its churches include the Agioi Anargyroi, an eleventh century edifice with murals from the eleventh and twelfth centuries; the eleventh century Agioi Taxiarchai, with some murals of the Serbian school; and the Church of the Dormition, or Koimisis Tis Theotokou, which has splendid examples of late Byzantine painting. Kastoria's prize, however, is the Church of Koubelidiki, a small charming building with a dome, whereas all the others are basilicas.

The town is built on a little promontory and water almost surrounds it, giving it a cool, restful atmosphere.

It is the fur-trading capital of Greece, exporting its experts to New York and London, or wherever else fine workmanship is needed.

IOANNINA AND METSOVO

HOW TO GET THERE

Either fly from Athens to Ioannina (95 minutes) or take the bus from Athens (10 hours).

Planes fly from Athens daily, except Sundays, cost $11.17 one way and $20.10 return.

Buses run once a day from Athens and cost $5 one way and $8.85 return. Buses from Ioannina to Metsovo run twice a day, and cost 81 cents one way, $1.44 return. From Athens there is one bus a day direct to Metsovo (11 hours) via Karditsa and Trikala, costing $5.50 one way, $8.90 return.

IOANNINA AND METSOVO HOTELS

Prices without meals: Category A, $3.93 single, $5.45 double; Category C, $3.20 single, $3.99 double; Category E, $0.70 single, $1.00 double.

Location	Category	Name
Ioannina	A ** (R)	Xenia
"	C *	Acropole
"	C *	Palladion
Metsovo	C *	Peripteron
"	E	Betouni
"	E	Foufa
"	E	Korka

WHAT TO SEE

IOANNINA AND DODONI

The fair Ioannina is an inland city with the appearance of a seaside resort, because it rests on the shores of the beautiful Pamvotis Lake with an island that once was the headquarters of the regional Turkish Pasha. You can see the Turkish influence in architecture—a Muslim fortress, mosques, and somber subterranean passages and dungeons on the Turkish Pasha's island residence.

But Greece's earlier history has left traces in the region too. Take the short ride from Ioannina to ancient Dodoni, seat of the oldest Greek oracle dedicated to Zeus. The oracle resided in an oak grove hung with vessels of brass, necessary, it was believed, to make Zeus's voice audible to man. Sometimes, however, Zeus's desires were made known by the rustling of leaves in this sacred grove.

To this day it can be a forbidding place in the winter, blasted by howling winds which must indeed have sounded like the voice of God to those men of old. Hercules and Odysseus came here to learn their fate, and so did the common man who left his question engraved on leaden tablets, some of which have been unearthed. A man called Agis, for example, asks whether his blankets and pillows were lost or stolen. And another, Lyssanias, asks whether the pregnant woman Nyla is carrying his child or someone else's.

The shrine was looted and destroyed in 219 B.C. and though rebuilt it declined steadily in influence. The Byzantines made it into a Christian church.

Just four kilometers from Ioannina is the enormous cave of Perama, one of the finest in the Balkans. It has many chambers and passages, is rich in stalactites, stalagmites, rock pillars and subterranean lakes. You can go nearly a quarter of a mile into the cave along well-kept, illuminated paths.

You can fish on Ioannina's lake, or swim during the warm summer months, and at night there is dancing at several restaurants.

METSOVO

Metsovo is probably the most scenic mountain hamlet in Greece. Throughout its long history it was a stronghold commanding the valleys and the many rivers that have their sources in the surrounding mountains. Its rich sons never forget their place of origin, and have donated pleasing parks and schools to Metsovo, while building for their own pleasure imposing homes, one of which is now a museum for local handicrafts. The little town's Byzantine Monastery of St. Nicholas has beautiful paintings and wood carvings. In the same tradition are the modern carvings of Metsovo's Church of St. Paraskevi whose holy vessels and unique mosaics are particularly ornate.

On July 20 there is a local fair followed six days later by another with feasting and dancing throughout Metsovo. Prizes are given for the best dancing.

But you visit Metsovo principally to be enchanted by its setting and commanding vistas which can be equaled only in the Alps.

VOLOS AND PELION

HOW TO GET THERE

Either fly from Athens to Larissa (70 minutes) and take a bus from Larissa to Volos (80 minutes); or take the bus direct from Athens to Volos (7 hours). From Volos there are numerous buses to various villages on Mount Pelion. (To give you an idea of times and costs, the bus from Volos to Tsangarada on the Aegean takes 90 minutes and costs 65 cents one way, $1.15 return.)

Planes fly from Athens to Larissa on Mondays, Tuesdays, Wednesdays and Saturdays, and cost $9.60 one way, $17.25 return. (Olympic Airways.)

Buses from Larissa to Volos run hourly, cost 81 cents one way, $1.43 return. From Athens to Volos there are four buses a day; they cost $4.33 one way, $7.33 return.

Private transportation. Taxis are available in Larissa or Volos for the trip to Mount Pelion, or you can rent a car, with or without driver.

VOLOS AND PELION HOTELS

Prices without meals: Category B, $4.22 single, $5.50 double; Category C, $1.80 single, $3.00 double.

Location	Category	Name
Volos	B * (R)	Aigli
"	B * (R)	Palace
"	B * (R)	Xenia
"	C * (R)	Avra

Volos	C * (R)	Kypseli
Pelion		
(Ai-Yannis)	C	Aigaion
"	C	Galini
Pelion		
(Tsangarada)	B ** (R)	Xenia
"	C	Hellas
Pelion		
(Portaria)	B ** (R)	Xenia

Village rooms can be rented in the Pelion region. For bookings see page 16.

VOLOS

Volos, the port of Thessaly, and a growing industrial center, is on the site of ancient Iolkos, the home of Jason, who brought to Greece the Golden Fleece.

Recent excavations have uncovered the remains nearby of three palaces of the Mycenaean period, the ruins of houses, household vessels, as well as 700 or so drinking cups of the pregeometric period. The museum of Volos has an excellent and unique collection of ancient tombstones that are painted rather than carved. They have miraculously retained their colors almost intact and are invaluable to the study of ancient techniques in painting. There is also a collection of fossils from about 500,000 B.C., plus ancient statues, statuettes, tools, ornaments and inscriptions.

From Volos you can visit the lovely Mount Pelion, with its beautiful beaches and fine restaurants where you can also dance.

PELION

This long thin mountain forms the Peninsula of Magnesia that protects the Pagassitikos Gulf from the open sea. Pelion's forests and gorges were the home of the mythical centaurs, half men and half horses (probably a primitive race of horse breeders). The most famous centaur was Cheiron who taught Asclepius, god of medicine, the use of herbs to cure the sick.

Today there are twenty-four villages on Pelion that grew almost imperceptibly through the centuries as men from the shores and plains climbed the mountain, taking refuge from foreign incursions and devastation. They eventually built some magnificent old mansions if they were rich, or picturesque flower-covered cottages if they were not, and charming chapels and monasteries with beautiful carved altar screens, set amid the lovely trees of these wooded slopes.

The mountain rises steeply from the sea and has a great many springs whose waters are considered among the finest in Greece.

With its lovely villages down by the blue sea or high up on the green slopes, its freshness and its gentle, civilized, hospitable people, Pelion is one of the prettiest and most welcoming areas of Greece and well worth a visit. It is also an excellent spot for hiking. You will not want to miss the village of Portaria which grew around the thirteenth century Byzantine Monastery of Theotokos Portares. From this village you can hike to the summit of Mount Pelion. The climb will take only one and a half hours, the views are arresting. Just below the peak is a cave said to be the home of Cherion. Another delightful village is Makrynitsa, the former stronghold of Pelion, built on difficult ground. Its old homes are particularly beautiful.

Zagora, one of the largest and richest villages of the region, looks out over the blue Aegean. It is a veritable orchard and has many churches, in particular St. Kyriaki, which has notable frescoes. Zagora was a center of Greek culture during the Turkish occupation and its famed library contains a rare edition of Homer. Rivaling Zagora is Tsangarada which is set in an apple orchard surrounded by a forest of chestnut trees. This too has several fine old churches, the best of which is Agia Trias, with excellent altar screens and frescoes. Then, right on the shore, is the captivating fishing village of Ai-Yannis with its lovely beaches. This is a favorite spot for campers.

If you want to explore Mount Pelion further, visit Milies on the western side of the peninsula. This was a seat of learning in the nineteenth century, with an interesting library still in existence. At the very southern tip of Pelion is the isolated village of Trikeri which communicates with the outside world mainly by motorboat and has thus preserved its native customs and traditions. This is a fine place for studying the folklore of the region as well as for skin diving, swimming and fishing in the beautiful bay.

KAMMENA VOURLA

HOW TO GET THERE

Take one of the nine daily buses from Athens for the 2½-hour journey, which costs $2.33 one way, $3.84 return.

KAMMENA VOURLA HOTELS

Prices without meals: Category A, $4.90 single, $6.90 double; Category B, $4.30 single, $5.90 double; Category C, $3.15 single, $4.03 double.

Category		Name
A *	(R)	Radium
B **	(R)	Galini
B *	(R)	Thronion
B *	(R)	Argo
B *	(R)	Flisvos

WHAT TO DO

This is a neat, manicured little spa with trim lawns, flowers everywhere and hotels which are set against the background of a wild cliff covered with dark green bushes. Here and there you will see the cliff's purple-gray rock which contains the minerals that make the medicinal waters so very effective, according to those who take the waters.

There are no ruins to speak of, as this was a swamp. Eventually it was found that the waters flowing from the cliff above the little town had great curative value for those who suffer from rheumatism or rheumatoid arthritis. There is another source called the Source of Aphrodite which is said to be particularly good for the skin.

You can also have "sand baths," "mud baths" or "air baths," and if you want something less exotic there are inviting sandy beaches nearby with very clear water where you can swim and simply relax. The place is very lush and through the woods nearby there is a walk so well hidden that it is known as "Lovers Lane."

CHALKIS

HOW TO GET THERE

Trains run from Athens five times daily, take 2 hours, and cost $1.60 first class, $1.10 third.

Buses run hourly from Athens, take 90 minutes, and cost $1.16 one way, $1.84 return.

CHALKIS HOTELS

Prices without meals: Category A, $4.75 single, $6.00 double; Category C, $1.80 single, $2.60 double.

Category	Name
A * (R)	Lucy
C	Ethnikon
C	Paliria

WHAT TO SEE

This town straddles the narrow passage between mainland Greece and the island of Euboea, connected at this point by a bridge. Here there is a local "wonder"—an unexplained tide that runs six hours in each direction through the passage, even though Greece has no tides elsewhere. Fishing is particularly good from the bridge and its surroundings. In ancient times Chalkis was a prosperous port, famous also for its skill in working copper, hence its name; *chalkos* means copper in Greek.

It is now a pleasing little town with a fine small archaeological museum and a medieval museum that once was a Turkish mosque. The Church of St. Paraskevi, a very well-known Byzantine basilica, is beautifully decorated.

SPORADES ISLANDS (listed alphabetically)

HOW TO GET THERE

Take the bus from Athens to Chalkis; there, take another bus to Kymi in Euboea (4 hours driving in all). From Kymi a ship sails to Skyros (1¾ hours) then continues to Skopelos (2 hours) and Skiathos (3½ hours).

Prepackaged tours to the Sporades are arranged by the Alcyon Agency, 98 Academias Street, Athens.

Buses run from Athens to Chalkis every hour. From Chalkis to Kymi there are several buses daily. The total trip costs $2.60 each way.

Ships sail from Kymi three times a week and cost from $1.33 first class to $1 tourist each way to Skyros; from $2.33 to $1.66 to Skopelos; and from $4.06 to $3.09 to Skiathos.

Schooners run daily from Kymi to the Sporades; they cost half as much as the ship and take twice as long.

SPORADES ISLANDS HOTELS

Prices without meals: Category B, $3.37 single, $5.06 double; Category C, $1.38 single, $2.07 double; Category D or E, $1.00 single, $1.50 double.

Address	Category	Name
Skiathos	C	Akti
"	D	Avra
"	D	Skiathos
Skyros	B * (R)	Xenia

Skopelos	E	Aktaion
"	E	Ameriki
"	E	Skopelos

THE SPORADES

This group of islands, north of the Cyclades, is full of spreading pines and ferns which frame small chapels, dazzling white houses and ruined castles. The Sporades are famed for their carved furniture and succulent lobsters.

The beaches are glorious. There are excellent spearfishing and skin-diving grounds.

SKIATHOS

This island has, perhaps, the most magnificent beach in the whole Mediterranean. Called Koukounaries, it is an hour and a half by motorboat from the main town on the northwestern tip of the island. Huge pine trees come right down to the beach, and the water, always a pure light blue, is rarely disturbed by a ripple.

SKOPELOS

Skopelos is famous for its fruit and an excellent local wine. Legend holds that the island was first colonized by Stafilus, son of Ariadne and either Theseus or Dionysus—the ancients never were quite sure who the father was.

The women of Skopelos are renowned for their weaving and exquisite embroidery.

In the main town, which is minute, there are 123 churches and chapels, each with its own variation of style and some with delightful murals and miniatures. The island also has twelve convents built during the seventeenth and eighteenth centuries and filled with treasures—skillfully carved altar screens, murals and rich holy vessels.

You may buy lovely pottery from a family called Rodiou which has been making fine vases for generations. They have a little shop at the beach nearest the main town.

SKYROS

The island of Skyros has given its name to the furniture produced in the Sporades. It is also known for its ponies, tasty fish and cheese.

On the hill that dominates the main town is an old acropolis, the best fortified in the whole Aegean in ancient times. It was the stronghold of Lycomedes with whose daughters Achilles hid, dressed as a girl, to avoid "call up" for the Trojan war.

Later Theseus, founder of Athens, is said to have been slain by pirates on the island. Kimon, the elected leader of the Athenians, who preceded Pericles, discovered an outsize tomb on Skyros with the skeleton of a very large man whom the Athenians believed to be Theseus.

The inhabitants of Skyros flock to their festivals and fairs dressed in local costume. They are hailed throughout Greece for their fine embroidery.

CYCLADES ISLANDS (listed alphabetically)

HOW TO GET THERE

Take one of the little ships that serve this island group from Piraeus or its neighboring small ports mentioned below. Schedules vary, so check with the shipping lines indicated after each island. Schooners make interisland trips, but these are not scheduled.

Prepackaged tours are available to some of these islands. (See Section I.)

Amorgos. Ships leave Piraeus twice a week, take from 9 to 21 hours depending on intermediate stops, which are not known in advance, and cost from $8.20 to $2.70. (Cavounidis, Typaldos lines.)

Andros. Take the bus from Athens to Rafina (45 minutes, 40 cents), then the local daily boat which takes 4 hours, and costs from $2.50 to $2.

Ios. Ships leave Piraeus three times a week, take 13 to 14 hours and cost from $7.35 to $2.66. (Lakoniki, Typaldos, Arkadiki, Foustanos lines.)

Kea. Take the bus from Athens to Lavrion (90 minutes, 60 cents) for the local daily boat, which takes 2 hours and costs 60 cents.

Milos. A ship leaves twice a week from Piraeus, takes 10 to 12 hours and costs from $6 to $3.50. (Cavounidis, Typaldos, Lagas lines.)

Naxos. Ships leave Piraeus daily except Sunday, take 8 to 9½ hours and cost from $5.66 to $2. (Foustanos, Lakoniki, Typaldos, Arkadiki, New Epirotiki lines.)

Paros. Ships leave Piraeus daily except Sunday, take 6 to 8 hours and cost from $5 to $2. (Foustanos, Lakoniki, Typaldos, Arkadiki, New Epirotiki lines.)

Santorini. Ships leave Piraeus twice a week, take from 14 to 16 hours and cost from $7.30 to $2.40. (Lakoniki, Typaldos, Arkadiki, Foustanos lines.)

Siphnos. Ships leave Piraeus three times a week, take 8 to 9 hours and cost from $5.15 to $3.12. (Lagas, Typaldos lines.)

Syros. Ships leave Piraeus daily, take 6 hours and cost from $3.70 to $1.70. (Typaldos, Foustanos, Lakoniki, Cavounidis, Nomikos lines.)

Tinos. Ships leave Piraeus daily, take 6 to 8 hours and cost from $5 to $3. (Foustanos, Nomikos, Lagas lines.)

CYCLADES ISLANDS HOTELS

Prices without meals: Category B, $4.00 single, $5.06 double; Category C, $1.60 single, $2.50 double; Category D, $1.00 single, $1.50 double.

Address	Category			Name
Amorgos	C	**	(R)	Micke
Andros	B	**	(R)	Likion
"	B	**	(R)	Xenia
"	C			Aigli
"	C			Avra
Ios	C			Aigli
Kea	B			Tzia Mas
Naxos	C			Apollon
"	D			Dionysos
"	D			Neon
Paros	B	*	(R)	Marpissa Guesthouse
"	B			Naoussa
"	B	*	(R)	Xenia-Meltemi
"	C			Pandrossos
Santorini	B	*	(R)	Atlantis

Siphnos	B ** (R)	Xenia
Syros	B * (R)	Hermes
"	C	Kykladikon
Tinos	C * (R)	Theoxenia
"	B *	Tinion
"	C	Flisvos
"	C	Possidonion

Village rooms can be rented in these islands. For bookings see page 16.

THE CYCLADES

This island group lies in the middle of the Aegean and its foremost islands are Mykonos and Delos. The islands are of all shapes and sizes, remnants of a great island that once linked Europe and Asia. They have been used, since time began, as steppingstones for the passage of men and ideas between these two continents. These tiny specks of land have nearly all had a history quite disproportionate to their size and it is rare indeed that one cannot boast of having given the world a philosopher, sculptor, poet, or some genius whose achievements have enriched us all.

Their history stretches back to the so-called Cycladic civilization which flourished between 3000 and 2000 B.C.

AMORGOS

Amorgos is the easternmost island of the Cyclades, and is dotted with miniature villages and even more miniature churches set among silvery olives, vineyards and almond trees. The cubist character of the Greek island architecture is particularly pure here and seems to have been arranged for the painter or photographer. The main settlement, Katapola, has a beautiful promenade flanked on either side by magnificent sandy beaches and very clear water.

At the bottom of a massive white cliff is a particularly fine monastery called Hozoviotissis, erected according to legend at the precise spot where an icon of the Virgin Mary was washed ashore.

ANDROS

This island was a Phoenician colony, later falling to the Egyptians, to the Cretans and finally to the Ionians. Like the rest of the islands in the Aegean, it was an ally of Athens, and after the population was converted to Christianity the island became a Frankish fiefdom. The Turks took it, and one Turkish sultan made a gift of the island to his favorite, a very rich Jew called Joseph Naze.

There are interesting traces of all these masters of Andros, and its museum has some very fine pieces from the classic and Hellenistic periods, in particular a sculpted woman's head, a head of Bacchus (Dionysus) and a statue of Aphrodite. Then there are many Byzantine churches and chapels to see. The village houses are brightly painted and surrounded with small gardens. Each village also boasts several substantial homes with arched verandas. If you want not only peace and quiet on a beautiful island, but also good eating, Andros is the island you should pick.

IOS

The people of this charming island claim that Homer died here and they will even point out his grave. Though most archaeologists would dispute this, the British Admiralty Mediterranean Pilot continues to mark Homer's grave on this spot. The island has always claimed kinship with Homer and its ancient coins are stamped with his head. This is another unspoiled little island, full of lovely coves, beaches and kindly people.

KEA

This minuscule island has not yet been developed for visitors but it soon should be since it is just 12 nautical miles from Attica. From the sea it looks arid and uninviting, but it actually has many trees, an abundance of springs and productive little valleys where the islanders have market gardens, grow vines and wheat. Its newly imported Swiss cattle have adapted themselves to the island and today are thriving.

The island has a proud history. Its ships fought against the Persians at the naval battles of Artemisium and Salamis. The famous poet Simonides came from this island as did the philosopher Theramenes and the physician Erasistratus.

There are two hundred chapels to explore today, many of them with fine murals, mosaics and icons.

The village of Hora has fifteen fine churches, many windmills and a castle on top of a hill. Wherever you go you will find little coves and beaches you will have to share with no one.

MILOS

The original home of the famous marble Venus (Aphrodite) that adorns the Louvre in Paris, Milos also has the distinction of being the home of the most ancient Aegean civilization, a civilization of which we know little except that it preceded that of Minos. One explanation for its prehistoric prominence was that it produced and exported stones for grinding corn, and also obsidian, which was in demand from the earliest times for making precision tools.

Milos is still rich in minerals; as you sail around it you can see white cliffs of caolin, the mineral used to produce porcelain. There is a huge gulf that almost cuts the island in two and forms a magnificent natural harbor ringed with delightful beaches and pretty villages. Near the main city of Plaka, there is a Frankish castle still bearing its founders' coats of arms. The church belonging to the castle, a basilica, is particularly fine and has superb wood carvings. The museum has a plaster cast of the Venus de Milo given by the Louvre. Nearby are some catacombs, underground corridors containing the graves of the island's first followers of Christ. There are also the ruins of an ancient theater.

The coast is very heavily indented and has many caves and oddly-shaped rocks.

NAXOS

This is the island of Dionysus, god of drink, who took Ariadne, the daughter of Minos, from Theseus when they were fleeing Crete after she had helped Theseus find his way through the Minotaur's labyrinth.

There are monuments as old as the legends, going back to 2400 B.C.; inscriptions carved on the mountains themselves; Byzantine churches; Venetian fortifications as well as large numbers of small chapels in remote valleys.

Naxos was always famous for its sheep, said to be under the special protection of Zeus. Large herds still roam the hillsides. From the milk of these herds the island produces some great cheeses, particularly myzithra and manouri. Living on the island is remarkably inexpensive. It has good fishing and beautiful beaches, making Naxos a delightful place for a long, restful holiday.

There is much to see: the archaic temple of Apollo; Mycenaean tombs; the museum, with an imposing collection for so small a place; the archives with documents from the Crusades; a Venetian fortress; some marvelous paintings by the Cretan Angelo, teacher of El Greco; the Church of Vlacherniotissa and that of St. Kyriaki, which is a veritable museum of Byzantine art; and the cathedral of Naxos which has a beautiful marble altar screen and paintings by the best artists the island has produced.

There are buses, or you can hire taxis, to visit all the parts of the island and it would be well worth your while to explore as much of Naxos as you can. In particular you should visit Halki, 17 kilometers from the main town, which has a fine Frankish castle plus some remarkable churches, such as that of St. George which contains excellent murals dating from the ninth, tenth and thirteenth centuries, two churches to the Virgin Mary, one called Damniotissa and the other called Drosiane, both with some very fine murals.

Naxos has quite a few festivals and fairs, the most imposing of which is held in the village of Tripodes on August 23. Everybody dresses up, there is much feasting and the local dancing is famed throughout Greece.

PAROS

Paros is a gentle, fertile island with good harbors and many beautiful little bays. It produces a fine wine, olive oil, figs, tobacco and honey. It also provided ancient Greek sculptors with excellent marble.

Fishing is good round this isle and this patient sport is particularly suitable to the mood of Paros. If you prefer sight-seeing, there are fine churches with excellent mosaics, murals and icons. The large cruciform Church of Ekatontapyliani—said to have been built by St. Helena in A.D. 326 while on her way to the Holy Land to discover the holy cross—was erected like so many others over the remains of an ancient temple. There are three particularly attractive little chapels inside and a small museum of Byzantine relics. Just behind the church is the archaeological museum, whose prize possession is a superb statue of the Wingless Victory by the famous Parian sculptor Skopas. Here, too, you can see parts of the Parian

Chronicle, discovered in 1627, containing the history of the island all the way back to 263 B.C.

Twenty-seven kilometers from the main town is the tiny village of Dryos, an engaging hamlet with three brooks whose water is collected in large cisterns and then used for irrigation purposes. At the village is an imposing guesthouse and a very fine restaurant, right next to one of the best beaches in the island.

SANTORINI

The original name of this island was Thera. It became known as Santorini under the Franks who took this sickle-shaped island during the Crusades. It is the rim of an ancient volcano, which gives it a spectacular coastline and a unique beach of black sand formed from lava. You land on the island at the foot of the cliff and climb up a path on mule or donkey.

The island is very dry. It rains there just once or twice a year and there are few wells. Nevertheless, its industrious inhabitants grow grapes—from which they make a fine local wine—and good early tomatoes. One wonders why people would stay on this island which has so often been destroyed by earthquake, yet they have, perhaps because of the great beauty of this rocky speck in the Aegean.

Santorini was once an outpost of King Minos; later it allied itself with Persia, which led to its seizure by Athens. There are ancient ruins and some captivating Byzantine churches. The island was at its peak in the fourth and third centuries B.C., if we are to judge by the large number of coins that were minted there at that time. Most of those found are of copper with heads of Zeus and Apollo. The museum has some fine pottery of the geometric period, sculpture from the Hellenistic period and some Byzantine finds. Near it is a winding little street ascending dizzily among the houses and lined with small shops where you can buy souvenirs to your heart's content.

It is a picturesque island with sparkling whitewashed houses along the gaunt rock, spectacularly painted boats, dainty churches, and breathtaking cliffs. Characteristic are the vaulted roofs of the island, and the very fine church steeples.

There are buses on the island to take you from village to village, and small boats ply to the islets in the gulf, the remains of the volcano's last great eruption, in 1866.

SIPHNOS

This was once the wealthiest place in Greece with a rich productive gold mine. The inhabitants used to divide the yield among themselves each year after putting away a sum for public works and monuments. It is said that the Siphnians once asked the oracle at Delphi how long their wealth would last. The answer was "Danger will come from a wooden host and a scarlet herald." From Samos, shortly thereafter, came a ship painted scarlet, seeking a loan. When the Siphnians refused, the Samians sacked the town and thus fulfilled the prophecy of the oracle.

Today the island is best known for its picturesque monasteries and chapels, its quiet beaches and an interesting collection of ruins ranging from ancient times to the Byzantine and Venetian periods.

However, this is not a place in which to study the relics of the past; it is another of the many little islands to discover and laze upon.

SYROS

Syros is the capital of the Cyclades, a tiny island which remained neutral under French protection during the war of independence in the last century and became thus an asylum for Greek refugees. It flourished, consequently, as one of the principal ports of Greece. The first known inhabitants were Phoenicians, from whom the island got its name. The Phoenician word *syr* means rock, or fort. From the Phoenicians, also, the island retained the worship of the god Pan. In the sixth century B.C. Syros produced Pherecydes, the teacher of Pythagoras, and some believe it was he who built on Syros the first observatory in Greece. Later, Syros became a member of the Delian league and had two flourishing cities, whose ruins can be seen to this day.

Its main town is set like an amphitheater around a little harbor with houses built along the waterfront and up the hill. Some of the buildings seem much too large and almost out of place for so small an island, but they are a measure of the importance Syros acquired as a commercial center during the last century. Its museum has some interesting finds from prehistoric times and from the classical era. Its Church of St. Nicholas, one of the largest in Greece, has a cemetery full of very handsome mausolea. On October 26 the Feast of St. Demetrius is celebrated with much Byzantine pomp and a miraculous icon is carried in procession around the town to cure the ailing.

TINOS

This is the holy isle of the Aegean, dominated by the Church of the Virgin Mary that houses a miraculous icon, famous for its cures. On Tinos the Feast of the Dormition of the Virgin Mary, August 15, is one of the most picturesque and imposing religious festivals in Greece. If you can possibly squeeze onto the island for the occasion you will see a unique manifestation of Greek Orthodoxy. The church is packed, and the uncountable ornaments in gold and silver, donated by those who have been cured by the Virgin, reflect the lights of the thousands of candles lit by the faithful. Large contingents of bishops and priests, splendidly robed, officiate, while all around the afflicted kneel, lie down, or sit waiting patiently for the miracle to cure them. It is an emotional, popular occasion, full of simplicity and faith. The church provides a magnificent setting since it is a brilliant example of typical island architecture, built with marble from Tinos and its neighboring islands.

SECTION IV

THE MOTORIST'S GUIDE

INTRODUCTION

The routes I have chosen for the motorist follow the pattern adopted in this guidebook as a whole. They take in most of the classical landscape described in Section II and include places less well known described in Section III.

For what it is worth, here is how I would tour Greece by car. (The sequence of the maps in this section fits my suggested tour.)

The ferry from Italy stops at Corfu, so stay over to visit the island. From Corfu take the ferry to Igoumenitsa on the mainland and drive to Ioannina (map 1). You might take the side trip to Metsovo, but on my plan I would be returning eventually to that spot from Kastoria for the ferry to Italy, so you will see it later anyway.

From Ioannina go to Arta (map 2) and then to Antirion (map 3) to catch the ferry to Rion, which is 8 kilometers from Patras in the Peloponnesus. From Rion you can either continue to Athens on the coastal road via Corinth (maps 4 and 11) or tour the Peloponnesus.

Map 5 takes you from Patras to Pyrgus on a road skirting the coast with its many fine beaches. From Pyrgus go to Olympia (map 6) and stay the night. Continue next day to Tripolis (map 6) over the mountains. Use Tripolis as the base for trips to Pylus (map 7) to visit the ruins of Nestor's palace, and to Sparta (map 8) and Mystras (3 miles west of Sparta) and, if you wish, to Monemvasia (map 8). From Tripolis go to Argos (map 9) and on to Nauplion and Epidaurus (map 10)—the side trip to Ermioni is very pleasant.

Return to Argos, take the road to Corinth, stopping at Mycenae (map 9). From Corinth continue to Athens (map 11).

Athens is your jumping-off point for island cruises and
tours. Most of the islands are small, have buses and taxis,
and I suggest you leave the car in Athens, except for Crete
which is large. From Athens ferries run daily to Crete. For
an itinerary in Crete see map 24.

To go to Delphi from Athens you pass Thebes (map 12),
continue to Levadia (map 13), where you turn off for Delphi
and Itea (map 14). From Delphi retrace your steps to Levadia
and proceed to Lamia (map 13) across the mountains, and
so on to Larissa (map 15). This is a lovely route across mountains to the plain of Thessaly. From Larissa go to Volos
(map 16) and Mount Pelion. From Larissa you can also drive
to Trikala and on to Kalabaka for the Meteora (map 17).
(This map also shows a side trip to Metsovo. If you lack time,
continue from Metsovo to Igoumenitsa—map 1. There is a
ferry to Italy.) Return to Larissa and take the coastal road
to Salonica (Thessaloniki) (map 18). Use Salonica as your
base to visit Mount Athos (map 19) and Pella (map 21).
From Salonica you can take the road that leads to Yugoslavia
if you wish to leave Greece that way (map 20). However, if
you are leaving Greece via Igoumenitsa for Italy, continue
from Pella to Edessa (map 21) on to Florina and Kastoria
(map 22), all through marvelous scenery. Stay in peaceful
Kastoria by its sparkling lake. From there, drive to Hani
Mourgani (map 23), proceed to Metsovo (map 17) and so
to Ioannina and Igoumenitsa.

The maps are reproduced by permission of AL-MA pub-
lications and the Automobile Touring Club of Greece. Their
book of road maps contains many more routes than those
given here. The maps are distorted in scale in order to clearly
indicate the route. Distances, however, are correct.

There are many more service stations for gasoline or repairs than mentioned in the descriptions beside each map. I have included just enough to reassure the anxious driver that if gas is low, he will not have far to go for a filling station. Gas is 80 cents a gallon in Greece; lubricants and parts are equivalently priced. The Greek mechanic is generally good and inexpensive and he is excellent at improvising, if you need parts that are locally unobtainable. He will keep you going until you reach a large town where parts can be bought. Road patrols of the Automobile Touring Club of Greece automatically assist any foreign car.

In towns the speed limit is 50 kilometers; outside towns the speed limit varies and is posted. All distances are given in kilometers, since this is the road measure used in Greece on road signs. One comparison that will help until you are acquainted with the kilometer is that 16 kilometers are roughly equal to 10 miles (0.62 miles = 1 kilometer).

Finally, I come to the problem of spellings of place names. Each country using the Latin alphabet has its own way of transliterating Greek place names. To please these countries, and every Greek scholar everywhere, Greece has, under pressure, burdened herself with a bewildering variety of Latin spellings. You may not always recognize them; for example, Thebes is given as Thivai or Thiva on road signs. So in this section, the first spelling given is that shown on the accompanying map. The second spelling, in parentheses, is the spelling you are most likely to recognize and that used throughout the rest of the book. Generally, the first spelling will be used on road signs in Greece, but in a few cases I have seen different road-sign spellings. If you encounter two or more different spellings, see if they sound more or less like your destination; if they do, take heart, you are not lost.

MAP INDEX

Note: (F) beside a place name indicates that this is a ferry-boat port.

DOMESTIC CAR FERRY SERVICES

Abbreviations: vv = vice versa. nm = nautical miles

Corfu to Igoumenitsa & vv (18 nm)
2 hours
Private cars $4.00
Passengers: 1st class   0.60
Passengers: 2d class   0.50

Egion to Itea & vv (27 nm)
3 hours
Private cars   4.32
Passengers   0.52

Patrai to Sami on Cephalonia & vv (58 nm)
3 hours; then to Ithaca & vv (17 nm) 1.30 hours
Private cars   6.70
Passengers   1.70

Piraeus to Hania (Canea, Crete) & vv (146 nm)
lv. 8 P.M. Mon. from Piraeus
ar. 7 A.M. Tues. at Hania
lv. 4 P.M. Tues. from Hania
ar. 5 A.M. Wed. at Piraeus
lv. 9 A.M. Wed. from Piraeus
ar. 8 P.M. Wed. at Hania
lv. 9 P.M. Wed. from Hania
ar. 11 A.M. Thur. at Piraeus
lv. 8 P.M. Thur. from Piraeus
ar. 7 A.M. Fri. at Hania
lv. 6 P.M. Fri. from Hania
ar. 7 A.M. Sat. Piraeus
lv. 8 P.M. Sat. from Piraeus
ar. 7 A.M. Sun. at Hania
lv. 6 P.M. Sun. from Hania
ar. 7 A.M. Mon. at Piraeus

Private cars: $10.00 each person
First class: $11
Second class: $10.40
Third class: $3.00

Ferries from Iraklion: Phone 220-429 or 236-351. Times and prices similar to those above from Hania to Piraeus.

Rion to Antirion & vv (15 nm)
15 minutes
Private cars   1.20
Passengers   0.04

Ferries from Kalamaki are small and fit their schedule to the traffic. They charge less than 50 cents a car and 3 cents a passenger.

FIRST-AID STATION

SHARP CURVE

OPEN CULVERT
OR DIP

CROSSROAD

GUARDED
RAILROAD CROSSING

UNGUARDED
RAILROAD CROSSING

BRIDGE

DANGER

THROUGH ROAD

INTERNATIONAL ROAD SIGNS

● Towns encountered on main routes
● Towns of importance
• Large villages
• Small villages
○ Villages not named
L Archaeological sites
δ Monasteries and old churches
⌂ Tourist pavilions
♠ Village hostels
↓ Inns

KEY TO MAPS

IGOUMENITSA. Gas, services.

VRATILA.

River Tyrias bridge.

River Thiamis bridge.

The Holy Virgin monastery.

Turn off for KARITSA (3.5 km) and ZITSA (6.5 km). The Zitsa plateau (alt. 1660 m) affords a superb view across the Thiamis Valley to which Lord Byron paid tribute in *Childe Harold*.

Junction for IOANNINA.

PERAMA, which has one of Europe's most beautiful stalactite caverns.

Monastery of the Holy Virgin on the banks of the Ioannina or Pamvotis Lake. The road follows the north shore, overlooked by Mount Mitsikeli.

MAZIA.

BALDOUMAS bridge.

VOUTONASSI. The road follows the right bank of the Arahthos River.

METSOVO.

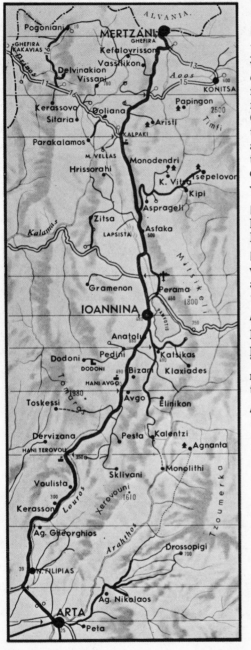

MERTZANI.

IOANNINA.

Junction for **DODONI** (14.5 km) with ruins on the site of the oracle of Zeus. **DODONI** flourished until A.D. 168, when it was destroyed by the Roman Consul Paulus Aemilius, but the sanctuary still functioned at the time of Constantine the Great, when it was converted into a church.

You see **MOUNT BIZANI.**

HANI AVGO (alt. 610 m), highest point on the drive. Restaurant.

HANI TEROVOU. Beautiful wooded spot with restaurants and a pleasant stop on road to **ARTA**. Gasoline.

AGIOS GHEORGHIOS.

Hydroelectric plant. Near the plant is an old Roman aqueduct 70 kilometers long. The road runs along the west bank of the River Louros.

ARTA.

3. ARTA, ANTIRION (172 kilometers)

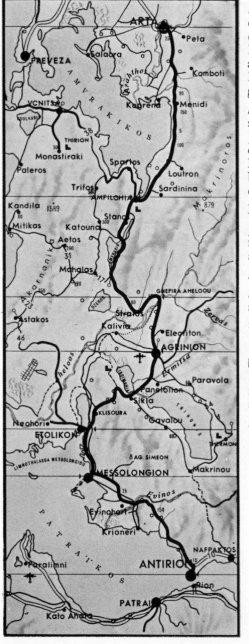

ARTA. In the fourteenth century, **ARTA** was the capital of the Byzantine despots of Epiros. There are fine churches and monasteries here. Restaurants, service stations, gasoline.

AMFILOHIA. Restaurants, service stations, gasoline. Just before the town, near the castle, are the ruins of ancient Limnae. Ten kilometers beyond the town are the ruins of ancient Amphilohikon Argos.

Bridge over **LAKE AMVRAKIA.**

Just off road is **STRATOS** with ruins of a castle, theater and a temple to Zeus.

AHELOOU bridge and dam.

AGRINION. Restaurants, service stations, gasoline.

SIKIA. Gasoline.

KLISOURA ravine.

MESSOLONGION where Lord Byron died, fighting for Greek independence. Restaurants, service station, gasoline.

ANTIRION. Ferryboat connection with **RION** and the Peloponnesus.

4. PATRAI, KORINTHOS (Patras, Corinth) (135 kilometers)

PATRAI. Ferries to Cephalonia and Ithaca. Junction for **RION**. Ferry to Antirion.

LAMBIRI. Small summer resort.

EGION. Ferry connection with Itea, port of Delfi (Delphi). Services, gas.

RIZOMILOS.

DIAKOPTON. Railway junction for **KALAVRITA**.

XILOKASTRON. Lovely little resort and beach. Gas, services. Junction for **ANO TRIKALA** (34 km), a pretty mountain resort with a ski area nearby.

KIATON (Sikionia). Gas. services. Junction for old **SIKION** (5 km) with its ruins and small museum.

Port of old Corinth. From here take road to **PALEA KORINTHOS** —old Corinth—a distance of 3.7 km.

KORINTHOS.

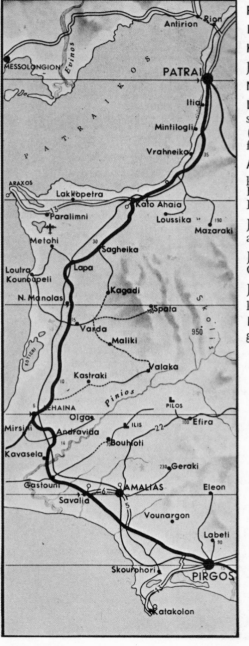

PATRAI westward.

ITIA. Beach, restaurant.

KATO AHAIA.

Junction for **ARAXOS** (13 km).

NEA MANOLAS. Gasoline.

LEHAINA. Gasoline, service station. Junction for Killini (12 km), a Frankish port, with ferry to Zakinthos.

ANDRAVIDA. Capital of the princes of Morea during the Frankish domination of the area. Bridge over the River Pinios.

Junction for Loutra Killinis, a spa. Restaurants, gasoline.

Junction for **AMALIAS** (6 km). Gasoline, service station.

Junction for **KATAKOLON**, the port of **PIRGOS**.

PIRGOS. Restaurants, gasoline, service station.

6. PIRGOS, OLIMPIA (Olympia), TRIPOLIS (156.2 kilometers)

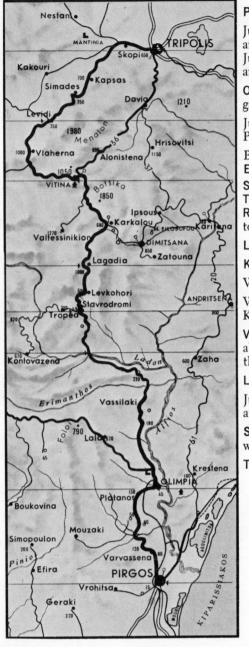

PIRGOS.

Junction for Kaiapha (25.5 km) and Kyparissia (60 km).
Junction for Kalavryta (102 km) and Patrai (118 km).

OLIMPIA, site of the ancient games.

Junction for Kalavryta and Patrai.

Bridge over **RIVER ERIMANTHOS.**

STAVRODROMI. Junction for **TROPEA** and the dam across the **RIVER LADON.** Winding road to Lagadia.

LAGADIA.

KARKALOU.

Water spring.

Winding road. Junctions for Kalavryta and Patrai.

VITINA. Mountain resort, with alternative route to **TRIPOLIS** through a fir forest.

LEVIDI.

Junction for site and ruins of ancient Mantinia (4 km).

SKOPI, where Epaminondas was killed.

TRIPOLIS.

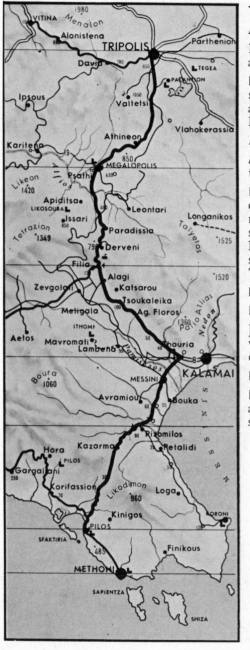

TRIPOLIS.

Ascent begins.

Kalogerikos pass. Descent begins along very winding road.

MEGALOPOLIS. Gasoline, service station. 1 km from town are ruins of ancient city. Restaurant.

ALAGI.

AGIOS FLOROS. Road continues through Messinean plain.

KALAMAI. Lovely views from old Venetian fortress. Hotels, restaurants, gasoline, service stations. Junction for Sparta and Mistras through marvelous scenic drive over Mount Taïyetos (62 km).

MESSINI.

RIZOMILOS.

Junction for Hora (15.2 km) with its ruins of the palace of Nestor.

PILOS. Gasoline, service stations.

METHONI. Delightful setting and Venetian castle. Gasoline, service stations.

TRIPOLIS.

Junction for **TEGEA** (1.5 km) with ruins of temple to Athena Alea. Also Byzantine Church of Episkopi with lovely mosaics. Restaurant, gasoline.

Delightful view of Lake Taka . Ascending, winding road.

Unique view of Mount Taïyetos and valley below. Descend on winding road.

HANI BAKOUROU. Restaurant.

SPARTI (Sparta). Junction for Mistras. From **SPARTI** continue south.

KROKEAI.

Vassilopitamos bridge over River Evrotas.

Junction for Githion (41 km).

SKALA. Gasoline, service station. Continue over bridge. Junction for **GERAKI** (17 km) with its fine old Byzantine churches and Acropolis.

Bridge of Apidia.

Gasoline.

MONEMVASIA. Gasoline, restaurants, service station.

9. TRIPOLIS, ARGOS, MIKINAI (Mycenae), KORINTHOS (Corinth)
(113.4 kilometers)

TRIPOLIS. Gas, services. Junctions for Sparta and Mistras (73 km); Kalamai (90 km); Pirgos (156 km); Patrai (Patras) (320 km).

AHLADOKAMPOS. Gasoline. Winding road descends.

Winding road up mountain.

MILI. Gasoline. Nearby are American School of Archaeology excavations.

Junction for **KEFALARI** (3 km). A beautiful spot, source of the River Erasinos. Restaurants.

ARGOS. Gasoline, service station. Junction for Nafplion (Nauplion) and Epidavros (Epidaurus) (see map 10).

Junction for **MIKINAI.** Restaurant.

FIHTIA. Gasoline.

Dervenaki gorge where in 1822 a celebrated battle was fought during the war of independence.

Junction for ancient **NEMEA** (5 km) with ruins of temple to Zeus Nemeios. Games took place in the valley in ancient times.

KORINTHOS.

10. ARGOS, EPIDAVROS (Epidaurus) (43.5 kilometers)

ARGOS. Junction for **NAFPLION** (Nauplion).

TIRINS. Ancient site with ruins. Gasoline.

NAFPLION. Junction for Epidavros.

Junction for **ERMIONI** (see below).

LIGOURION. Junction for small port serving **EPIDAVROS** (13.7 km).

EPIDAVROS.

ARGOS, ERMIONI
(88.7 kilometers)

ARGOS.

Junction for **ERMIONI.**

Junction for **ASSINI** (1.5 km), a lovely fishing village; and **TOLON** (4.3 km), a resort with magnificent beach.

The Bay of Drepanon with its lovely beach and Mount Avgo overlooking the bay. The road up the mountain is poor.

KRANIDI. Junction for **PORTOHELI** (7 km) on a picturesque bay. Gasoline, service station.

ERMIONI. Gasoline, service stations.

11. KORINTHOS, ATHINAI (Corinth, Athens) (86 kilometers)

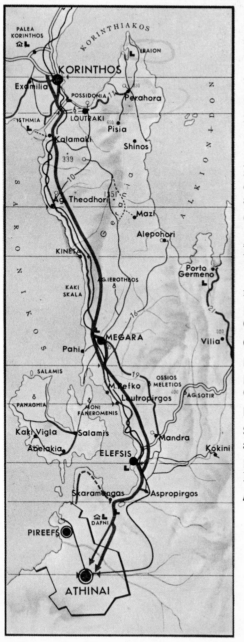

KORINTHOS (Corinth). Old Corinth harbor is 4.2 km distant; from there turn left 3.7 km for the old city.

Junction for **POSSIDONIA** (Poseidonia) (2 km) where you can see parts of the ancient slipway used to haul ships between the Corinth and Saronic gulfs.

Junction for **ISTHMIA** (6 km), site of ancient games. Ruins of temple to Poseidon and a sanctuary of Palaimon.

Corinth Canal. Gas, services.

Junction for **LOUTRAKI** (6.5 km), a little resort; **PERAHORA** (17 km); Vouliagmeni Lake (19 km) and Iraion with its ruins of temple to Akraia Hera.

KALAMAKI. Ferry across Corinth Canal.

Gas. Restaurant.

KINETA beach.

MEGALO PEFKO. Restaurant. Gasoline.

ELEFSIS (Eleusis). Gas, services.

SKARAMANGAS. New arsenal and ship repair workshops.

DAFNI (Daphne). Monastery. Restaurant.

ATHINAI (Athens).

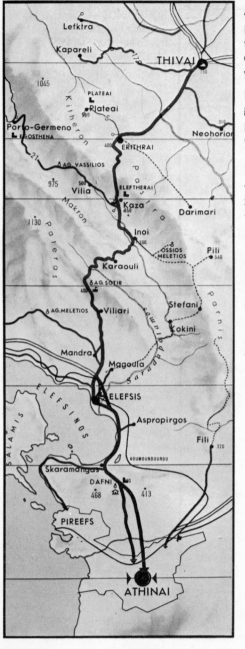

ATHINAI.

ELEFSIS (Eleusis). Continue to **MANDRA**, after which road climbs to **VILIARI**.

VILIARI.

KARAOULI. Restaurants, gasoline.

INOI. Ancient watchtower. Gasoline.

Junction for **VILIA** (4.3 km) and **PORTO-GERMENO** (21 km) with its ruins of the ancient fortress **EGOSTHENA**.

Winding road to **KAZA.** Restaurants, gasoline. Take the ten minute walk to **ELEFTHERAE**, an ancient fortress that dominated the road to the plain of Athens.

Cithaeron pass.

ERITHRAI. Gasoline, service station.

THIVAI. Gasoline.

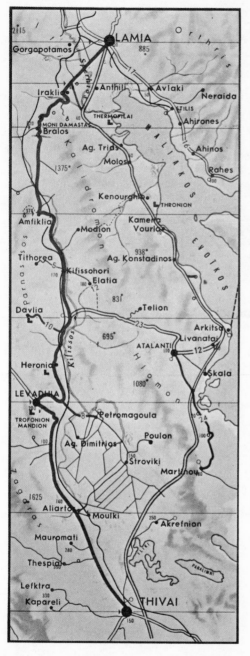

THIVAI.

On the right Mount Sphingion, seat of the legendary Sphinx.

ALIARTOS. Restaurant, gas. Junction for Kastro Goula (11 km) with ruins of Mycenaean palace and Cyclopean wall.

LEVADHIA. Gas, services. Junction for Delfi (Delphi). Junction for Skripou (4 km) with ruins of Orchomenos, an ancient Boeotian city.

HERONIA (Chaeronea) birthplace of Plutarch, site of Philip of Macedonia's victory over **THEBES** and Athens.

Junction for **ATALANTI** (23 km) and **ARKITSA** with ferry to Aedipsos.

BRALOS. Gasoline.

Mount Kallidromon pass. Winding road descends.

Junction for **THERMOPILAI** (Thermopylae) (9 km) and **KAMMENA VOURLA** spa (35 km).

Bridge over **RIVER SPERHIOS.**

LAMIA, and its port of **STILIS** 6 km away. Gas, services.

14. LEVADHIA, DELFI (Delphi) (70 kilometers)

LEVADHIA.

KORAKOLITHOS. Restaurant.

Junction for **DISTOMON** (5.7 km) and **OSIOS LOUKAS** monastery (7.5 km).

Ascent begins along winding road to **ARAHOVA.**

ARAHOVA.

DELFI. Descend to the port of **ITEA** along winding road.

Junction for **ITEA** and the ferryboat to Egion in the Peloponnesos. Service station and gasoline.

15. LAMIA, LARISSA (113 kilometers)

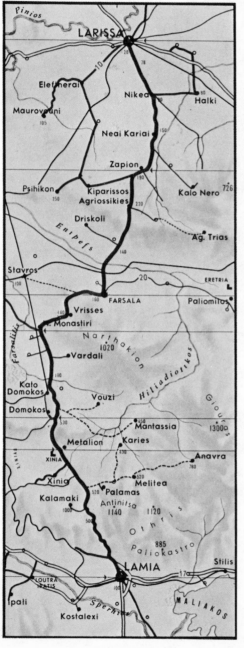

LAMIA. Just outside the city a winding road begins ascent to **MOUNT OTHRIS.**

Chapel of St. Catherine. Water spring.

On the right **METALION**, the richest chromium mine in Greece. Gasoline.

DOMOKOS (1 km off main road), the ancient city of Thaumakoi, with its magnificent view of the plain of Thessaly. Gasoline, service station. The winding road begins its descent to the plain, the largest in Greece. The plain of Thessaly is surrounded by mountains: Mount Olimpos (Olympus) to the north, Othris to the south, Agrafa southwest, Pindos to the northwest, and Ossa northeast.

NEON MONASTIRI. Junction for Karditsa (38 km) and Trikala (65 km).

FARSALA. Gasoline, service station.

Bridge over **RIVER ENIPEFS.**

ZAPION.

LARISSA. Restaurants, gasoline, service stations.

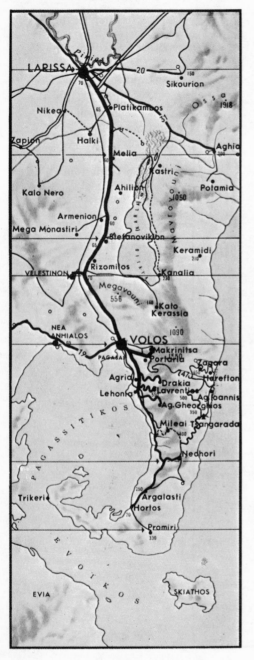

LARISSA.

Junction for **VELESTINON**
(2 km), site of ancient acropolis
and alleged home of Alcestis,
Euripides' heroine.

VOLOS. Gas, services.
From **VOLOS** two roads lead
to the various parts of
Mount Pelion.

Drive A. **VOLOS** *to* **HOREFTON**
(55 kilometers)

Ano Volos (4 km), legendary
birthplace of Jason, leader of
the Argonauts. **PORTARIA**
(14 km), a village resort.
From here the climb to Pelion's
peak (alt. 1618 m) takes one
and a half hours. **MAKRINITSA**,
1.5 km away, a picturesque
village with a fine medieval
church. Restaurant (20 km).
Road descends to coast. Hotel
(45 km). **ZAGORA** (47 km).
Hotel, gas. **HOREFTON** (55 km).
Gas, services.

Drive B. **VOLOS** *to* **AGRIA** *and*
LEHONIA *and down the west*
coast (31.5 kilometers)

Junction (20 km) for
MILEAI (11 km) with a famed
library at St. Athanasius Church.

Junction (31.5 km) for
NEOHORI (4 km);
TSANGARADA (24 km);
AGIOS IOANNIS (**AI YANNIS**).

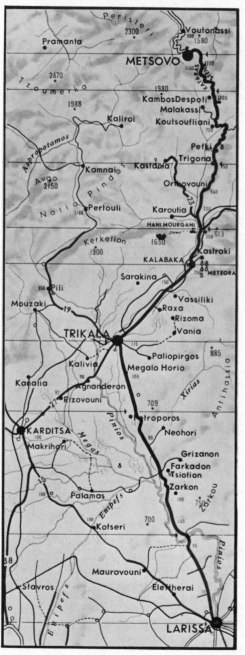

LARISSA.

Bridge.

Fork right until you reach the national road between Tirnavos and Elasson. From **PETROPOROS** village (49.2 km) the road continues straight across plain.

TRIKALA. Built on the site of a temple to Asclepius. The inhabitants were famous riders and bred a fine race of horses, models for the carved Parthenon friezes. Services, gas. From here visit Stena Portas (19 km) on Mount Pindos with its fine Byzantine architecture and old acropolis. From **TRIKALA** to **KALABAKA** the road is straight and tree-lined.

KALABAKA. Small town below the **METEORA.** Services, gas.

Junction for **KASTRAKI** and the **METEORA.** From **KALABAKA** to **HANI MOURGANI** the drive is beautiful.

HANI MOURGANI.

Junction for picturesque **KASTANIA** (22.5 km).

KAMBOS DESPOTI (alt. 1300 m). A good place to rest. Restaurant.

KATORAS PASS (alt. 1705 m) has a magnificent view of the Thessaly plain and surrounding mountains.

Junction for **METSOVO.**

METSOVO (alt. 1200 m). Gasoline.

18. LARISSA, THESSALONIKI (Salonica) (186 kilometers) Coastal road.

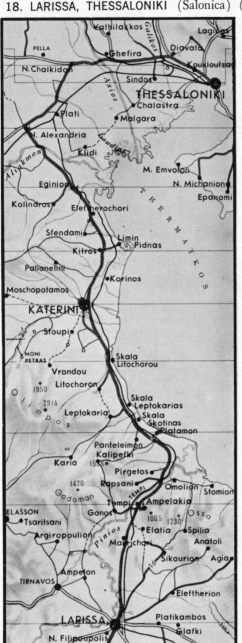

LARISSA.

Follow new road which runs close to railway line.

TEMPI.

Bridge. Railway station.

PANTELEIMON. Site of ancient Heraklion. Ruins of medieval fortress. Lovely long sandy beach.

LEPTOKARIA.

PORT OF LITOCHORON. Gasoline.

KATERINI. Junction for road to Mount Olimpos (Olympus). Restaurants, service stations, gasoline.

KITROS. Site of ancient Pidna, where the Roman Consul Paulus Aemilius destroyed the army led by Perseus, last king of Macedonia.

EGINION.

NEA ALEXANDRIA. Junction for Veria and Kozani.

RIVER LOUDIAS bridge.

NEA CHALKIDON (Halkidon). Junctions for Ghiannitsa (Yannitsa), Edessa, Florina, Prespa, and nearby PELLA (9 km), ruined capital of Alexander the Great.

RIVER AXIOS bridge.

AXIOS dam.

Junction for **GHEFIRA** (1 km) and Evzoni (51.5 km) on the Greek-Yugoslav frontier. Gas.

RIVER GALIKOS bridge.

Junction for Kilkis (43 km).

THESSALONIKI, capital of Macedonia.

THESSALONIKI. Follow road to **THERMI.**

THERMI. A little spa.

VASSILIKA. Gasoline.

One kilometer off road is Monastery of **ST. ANASTASSIA.**

GALATISTA. Summer resort in mountains.

Mountain pass and road begins to descend.

ARNEA. Gasoline.

PALEOHORION.

STAGIRA. Small town near site of ancient Stagira, birthplace of Aristotle.

IERISSOS. Stop here for **MOUNT ATHOS.** Restaurants, gasoline.

20. THESSALONIKI (Salonica), EVZONI (on Greek-Yugoslav border)
(79.1 kilometers)

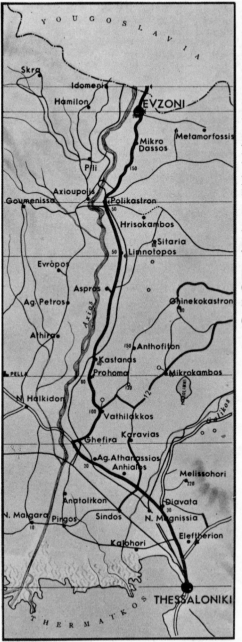

THESSALONIKI (Salonica).

Drive towards **GHEFIRA**. The road continues north along the east bank of the **AXIOS**, the largest river in Macedonia. Its source is in Yugoslavia and it flows into the Gulf of **THERMAIKOS** (Salonica) 20 km southwest of the city. It is 300 kilometers long. The **AXIOS** valley has always been the passage into Greece for invaders from the north.

LIMNOTOPOS. Gasoline. Junction for Kilkis (33 km).

POLIKASTRON. Gasoline. Water spring.

EVZONI. Restaurant, gasoline. Customs and passport formalities.

GREEK-YUGOSLAV border.

21. THESSALONIKI (Salonica), EDESSA (90.5 kilometers)

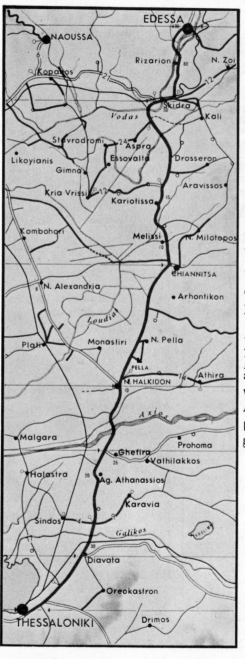

THESSALONIKI. Follow the Kozani-Athens road.

Junction for Kilkis (43 km).

Junction for **GHEFIRA** (1 km) and Evzoni (52 km) on the Greek-Yugoslav border. Gasoline.

Bridge over **RIVER AXIOS.**

NEA HALKIDON (Chalkidon). Junction for Ghiannitsa (Yannitsa)-Edessa. Continue on Kozani-Athens road.

Bear right for **NEA PELLA** (1.6 km) with its nearby ruins of the old capital of Alexander the Great.

Junction for Goumenissa (23 km) and Idomeni (66 km) on Greek-Yugoslav border.

Bear right for **GHIANNITSA** (1 km). Service station, gasoline.

Junction for Gida (17.5 km).

Junction for **NAOUSSA** (17 km) and Verria (32.5 km).

VODAS bridge. Junction for Aridea (29.5 km).

EDESSA. Service stations, gasoline.

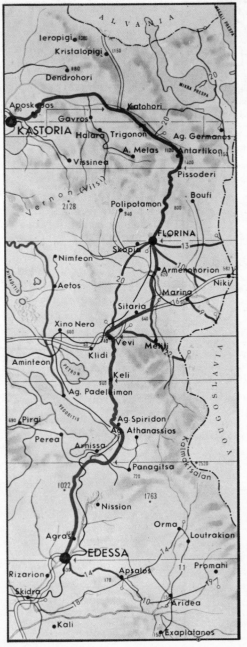

EDESSA.

AGRAS hydroelectric plant.

AGRAS.

Railroad junction.

Two kilometers off main road is **ARNISSA**, a resort town on **LAKE VEGORITIS.**

Winding road ascends for 19 kilometers.

VEVI. Gasoline.

Water spring.

Junction for Ptolemais (30.5 km) and Kozani (58.5 km).

Junction for **NIKI** on the **GREEK-YUGOSLAV** border (15.5 km).

FLORINA, a Byzantine town also known as Chloros, meaning green, because of its rich woods. Services, gas. From **FLORINA** the road ascends toward **PISSODERI.**

PISSODERI pass.

The village of **PISSODERI** with a magnificent view of **THE PRESPA LAKES.**

ANTARTIKON.

Junction for Prespa, on the **YUGOSLAV** border (23 km), and for the **ALBANIAN** border (37 km).

Junction for Kristalopigi and the Albanian border (13 km).

KASTORIA on Lake Kastoria (Lake Orestias), allegedly founded by Orestes, son of Agamemnon, in honor of his sister Electra. The town has seventy churches, both Byzantine and modern. Services, gas.

HANI MOURGANI.

AGHIOFILON. From here to **KASTORIA** the drive is at an altitude of between 500 and 700 meters.

Junction for Deskati (30 km). The road runs between the ranges of Mount Hassia, right, and Mount Pindos, left.

GREVENA. Services, gasoline.

VATOLAKKOS.

RIVER ALIAKMON bridge. Bear left for **KASTORIA**. (Bear right for **SIATISTA**, 6 km, and Kozani, 2 km.)

RIVER ALIAKMON bridge.

NEAPOLIS.

Bridge over **RIVER ALIAKMON.**

VOGATSIKON. Built on seven small hills, this is a beautiful spot surrounded by woods.

HANI MITIKA. Restaurant.

ARGOS ORESTIKON.

Junction for Lekhovon (33 km); Florina (56 km); and Edessa. Road follows the southwest bank of **LAKE KASTORIA** (Lake Orestias).

KASTORIA. Services, gas.

HANIA (Canea), RETHIMNON,
IRAKLION (Heraklion)
(151 kilometers)

HANIA (Canea).

VRISSES. Junction for Askifos
plateau; Nimbros ravine;
HORA SFAKION (57 km)
on the south coast.

Junction for TILISSOS (14 km),
ANOGHIA (23 km), and view
of MOUNT IDI (alt. 2456 m).

RETHIMNON. Gas services.

Branch right for ARKADIOU
MONASTERY.

IRAKLION (Heraklion). Gas,
services. 5 km southeast
is KNOSSOS.

HANIA (Canea), KASTELI
(Castelli) (42 kilometers)

HANIA (Canea).

Junction for orange and lemon
grove valley leading to
ALIKIANOU village (11 km)
with its Venetian ruins;
OMALOS (40 km) on the White
Mountains plateau (alt.
1100 m); the south coast's
deep Samaria ravine.

MALEME airport.

TAVRONITIS. Junction for
KANDANOS (42 km) and
the south coast town of
PALEOHORA (60 km).

Junction for the two great
SPILIA caverns.

KASTELI (Castelli). Gas,
services.

SECTION V

THE YACHTSMAN'S GUIDE

INTRODUCTION

For those who love the sea, a holiday by yacht in Greek waters, the most varied and beautiful in the world, will be an unforgettable delight and a great way in which to see Greece. It need not be too expensive either.

You are hardly ever out of sight of an island or the mainland, and since Greece is so small you have open to you not only the main classical sites, but also a whole world of seductive islands and secluded coves for safe anchorage. In fact Greece, with its 15,000 kilometers of coastline, 1425 islands, marvelous climate and incomparable scenery, is a yachtsman's paradise.

The cruising season lasts from the middle of April until late November with brilliant sunshine nearly every day. There are fine periods of sailing weather throughout the winter too, and some owners keep their yachts in commission the year round.

HOW TO CHARTER A YACHT
AND HOW MUCH IT WILL COST

If you count the cost of hotels and transportation, yachting in Greece need not be more expensive than living in a class A or a class AA hotel, depending on the type of yacht you rent. With a yacht you have the added advantage of mobility, so that your itinerary can be guided only by whim in your search for lovely secluded coves. You do not have to rely either on public transportation schedules or on hotel bookings. If you don't get seasick, there is no better way of enjoying Greece. It should not be too difficult to convince a sufficient number of your friends that they should join you for a yachting cruise in Greek waters, so that a group of you can rent a yacht and manage on about $30 a day each.

Personally I would charter a yacht that has been recently built, although many old salts will tell you that modern construction does not compare with that of pre-World War II. And a "good buy" would be a spacious yacht built within the last five years with accommodations for ten persons, in two-berth cabins, with at least three showers and toilets, a modern diesel engine, good radio equipment, an experienced crew with at least one linguist. Such yachts charter for about $200 a day which includes the salary and food of the crew, fuel for about eight hours of navigation daily, plus all port charges. The passengers' food is extra, costing between $4 and $5 per person a day, depending on the menu.

This is not the only sort of yacht available. You can get one for considerably less but with fewer amenities.

The best way to charter a yacht is to have a look at it before committing yourself. If you want to charter by correspondence, however, ask for full details, including the date the yacht was built, the characteristics of the engine, the date of last overhaul, type of insurance carried, plus a full rundown on accommodations and plumbing. Do not forget to find out what sort of radio equipment is carried.

If you have any doubts about a certain yacht, don't charter it, or else get some friend in Greece to look it over. You can also write to the National Tourist Organization, 4 Stadium Street, Athens, and ask them if the yacht is known to have been in an accident recently or has ever suffered extensive damage, or whether there have been complaints against the broker.

In the Classified Directory on page 343 you will find the yacht brokers listed by the National Tourist Organization of Greece. Here are some types of boats they are offering:

For $55 a day you get a little sailing vessel with one two-berth cabin and a saloon that converts into a four-berth cabin, one toilet and shower and an auxiliary 60-horsepower diesel engine. This is advertised as rebuilt in 1964 and it displaces 24 tons. Quarters are cramped, but you would not be spending much time below anyway.

A slightly larger boat, built like a Greek caique, rents for $70 a day, has one two-berth cabin and a dining room that converts into a two-berth cabin. It displaces 25 tons, is 50 feet long, has a beam of 16 feet and a draft of 5 feet. It has an auxiliary diesel engine of 85 horsepower that gives it the speed of 8 knots. This particular boat was built in 1961 and its whole configuration fits the Greek sea and movements.

For $120 a day you charter a schooner built in 1931, about 60 feet long with a beam of 14 feet, a draft of 10 feet, a 75-horsepower auxiliary diesel engine, complete set of sails, three

double cabins, a large saloon with two berths and two W.C.'s
—which seems a bargain. But here I would look closely, studying the condition of the hull and deck.

For $140, one of the brokers advertises a caique built in
1950, displacing 65 tons, 62 feet long with a beam of 18 feet
and a draft of 7 feet, with an auxiliary diesel engine of 70
horsepower that gives it a speed of 8 knots. The boat is said
to be of strong construction, accommodates 12, has a dining
saloon and six double cabins with two toilets and showers.
This would seem a good buy, inexpensive for what it offers,
but look closely at this one too.

For $140 a day there is another boat on the market, a two-
masted schooner, displacing 126 tons, 85 feet long with an
18-foot beam and a draft of 10 feet. It has an auxiliary diesel
engine of 225 horsepower that gives it a speed of 9 knots. The
broker claims this will accommodate 14 people in seven cabins with three toilets and showers. But it was built in 1931
and judging by the standard I have set of $200 a day for a
yacht that sleeps 10, this is another that bears close examina-
tion before chartering.

For $220 a day, you can rent a boat built in 1957 displacing
110 tons, 77 feet long with a beam of 20 feet, a draft of 10
feet and a diesel engine that gives it 8 knots. It accommodates
6 in two double and two single berth cabins, with two toilets
and showers. It is advertised as exceptionally well adapted to
Greek sea conditions and it looks like a local construction
job, very sturdy, probably a good sea boat, but bordering on
the expensive. On the other hand, another advertised for the
same price is marked down as a high-class yacht and is given
a Lloyd's rating of 100-A-1. It was built in 1930, probably for
some millionaire, and the prospectus claims it was rebuilt in
1957. It displaces 159 tons, is 96 feet long, has a beam of 16½
feet and a draft of 7 feet 3 inches. Its 120-horsepower diesel

engine gives it 10 knots and it accommodates 6 in two double and two single cabins with two bathrooms. Certainly 100-A-1 at Lloyd's is just about as safe as you can get, but if it is a luxury yacht, why does it charter for so little?

Another yacht is advertised for $285 a day, this one built in 1940 and displacing 85 tons. It is 85 feet long with a 19-foot beam, a draft of 6 feet and two diesel engines of 150 horse-power each, which give it a speed of 10 knots. It will accommodate 7, has a saloon, a dining room, three cabins, one bath and one toilet. This is on the expensive side.

For $300 a day you can charter a converted patrol boat, displacing 155 tons, 112 feet long with an 18-foot beam and a 7-foot draft. Its two diesel engines give it a speed of 11 knots and it will accommodate 12 in six two-berth cabins with three bathrooms and one toilet. These converted patrol boats, if the conversion is well done, are seaworthy vessels.

Another yacht is offered as one of the world's "first class" boats for $380 and it is said to have been rebuilt in 1957. It displaces 96 tons, is 104 feet long, has a beam of 21½ feet, a draft of 14 feet and a diesel engine of 155 horsepower which gives 8 knots. It will accommodate 12 in five two-berth cab-ins, plus an owner's cabin. It has five baths and showers, a spacious deckhouse plus a modern bar. It is fitted out as a schooner with a mainmast, a mizzen and two foresails and should be fun to sail. I would check on the insurance rating, however, since it is advertised as "rebuilt."

For $400 a day one of the brokers will let you have a 240-ton motor yacht built in 1930, 112 feet long with a beam of 22 feet, a draft of 11 feet, two diesel engines of 360 horsepower each which give it 11 knots. It accommodates 8 in two double and four single cabins, has three baths, is air-conditioned throughout, has a deck lounge and dining room, but since it is old I would check its insurance rating.

For $1000 a day you can rent a 345-ton yacht built in 1958 with a Lloyd's rating of 100-A-1. Her length is 136 feet, her beam is 25 feet, her draft is 13 feet and she has two 720-horsepower diesel engines that give her a speed of 15 knots. She will accommodate 10 with separate lounge and dining room and five two-berth cabins. She has three baths and is luxurious throughout.

YACHTING FACILITIES IN GREECE
(See endpaper map.)

At all the ports underlined on the map of Greece, permission is granted to enter and clear Greece.

Harbors marked ● have a reserved section of the quay where yachts may moor, and dockside facilities for engine repairs and hull maintenance. They also supply water, fuel, provisions, electricity and telephone connections, as well as space for yachts to lie up for the winter.

Harbors marked ○ provide all the above facilities, but no engine repairs or hull maintenance for large yachts.

Locations marked ■ offer only water, fuel and provisions.

Locations marked □ supply water and provisions, but no fuel. (The last two categories do not have reserved anchorage for yachts, but the harbormaster will show you where to anchor.)

YACHTING FACILITIES NEAR ATHENS

VOULIAGMENI MARINA (6 miles southeast of Piraeus)

This is reserved for yachts and is safe the year round in any weather. It supplies fuel, water and provisions and is a point of entry and exit. The basin has depths of 4 or 5 meters by the quay which is 310 meters long. Forty-one yachts can fit alongside the jetty and there are four mooring buoys for smaller craft. There are six special berths for larger craft of up to 55 meters. Yachts must moor and are not allowed to use their own anchors. Yachts are helped to their berth by the marina's personnel.

The marina pavilion has an office for port and customs authorities; an information and service bureau; a clubhouse which is an annex of the Royal Yacht Club; a laundry; a transit storehouse for the use of yachtsmen.

Vouliagmeni is a lovely spot away from the hustle and bustle of Piraeus, and only 26 kilometers from Athens.

PORT DUES AT THE MARINA

The first 15 days are free.

After this, yachts of over 8 registered tons pay a weekly charge of 1 drachma (3.3 cents) per R.T. per week.

ZEA MARINA (2 miles east of the entrance to Piraeus' main harbor)

A much larger harbor than that at Vouliagmeni, Zea can

accommodate 250 yachts. It has all the facilities and amenities of the Vouliagmeni Marina, plus installations for engine
repairs and hull maintenance. The fees are the same as at
Vouliagmeni.

WATER AND FUEL CONNECTIONS

The position of water and fuel connections on the quays is marked with slanting yellow and blue stripes and a staff flying a triangular pennant. The sea at those points is at least three meters deep. Yachts are expected to secure stern to.

When there isn't enough depth at the quayside, supply buoys are provided at a depth of at least four meters. These too are painted with yellow and blue slanting stripes.

FORMALITIES FOR YACHTS
ARRIVING FROM ABROAD

At the port of entry the yacht will go through customs, port police and health control and the captain will be given an information bulletin listing passport and currency regulations, as well as Greek rules for underwater fishing and exploration.

The captain will be asked to complete a transit log in triplicate. After the ship is inspected, two copies of the log will be kept by the authorities and one will be kept by the yacht's captain. The yacht is then free to move in Greek waters.

If at an intermediate port there is a change in crew or passengers, this must be noted in the log and certified therein by the port authorities. If the yacht receives goods in transit, these must be entered in the log and the entry shown to customs. If a yacht refuels in transit, the supplier's receipt must be checked by the port authorities and the amount of the transaction entered in the transit log. On arrival in port, after the yacht has berthed, the captain must show his transit log to a port official, who will record the ship's name and flag in the port register.

Before the ship leaves its last port of call in Greece the captain must fill in the final section of the transit log and give this to the local customs officer. The yacht is then free to leave Greece.

If exceptional circumstances prevent a yacht from reaching its last port of call in Greece, the captain must mail the transit log to the customs authority of that port after completing the last section and explaining the circumstances.

NAVIGATIONAL CONDITIONS IN GREEK WATERS

Navigation in Greek waters presents no special problems to the yachtsman. Shores are steep-to and rocks and ledges infrequent. Fog is practically nonexistent and if it occurs at all it is burned off by the rising sun. The coast and islands have innumerable small coves and anchorages which can be chosen at random from the charts. When anchoring for the night keep in mind that the prevailing wind is northerly.

In nearly all cases the water is so clear you can see the bottom at depths of up to eight or ten fathoms. Sand bottom is the rule, but where a thick matting of grass and weed can be seen it usually means poor holding ground.

Hazards to navigation such as ledges and rocks are not numerous. They are shown on the charts and are easily seen through the extremely clear water; but they are rarely marked by buoys in Greek waters. Cruising at night through the islands is easily managed for there are numerous lighthouses and flashers. Also, as the islands are high, they stand out clearly at night on the horizon, and many can be seen from a great distance in the clear atmosphere, even on moonless nights.

WEATHER CONDITIONS

Average Throughout Greece	April C° F°	May C° F°	June C° F°	July C° F°	Aug. C° F°	Sept. C° F°	Oct. C° F°
Temperature of atmo- sphere	16 60	18 65	22 72	26 80	26 80	22 72	18 65
Sea tempera- ture	16 60	18 65	21 70	24 75	25 77	23 74	21 70
Wind strength in Beaufort scale	0.8–4	0.7–3.5	0.7–3	0.8–3.5	1–3.5	0.8–3.5	0.5–3.5
Direction of prevailing winds	S-W	S-NW	N-W	NE-NW	N-NW	NE-NW	NE-NW

WINDS

The yachtsman can be assured of fine cruising in Greek waters if he plans his voyage so as to visit the right cruising grounds in the most suitable months. Weather conditions he is likely to meet while on any of the suggested cruises (page 284 on) are given for each cruise. In general, during the cruising season there are two prevailing winds: in the Ionian the Maistros, a gentle northwest breeze that comes up in the afternoon, drops in the evening and almost never interferes with yachting plans; in the Aegean the Meltemi, a strong northerly wind which can last two or three days. The Meltemi season is considered to last from mid-July until mid-September. During blows there is no fall in the barometer and skies remain clear, except for low-hanging white clouds over the high peaks of the islands. The wind can draw down off the mountains in heavy gusts and it is well to stand off from under the leeward shore of the high islands and coast. The winds vary from force 6 to force 8 on the Beaufort scale at times and are occasionally accompanied by short, rough, steep seas. Although a blow may last two or three days it generally abates considerably after sundown, so you can dodge the Meltemi even at its worst by island-hopping at night.

There is good sailing, even in Meltemi weather, in the Saronic Gulf which is sheltered by the mass of Attica. The Gulf of Nauplion is similarly sheltered. A west wind, the Pounente, prevails in the Gulf of Corinth, but it rarely reaches great velocity.

ESSENTIAL INFORMATION FOR
YACHTSMEN

Assistance. For assistance always contact the port authorities.

Airplanes. You can fly to Athens from Corfu, Kalamai, Heraklion, Volos, Salonica, Kavalla, Rhodes, Patras, Lesbos (Mytilene), Samos, Alexandroupolis, Cos, Preveza, Canea, Lemnos.

Charts. An up-to-date chart of the Greek coastal areas, showing all yacht supply stations, can be bought for 20 drs. ($0.66) at yacht supply stations and offices of the port control officers. You should have the British Admiralty charts of your cruising area and the British Admiralty Pilot, Volume IV, which contains all the information a yachtsman may require.

Correspondence should be addressed to the yacht by name, care of the local port authority, where it will be held pending the yacht's arrival.

Coves. Quiet and peaceful coves can be found everywhere. If you are chartering a yacht keep this in mind as most captains naturally prefer to stay in ports to be with friends, whereas for the passenger the hustle and bustle of a port can have its drawbacks.

Credit cards for fuel issued by B.P., Caltex, Mobiloil, Purfina and Shell will be honored at any yacht supply station, even if that station is not run by the company issuing the card, but by one of the others mentioned above.

Customs brokers will be found for you by local officials to assist in formalities when taking on provisions.

Electric current in Greece is AC 220/380 V, 50 cycles. Maximum line current 25A. To use this current the craft should have a transformer for DC. You pay 30 drs. ($1) at yacht harbors for the connection plus 6.3 cents per kilowatt. The price per kw decreases if you use large quantities. The lowest rate is 2.3 cents per kw.

Fishing. Beside net, rod and line fishing, spear fishing is a great sport. Through the Royal Yacht Club you can get in touch with amateur fishing associations for advice on the best fishing grounds.

Fuel is sold at transit prices which vary from one supply station to another (depending on the distance from Athens) from $46.66 per ton in Piraeus to $70.33 per ton in Castellorizo.

Paid hands. Excellent professional sailors are readily available to sign on as crew. The yacht supply station will help you with the hiring.

Provisions. Yachts should take on provisions in the larger harbors, where a greater range of supplies is available. The agents in charge of yacht supply stations will help you avoid being overcharged. The port control officer exercises a benevolent watching brief over such transactions.

Radio communication. At any port with a yacht supply station the port control officers will provide a leaflet giving details of wavelengths and times of transmission of the shore radio-telephone service, weather forecasts, emergency traffic, medical service and radio beacons, also a MAFOR code which gives the international code lettering for weather forecasts.

Royal Hellenic Yacht Club. This club is located at Tourkolimano, a small harbor near Piraeus. It offers many facilities to small racing yachts of all international classes; quite a number of these participate in the many winter and summer regattas at Phaliron Bay. Through the Royal Yacht Club the yacht racing enthusiast may join any of the other sailing clubs in the area, use any of the club's boats or have his own boat serviced.

Telephones cost $1 a week for the connection at yacht harbors. See pages 29 and 30 for inland and overseas telephone rates in Greece.

Water at yacht supply stations costs 66 cents per cubic meter.

WEATHER REPORTS

Weather reports are given in English twice daily in MAFOR code over Athens radio at 1001 and 2215 GMT (1201 and 2415 Local Greek time). Radio Athens has a calling frequency of 2182 KC and a traffic frequency of 2590 KC. Emergency warnings of rough weather are given in English in MAFOR code over these frequencies. For a weather forecast before leaving any harbor in Greece, phone Athens 980134 for a special report in either Greek or English.

SHORE RADIOTELEPHONE STATIONS - WEATHER FORECASTS - EMERGENCY
TRAFFIC - MEDICAL SERVICE - RADIO BEACONS

| Shore Station | Hours of Operation (G.M.T.) | Call Sign | Frequencies in KCS | | Traffic Lists* | Remarks |
			Calling	Traffic		
Athens-Radio	Continuous	SVN	2182	2590	5'	Weather Forecasts by This Station Only A) In MAFOR code at 1015 and 2215 GMT B) In Greek plain language 0945 and 2145 GMT C) Special weather warnings in Greek and English.
Chios-Radio	0600–2000	SVX	2182	3743	3'	

Shore Station	Hours of Operation (G.M.T.)	Call Sign	Calling	Traffic	Traffic Lists*	Remarks
Iraklion-Radio	Continuous	SVH	2182	2799	20'	
Kerkyra-Radio	0400–0001	SVK	2182	2607	10'	
Patras-Radio	0530–1930	SVP	2182	2792	25'	
Rodos-Radio	0600 through midnight to 0300	SVR	2182	2624	3'	
Thessaloniki-Radio	Continuous	SVS	2182	2730	15'	

The header "Frequencies in KCS" spans the Calling and Traffic columns.

* NOTE Traffic lists are transmitted at the number of minutes past the hour as indicated in the above column.

EMERGENCY TRAFFIC on 2182 kcs.

MEDICAL SERVICE in English plain language by Athens Radio only; throughout the 24 hours.

RADIO BEACONS (Continuous 24 hours service)

Name and Position		Call Sign	Type of Emission	Frequency
Thessaloniki (Salonica)	40° 37' N 22° 57' E	TMS	A2	308
Araxos (near Patras)	38° 10' N 21° 26' E	SWX	»	326
Glyfada (Athens Area)	37° 52' N 23° 45' E	HN	»	372
Iraklion (Crete)	35° 20' N 25° 10' E	SWH	»	259
Kerkyra (Corfu)	39° 26' N 19° 55' E	SWK	»	403

SUGGESTED CRUISES

The cruises described take in most of the areas that can be visited by yacht. By combining features of these cruises there are endless possibilities for working out special itineraries to suit the sportsman, the archaeology buff, the Byzantinologist, or the man who merely wants to laze and drift on a lovely sea amid beautiful scenery.

Descriptions of places of interest on the cruises suggested below can be found in Sections II and III. Consult the index.

We do not tell you here how long any voyage will take. This is for you to decide, taking into account the speed of your boat, the course you set and weather. So get out a chart and your dividers, measure the distance in minutes of longitude between your ports of call, consult the British Admiralty Pilot, Volume IV, and work out your estimated times of arrival.

CRUISE 1

Northwest Greece. Ionian Islands, northwest coast of the mainland, coasts of the Patras and Corinth Gulf. This will take in Corfu, Mourtos, Paxos, Parga, Preveza, Lefkas, Ithaca, Cephalonia, Patras, Naupactus (Lepanto), Itea, Corinth and Piraeus. (British Admiralty Charts nos.: 203, 206, 221, 1450, 1557, 1600, 1609, 1620, 1676, 1939, 3485, 3496)

Weather. Fine for the whole cruising season. The prevailing wind is the Maistros, a gentle northwest wind. In the Gulf of Corinth you may encounter the Pounente, a westerly wind which kicks up white horses but raises no swell to speak of.

Corfu. The town of Corfu is a point of entry and exit. Yacht supply station for fuel, water, provisions and repairs. Depth by the quay, 6 meters. Local yacht club. *Alipa* at Paliocastritsa, on the northwest part of the island, has a yacht supply station for fuel and water. Yachts secure to a supply buoy at a depth of 4 meters. (If a yacht coming from the west reaches Alipa as its first stop in Greece and needs to refuel, it can do so provided it then proceeds directly to the port of Corfu for the entry formalities.) Near Alipa is a pavilion with restaurant and telephone.

Gouvia Bay is 3½ miles N.N.W. of the port of Corfu. Fully protected from all winds this bay is 5 meters deep at the center and is a perfectly peaceful spot for yachts planning long stays or for wintering. It has a yacht supply station for fuel, water and provisions. Yachts secure to a buoy at a depth of 4 meters.

Mourtos. Opposite the southern point of Corfu on the mainland coast of Epirus in a small bay is the village of Mourtos, a yacht supply station for water and basic food. Depth, 3 meters. From Mourtos you can hire a car or take a bus to Ioannina.

Paxos. South of Mourtos is Paxos island with its picturesque Bay of Gaios. A yacht supply station for water and basic food. Depth, 3 meters.

Parga. South from Mourtos on the coast of Epirus is the small town of Parga with a yacht supply station for fuel, water and provisions. Depth, 2.5 meters. Marvelous sandy beaches for swimming flank this town.

Preveza. South along the Epirus coast and at the entrance to the Amvrakikos Gulf is the small town of Preveza, a yacht supply station for fuel, water and provisions. Depth, 3.5 meters and over. Point of entry and exit. Cruise around the beautiful gulf. Take the fifteen-minute car trip to Nicopolis and to Arta which has lovely Byzantine churches.

Lefkas. This island is south from Preveza. The port has a yacht supply station for fuel, water and provisions. Depth, 4 meters. Sail through the straits of Lefkas with its medieval fortress and stop at some of the delightful islets off the east coast. Sail south to Ithaca.

Ithaca. At its port of Vathi is a yacht supply station for fuel, water, provisions and small repairs. Depth, 4 meters. Local yacht club. Some pre-Mycenaean ruins, locally believed to be the palace of Odysseus. Sail south.

Cephalonia. (See also Cruise 1a). The main port, Argostoli, has a yacht supply station for fuel, water, provisions and minor repairs. Depth, 6 meters. Point of entry and exit. Local yacht club. A drive across the island is recommended. From Argostoli sail west through the Patraikos Gulf.

Patras. Yacht supply station for fuel, water and provisions and major repairs. Point of entry and exit. Depth, 3 meters. Local yacht club. Fine beaches nearby. Sail N.E. to Naupactus (Lepanto). This is a small port that dates from the Middle Ages. A yacht supply station for fuel, water and provisions. Depth, 3 meters. From here you can take a car to Messolongi where Lord Byron died. Continue along the north coast of the Gulf of Corinth to Itea.

Itea. A yacht supply station for fuel, water and provisions. Depth, 3.5 meters. Point of entry and exit. While in this area visit Delphi, then enter the bay of Antikiros, opposite the village of Aspra-Spitia, for a visit to the Byzantine monastery of Osios Loukas. Now sail along the north or south coast of the Gulf of Corinth. Both are lovely, the south green and populated, while the north coast has numerous little bays and inlets.

Corinth. Yacht supply station for fuel, water and provisions. Depth, 2.5 meters, marker buoys indicate where the water is 3 meters. Visit old Corinth harbor and the Akrokorinthos—the fortress. Anchor in the small harbor at the western end of the Corinth Canal until the Canal authorities give you permission to pass.

CORINTH CANAL DUES

Yachts arriving from or proceeding to a foreign port:

0– 50 tons	600 drachmas
51–100 "	980 "
101–150 "	1,500 "
151–200 "	2,100 "
201–250 "	2,800 "
251–300 "	3,220 "

Yachts moving in Greek territorial waters:

0– 25 tons	102 drachmas
25– 50 "	177 "
51– 75 "	237 "
76–100 "	327 "
101–125 "	417 "
126–150 "	507 "
151–175 "	597 "
176–200 "	687 "
201–225 "	777 "
226–250 "	867 "
251–300 "	972 "

Pass through the canal and sail for Zea, the yacht marina at Piraeus, or for the yacht marina at Vouliagmeni.

CRUISE 1a

Zakinthos, the West and South Coast of the Peloponnesus.
This is an alternative cruise round the Peloponnesus, taking
in the island of Zakinthos, the ports of Katakolon, Pylus,
Methoni, Kalamata, Limenion, and Githion. If you wish to
continue round the coast of the Peloponnesus to Piraeus,
simply reverse the itinerary described in Cruise 2. (British
Admiralty Charts nos.: 207, 335, 682, 1436, 1685, 3342, 3372)

Weather. Ideal cruising weather. Sailing enthusiasts should
go round the Peloponnesus from West to East. In the Ionian,
the gentle northerly Maistros prevails—a breeze that comes
up in the early afternoon and dies down at sunset. The west
and southern coast of the Peloponnesus is protected during
the cruising season as the south winds one encounters there
are rarely strong. However, around Cape Malea, navigate with
care for when N.W. and N.E. winds are blowing they generate
strong currents there.

From *Cephalonia* sail due south to Zakinthos. From *Patras*
sail S.W.

Zakinthos. A yacht supply station for fuel, water and provisions. Depth, 4 meters. Point of entry and exit. Drive around
this lovely island, called the "Flower of the Levant" by the
Venetians. Sail S.E. from Zakinthos to the mainland.

Katakolon. This port has a yacht supply station for fuel,
water and provisions. Depth, 3.5 meters. Point of entry and
exit. The bay is protected in all weathers. From here take the
bus or hire a car and visit Olympia, 32 kilometers away. Proceed south from Katakolon sailing near the coast which is
full of lovely beaches, lush fields and orchards set against a
beautiful chain of mountains in the background.

Pylus (Navarinon). Yacht supply station for fuel, water

and provisions. Depth, 4 meters. Point of entry and exit. Lovely town and bay. By road one hour from Kalamai and 30 minutes from Methoni. Visit the ancient palace of Nestor, 10 kilometers away. Proceed southward.

Methoni. Yacht supply station for fuel, water and provisions. Depth, 3 meters. Lovely bay and sandy beaches. Continue southward toward Kavo Akrita and follow the west coast of the Messiniakos Gulf to Kalamai.

Kalamai. Yacht supply station for fuel, water, provisions, wintering and major repairs. Local yacht club. From Kalamai you can visit Mystras and Sparta by road over the Taïyetos Mountains, a fine drive. You can also visit the Frankish fortress of Koroni, or the ancient Greek site at Ithome. From Kalamai sail south and continue round the Mani peninsula, distinguished for its wild beauty and many old towers. Between Kalamai and Cape Tenaron, the only protected bay is at Limenion on the Mani peninsula.

Limenion. Yacht supply station for fuel, water and provisions. Depth, 3 meters. Now sail southward staying as close as possible to the coast, round Cape Tenaron (Matapan) and then sail due north.

Githion. Yacht supply station for fuel, water and provisions. If you missed the drive over the mountain from Kalamai to Sparta and Mystras you may drive there from Githion. From Githion you can follow the eastern coast of the Gulf of Laconia and spend the night at Elafonissos, a perfectly protected small bay.

CRUISE 2

From Attica sailing S.W. round the Saronic Gulf and islands, taking in Salamis, Aegina, Palea Epidaurus, Poros,

Hydra, Spetses, Nauplion and then Monemvasia. (British Admiralty Charts nos.: 1308, 1436, 1518, 1685)

Weather. Ideal cruising the whole year round except for a rare winter storm. Protected from the Meltemi.

Salamis. Sail around the island to see its little bays and coves. Because of the shipyard and naval base, traffic is heavy so keep an eye out.

Aegina. At the small port on the N.W. tip of the island is a yacht supply station for fuel, water provisions and small repairs. Depth by the quay, 2.5 meters. On the N.E. of the island is the ancient temple of Aphaea Athena.

Palea Epidaurus. Sail westward to this pleasant bay and visit the ancient theater of Epidaurus. Yacht supply station for fuel, water and provisions. Depth, 3 meters. Sail S.E. along a beautiful stretch of coastline to Poros.

Poros. Yacht supply station for fuel, water and provisions. Excellent bay for sailing and water-skiing. Sail southward.

Hydra. Yacht supply station for fuel, water and provisions. Continue S.W. to Spetses.

Spetses. Yacht supply station for fuel, water, provisions and minor repairs inside the old harbor, not far from the lighthouse. Depth, 3 meters. Sail N.W. to Nauplion.

Nauplion. Yacht supply station for fuel, water, provisions and minor repairs. Point of entry and exit. Depth, 6 meters. Visit Mycenae and Tiryns. Sail directly south to Monemvasia.

Monemvasia. Yacht supply station for fuel, water and provisions. Secure to a supply buoy anchored at a depth of 4.5 meters. Visit Sparta and Mystras.

CRUISE 3

South Aegean area, Kithira, Crete, Carpathus, Rhodes, Castellorizo. (British Admiralty Charts nos.: 236, 1533, 1555,

1604, 1658, 1667, 1685, 1886, 2188, 2536a and 2536b, 2824, 3928)

Weather. If you are cruising in this area during the Meltemi season (mid-July to mid-September) you may face fairly stiff blows; but the winds drop considerably after dark and since visibility is good even on moonless nights, cruising at night presents no difficulties.

Sailing S.W. from Monemvasia you come to the island of Kithira.

Kithira and its bay of Kapsali are fully protected from the north wind. Yacht supply station for fuel, water and provisions. Depth, 3 meters. The whole island is attractive and worth a visit. Sail S.E. toward Crete.

Crete. The first port is Canea, a NATO base, and administrative capital of the island. Port of entry and exit. Yacht supply station for fuel, water and provisions. Depth, 3 meters. Continue eastward round the Akrotiri peninsula to Rethimnon.

Rethimnon. Yacht supply station for water and provisions only. Depth, 5 meters. Continuing eastward you arrive at Heraklion.

Heraklion. Point of entry and exit. Yacht supply station for fuel, water, provisions and minor repairs. Depth, 6 meters. Greece's second largest commercial port. Visit Knossos and Phaestos. The trip by land to Agios Nikolaos is through some breathtaking scenery. From Heraklion sail eastward to the perfectly protected bay of Agios Nikolaos.

Agios Nikolaos. A yacht supply station for fuel, water and provisions and minor repairs. Depth, 3 meters. Point of entry and exit. There are lovely sandy beaches and nearby the small island of Spinalonga with its Venetian fortress. The trip by land to Sitia, 73 kilometers away is superb. Sail east to *Sitia*, a yacht supply station for water and provisions only. Depth,

3 meters. From Sitia follow a N.E. course to pass Cape Sidero, the easternmost tip of Crete. (Sail around the southern coast of the island only if the weather is good. Keep in mind this coast has no safe ports or bays.)

Weather note. The sea in the Crete-Kassos channel is often rough and requires careful navigation. On the south point of Kassos is the small bay of Avlaki, a safe refuge. The prevailing wind in that area is from the west.

Carpathus. At the small port of Pigadia is a yacht supply station for fuel, water and provisions. Depth, 4 meters. The beaches on the island are marvelous and the scenery a delight. Sail N.E. for Rhodes.

Rhodes. Follow the eastern coast and stop at *Lindos,* a yacht supply station for fuel, water and provisions. Depth, 3 meters. Visit the acropolis. Sail north to the capital, *Rhodes,* whose harbor, Mandraki, in the city, is well protected. Yacht supply station for fuel, water, provisions and repairs. Depth, 4 meters. Rhodes is a perfect place from which to cruise along the Turkish coast or to the many small islands round about. Sailing S.E. from Rhodes you come to Greece's southernmost island, Castellorizo.

Castellorizo. Yacht supply station for fuel, water and provisions. Depth, 3 meters. Castellorizo is not a point of entry or exit, but yachts arriving from the east can refuel and also make a short stay on the island provided they then proceed to Rhodes for the necessary entry formalities. This island is worth a visit for its delightful scenery and beaches. Also for its extraordinary grotto, a quarter of a mile from the harbor, best seen at sunrise when its blue coloring is most intense.

CRUISE 4

Rhodes, Symi, Cos, Kalimnos, Leros, Patmos, Samos, Chios, Andros, Kea, Piraeus. (British Admiralty Charts nos.:

1522, 1526, 1530, 1533, 1537, 1566, 1568, 1604, 1617, 1645, 1657, 1669, 1820, 1833, 1867, 1898, 2682 and charts 3923 through 3928, 3466)

Weather. This itinerary is on the whole protected during the Meltemi season, being under the lee of Asia Minor. Once you leave Chios for islands in the central Aegean (Andros and Kea, in this itinerary) it is advisable to go through the Andros-Tinos channel to avoid the strait between Southern Euboea and Andros, an area specially exposed to the north-easter. Also, by going as far north as Chios along the Turkish coast, before turning toward the central Aegean, you will then sail before the wind in the Meltemi season.

From *Rhodes* sail N.W. to *Symi*. Visit the Panormiti monastery in the bay on the southern part of the island. The small town of Symi has a splendid deep natural harbor. From Symi, keeping close to Cape Krios, sail northwest to Cos.

Cos. Yacht supply station for fuel, water and provisions. A marker buoy indicates a depth of 3 meters. Point of entry and exit. Birthplace of Hippocrates. Visit the archaeological sites and take a trip across the lovely island. Sail on a westerly course to Kalimnos.

Kalimnos. Yacht supply station for fuel, water, provisions and minor repairs. Depth, 3 meters. Here are lovely beaches, an original island architecture and a flourishing fleet of sponge divers. Sail along the west coast of the island on a northerly course to Leros.

Leros. At the port of Laki is a yacht supply station for fuel, water, provisions and repairs. Depth, 3 meters. Excellent and well protected natural harbor. From Laki sail along the west coast of Leros on a N.N.W. course for Patmos.

Patmos. At the port of Scala is a yacht supply station for fuel, water and provisions. Depth, 3 meters. Visit the Byzantine monastery, the museum and library. Following the eastern coast of Patmos sail in a N.E. direction for Samos.

Samos. The port of Tigani has a yacht supply station for fuel, water and provisions. A depth of 3 meters is indicated by marker buoy. Point of entry and exit. Visit the ancient ruins near Tigani and take time to explore the interior of this island. From Tigani sail through the channel between Samos and the Turkish coast along the eastern side of the island and proceed N.W. to Chios.

Chios. Yacht supply station for fuel, water, provisions and repairs. A depth of 3 meters is indicated by marker buoy. Point of entry and exit. Local yacht club. Now proceed to Andros on a S.W. course.

Andros. The port of Kastron in the center of the east coast of the island has a yacht supply station for fuel, water, and provisions. Continue down the east coast of the island and up the west coast to Batsi in Gavrion Bay where there is a yacht supply station for water and provisions. You might wish to take the 30-minute drive to Batsi across the island instead. Marvelous beaches. From Batsi sail S.W. for Kea.

Kea. A yacht supply station for fuel, water and provisions. Depth, 3 meters. From Agios Nicolaos, its port, passing Cape Sounion, sail into the Piraeus area.

CRUISE 4a

Islands in the central Aegean. Here we take in alternative islands between Piraeus and Rhodes—Soros, Tinos, Paros, Naxos and Amorgos. When sailing from the Piraeus area to Rhodes this is the most usual course, but the multitude of islands gives endless possibilities for exploring along the way. (British Admiralty Charts nos.: as in Cruise 4)

Weather. This area is exposed to the Meltemi from mid-July to mid-September, but the winds do not blow continuously and generally drop at night. Moreover, since the distance between one island and the next is small, plan your course so as to be protected during the hours when the wind is at its greatest strength. In this way you may find the winds, if anything, favorable to sailing. Also during the Meltemi season it is advisable to leave Piraeus on a S.E. course and return on the itinerary described in Cruise 4.

Leave Piraeus on a S.E. course and pass *Anavissos* on the coast of Attica where there is a yacht supply station for fuel, water and provisions. Depth, 3 meters. From Anavissos sailing close to the coast you can reach *Cape Sounion* and anchor for a visit to the temple. From Cape Sounion on a S.E. course pass the southern point of Kea and sail on past the northern point of Kithnos to the island of Syros.

Syros. The port has a yacht supply station for fuel, water, provisions and repairs. Depth, 3 meters. Point of entry and exit. Visit the island. Sail on a N.E. course to the nearby island of Tinos.

Tinos. Yacht supply station for water, fuel and provisions. Depth, 3 meters. Visit the famous church of the Virgin with its miraculous icon. If you can, stop at the island August 15 to see the Feast of the Dormition. From Tinos take a S.S.E. course to Mykonos.

Mykonos. Yacht supply station for fuel, water and provisions. Depth, 3 meters. As the port of Mykonos is exposed to the north wind, anchor at the nearby bay of Ornos on the S.W. coast, about 3 kilometers from the port. Swim at the beach and visit the town. From Mykonos continue southward.

Paros. The port of Parikia has a yacht supply station for fuel, water and provisions. Depth, 3 meters. Visit the grotto on the islet of Antiparos. From Parikia sail along the north coast of Paros to the island of Naxos.

Naxos. Yacht supply station for fuel, water and provisions.

A depth of 3 meters is indicated by a marker buoy. Stay awhile to visit the island. Sail through the Paros-Naxos channel, passing the Schinoussa islands on the way and arrive at Amorgos.

Amorgos. Katapola port has a yacht supply station for fuel, water and provisions. Depth, 3 meters, but ten meters from the quay the depth increases to 4.5 meters. Marvelous beaches and good spear-fishing. From Amorgos, by way of Astypalaea, and sailing between Nissiros and Tilos, proceed to Rhodes.

CRUISE 4b

Islands in the central Aegean. Here is yet another route from Piraeus to Rhodes taking in the islands of Siphnos, Milos and Ios. (British Admiralty Charts nos.: 1526, 1542, 1657, 1682, 1815, 1817, 1832, 1833, 1837, 1898, 2043, 2051, 2753, 3922)

Weather is as described in Cruise 4a.

Proceed from Piraeus past *Cape Sounion* and sail first round the east coast of Kithnos and then along the west coast of Serifos, which is worth a visit for its pretty town overlooking the delightful small bay. Sail to the island of Siphnos.

Siphnos. Its port of Kamares has a yacht supply station for fuel, water and provisions. Depth, 3 meters. Visit the picturesque island and swim on its beautiful beaches. Take a S.S.W. course and pass along the south coast of Kimolos till you arrive at Adamas, the port of Milos.

Milos. Yacht supply station for fuel, water and provisions. Depth of 3 meters is indicated by a marker buoy. Visit the capital of the island noted for its magnificent setting and nearby catacombs. Sail around the north coast of Milos through the Kimolos-Milos channel, along the north coast of Poliaigos and continue to Ios on an easterly course.

Ios. Yacht supply station for fuel, water and provisions. Depth, 3 meters. Well protected harbor. Stay here and take a side trip to Santorini, the volcanic island nearby. (Santorini has no anchorage because its waters are so deep, and it is exposed to north winds, but you can secure to a buoy while visiting the town.) If you do not wish to return to Ios for the night you can sail northward and anchor at Scala, 3 miles S.W. of Kavo-Malta, on the islet of *Sikinos.*

From Sikinos follow an easterly course, by the south coast of Astypalaea and through the Nisiros-Tilos channel to Rhodes.

CRUISE 5

N.E. coast of Greece, Euboea, Sporades, Haldidiki, Thasos, north coast of Greece, taking in Lavrion, Chalkis, Kammena Vourla, Volos, Skiathos, Skopelos, Skyros, Kymi, Salonica, Paliouri, Porto-Koufo, Agios Nikolaos, Ouranoupolis for Mount Athos, Ierissos, Eleftere, Kavalla, Thasos, Porto-Lago, Alexandroupolis. (British Admiralty Charts nos.: 1086, 1568, 1659, 1661, 1664, 1665, 1668, 1672, 1891)

Weather. This whole area is protected from the Meltemi, except for the section from Skiathos and Skopelos up to Salonica in this itinerary. If you take this cruise during the Meltemi season, before leaving either Skiathos or Skopelos on a north course, consult the meteorological bulletin or phone Athens 980134, for a special weather report. Best sail from Skiathos after sunset when the wind drops and reach a protected area before dawn. Leave Piraeus for Cape Sounion and then take a N.N.E. course for Lavrion.

Lavrion. Yacht supply station for fuel, water and provisions. Depth, 3 meters. Point of entry and exit. From Lavrion northward, sail either along the lovely east coast of Attica or toward the small town of Karistos in a delightful bay of southern Euboea, pass among the Petalii islets and proceed north in the Evoikos Gulf.

Chalkis. Here are two yacht supply stations for fuel, water and provisions, one to the north and one to the south of the bridge that connects Euboea and the mainland. The depth is 3 meters. The strait has a strange local tide that changes course from north to south, every six hours. At its peak, in the middle of the six-hour period, it reaches a velocity of 6 knots. The bridge between Euboea and the mainland opens for the passage of ships at the time the tide changes. The two yacht supply stations have been so located that yachts can refuel while waiting for the bridge to open. To visit Chalkis, anchor in the bay just N.W. of the straits. Continuing on course through the north Evoikos Gulf, you sail between pleasant coastlines on both sides. But keep a sufficient distance from the shore because in a strong blow near the mountains, whirlwinds are apt to form. You can stop to visit the pretty bay of Aedipsos on Euboea with its little spa, then cross S.W. to the mainland and Kammena Vourla.

Kammena Vourla. Yacht supply station for water and provisions only. From here you can drive to the pass of Thermopylae. Sail along the north coast of Euboea through the Trikeri channel into the Pagassitikos Gulf.

Volos. Yacht supply station for fuel, water, provisions and repairs. Depth, 3 meters. Point of entry and exit. Local yacht club. From Volos drive to Mount Pelion. Sail south from Volos across the Pagassitikos Gulf to Trikeri and turn east for the island of Skiathos.

Skiathos. Yacht supply station for fuel, water and provisions. Depth, 3 meters. If you wish to visit the various islands of the Sporades make this your base. All the islands are worth seeing, even the northern islands that are uninhabited. Serene, beautiful beaches.

Skopelos. Yacht supply station for fuel, water and provisions. Depth, 3 meters. Proceed to Skyros.

Skyros. Anchor at the port of Linaria. Yacht supply station for fuel, water and provisions. Depth, 3 meters. Visit the picturesque little town of Skyros. From Skyros you may wish to visit Kymi on the coast of Euboea.

Kymi. Yacht supply station for fuel, water and provisions. Depth, 3 meters. Sail back to the island of Skiathos.

Weather note. At Skiathos, if the Meltemi is blowing, consult the meteorological bulletin and leave at night on a N.N.W. course across the Thermaikos Gulf to Salonica.

Salonica. Yacht supply station for fuel, water, provisions and repairs. Depth, 3 meters. Point of entry and exit. Local yacht club. Visit the superb Byzantine churches of the area and ancient Pella, 30 kilometers away, capital of Alexander the Great. Sail across the Thermaikos Gulf toward the Halkidiki peninsula which ends in three prongs, called respectively from west to east, Cassandra, Sidonia and Athos. Stop at Paliouri on the S.W. point of Cassandra.

Paliouri. Yacht supply station for water and provisions. Depth, 3 meters. You can sail direct to Porto-Koufo on the next prong, but the coast of the Toroneos Gulf between Cassandra and Sidonia is so calm and peaceful that it is worth meandering here.

Porto-Koufo. A perfectly protected natural harbor. Yacht supply station for fuel, water and provisions. Depth, 3 meters. From here sail round Drepanon point and follow the eastern coast of Sidonia.

Agios Nikolaos. Yacht supply station for water and provisions only. Depth, 3 meters. Make a short stay in this idyllic bay to cruise among its multitude of islands and islets. Ideal fishing. Now follow the north coast of the Singiticos Gulf to Ouranoupolis.

Ouranoupolis (Pyrgus). Yacht supply station for fuel, water and provisions. Depth, 4.5 meters. From here visit Mount Athos.

Weather note. The sea is generally calm during the summer on the western coast of the Athos peninsula. The eastern coast is more exposed to the north wind. Navigate the southern point of the peninsula with care, as the sea can get rough at times. If you plan to cruise along the eastern side keep in mind that it has no natural harbors. The only natural harbors really protected from all winds are the small cove near the lighthouse of the islet Amouliani and the small bay south of Akra point, 5 miles N.N.E. of Ierissos.

Ierissos. Yacht supply station for fuel, water and provisions. Depth, 3 meters. The harbor is not adequately protected from strong winds. Use it only as a supply point and anchor at the small bay south of Akra point. From here sail around the serene Strimonikos Gulf, but look out for shallows in the northern parts of the gulf. Proceed to Elefthere.

Elefthere (near Perama). Yacht supply station for fuel, water and provisions. A depth of 3 meters is indicated by a marker buoy. Spend the night at the perfectly protected harbor. Proceed on a N.E. course to Kavalla.

Kavalla. Yacht supply station for fuel, water and provisions. Depth, 5 meters. Local yacht club. Visit Philippi, 25 kilometers away. Proceed to Thasos.

Thasos. Yacht supply station for fuel, water and provisions. Continue on a N.N.E. course.

Porto-Lago. Yacht supply station for fuel, water and provisions. A depth of 3 meters is indicated by a marker buoy. The bay is perfectly protected in all weathers, but requires careful sailing as it is shallow in parts. Stay in the channel marked with buoys. Now sail along the coast of Thrace, making sure you avoid the shallows.

Alexandroupolis. Yacht supply station for fuel, water and provisions. Depth, 4 meters. Point of entry and exit.

CRUISE 5a

Northern Aegean Samothrace, Lemnos, Lesbos (Mytilene). This cruise starts at Alexandroupolis and takes in Samothrace, Lemnos and its southern bay of Moudros, then Lesbos from which you proceed to Piraeus. (British Admiralty Charts: same as for Cruise 5)

Weather. As described in Cruise 5. Sail from Alexandroupolis on a S.S.W. course for Samothrace to visit the archaeological sites there.

Samothrace. The Kamariotissa bay is not protected from the north wind and it is too deep for anchoring. However, there is a mooring buoy for yachts. From Samothrace continue on a S.S.W. course to Lemnos.

Lemnos. The port of Mirini is a yacht supply station for fuel, water and provisions. Depth, 3 meters. Point of entry and exit. Yachts sailing through the Dardanelles to Istanbul use this port. If you are in the area in August you will see the extraordinary sunsets behind Mount Athos, when the peak seems to be on fire. From Mirini sail S.E. round the southern coast of Lemnos to the lovely natural bay.

Moudros. Yacht supply station for water and provisions only. From Moudros on a S.S.E. course pass through the channel north of Lesbos following the N.E. coast to arrive at the port Mytilene on Lesbos.

Lesbos (Mytilene). Yacht supply station for fuel, water and provisions. Depth, 4 meters. Point of entry and exit. Visit the petrified forest. Sail along the southern coast of the island on a S.W.W. course. You can stop at the small island of *Psara*, and return to Piraeus either through the channel between South Euboea and Andros if there is no Meltemi, or through the Andros-Tinos channel.

SECTION VI

A glimpse at the essence of Greek mythology, history, religion, and culture

MYTHOLOGY AND HISTORY

Since this is not a history book, I am giving you here what I consider to be the essence of Greece's contribution to history. I feature Athens above all other ancient Greek cities, because I think it is fair to say that Athens is representative of what ancient Greece gave to the world.

In the dim mists of prehistory, Athens was a group of huts huddled around the Acropolis, a steep hill with a water supply. Gradually it grew stronger, favored by two gods—one, Athena, goddess of wisdom and daughter of Zeus from whose head she emerged fully grown and fully armed, the eternal virgin; the other, Poseidon, brother of Zeus, god of the sea. Each offered a tremendous gift to the Athenians: Poseidon struck the rock of the Acropolis with a trident and out sprang a horse; Athena struck the rock with her spear and an olive tree grew instantly. The Athenians chose Athena's gift and gave her name to their city.

With such protectors, Athens prospered, extending her domain to neighboring villages. Fabled Theseus, for whose existence there is no historical evidence, united the whole of Attica into one kingdom, a federal union, governed by delegates from each part. Theseus is reputed to have invited his fellow Greeks to become Athenians, originating a policy that was to be one of the political glories of Athens. He is also said to have resigned as king in the twelfth century B.C. to further the cause of democracy.

Mythology apart, there seems little doubt that Athens was

first governed by kings, then by aristocrats who lorded it over the farmers and artisans, the other two classes of the society. Gradually the ruling aristocrats had to submit to elections and their terms of office were reduced, at first from life to ten years and, in 683 B.C., to one year.

In 594 B.C., a great date in the history of democracy, the laws of Solon were enacted. An impoverished nobleman, Solon was forced to engage in trade and therefore to travel, especially in Ionia, the western coast of what is Turkey and was then a thriving part of the Greek world. Solon, a poet and philosopher as well as a gifted trader, used his poetry to preach his philosophy to the Athenians. He preached that injustice could be eradicated by law and told scoffers that men would keep even verbal agreements once they learned it was to their advantage to do so.

Having gained an envied political reputation by extending the territory of Athens and by his performance as negotiator in disputes with other states, Solon was given broad powers in 594 B.C. to prevent a threatening civil war over the extreme wealth of the rich and the abysmal misery of the poor.

On assuming office, Solon decreed that no one could be enslaved for indebtedness. He put a limit on the area of land that could be owned by one person. He curtailed exports of grain so that enough food was left to feed the populace. His laws encouraged trade and manufacture. He divided the people into four classes according to wealth, and each class was taxed in accordance with its ability to pay. He extended the franchise, so that the aristocrats had to share their power with people of other classes and he stipulated that all classes participate to some degree in the administration of justice. Public officials became answerable to the courts. He even passed a law disfranchizing citizens who refused to take sides in the

Assembly—thus compelling all Athenians to take part in government.

No one was quite satisfied with Solon's laws. The poor had expected more, the rich could not bear to lose their privileges. There was unrest and "tyrants" took over—tyranny, then, simply meant one-man rule. The tyrants were overthrown by Clisthenes, the leader of a great noble family, the Alkmeonids. Clisthenes produced a new constitution which turned Athens into the world's first pure democracy: popular assemblies of all male citizens made the laws and elected the executive. Foreigners living in Athens acquired the right of naturalization.

The city meanwhile grew in power. Its proud, free citizens felt themselves second to none. They even challenged mighty Persia when she attacked Greek territories in Asia Minor. Thus provoked, the Persian emperors invaded Greece, only to be soundly defeated under Athenian leadership at Marathon, Salamis and Mykali.

These wars, and the Athenian Confederacy of Greek states which emerged from the wars, laid the foundation for Greece's Golden Age, a period which coincided with the life of one man, Pericles (495 to 429 B.C.) nephew of Clisthenes the Alkmeonid.

There is evidence for and against the verdict that Pericles was the model statesman of all time. In the nineteenth century the great British historians and scholars praised him as the prototype of the English gentleman who entered public life and ran his country with dignity, enlightenment and success, the perfect blend of popular politician and great aristocrat, patron of the arts, a majestic orator with lofty sentiments filling quotation books forever after. ("Ask not what your country will do for you, ask rather what you can do for your country," is a not too far-fetched translation of a Periclean passage.)

Yet, when he first took power, Pericles launched an over-ambitious expedition against Egypt, an operation which lasted ten years and decimated the manhood of Athens. Pericles asserted publicly and to his allies, that Athens had a moral superiority which no one could match, and therefore deserved to lead the alliance. He tried to extend the territories of Athens and transformed her allies into vassal states without right to secede from the Athenian alliance.

Finally, he led Athens into the Peloponnesian Wars against Sparta's alliance, and Nemesis, the goddess of retribution, struck. Athens was hit by the plague. Pericles contracted the disease and died in the first year of the war, never having recovered his full powers. The war, begun under his rule, lasted thirty years and Athens emerged a second class power, with Sparta, her enemy, leader of Greece. One possible reason why Athens declined in power was the Periclean law denying citizenship to those not legitimately born of citizen parents on both sides. Until then, Athens had been a symbol of panhellenism, the city to which Greeks everywhere could be loyal because they knew they could become its citizens. After Pericles's law was passed, Athens could not renew itself with the blood of new citizens. Yet Pericles is revered as a superb statesman, perhaps because he was an imperialist, as were the English scholars who felt so close an affinity with him in the new classical era of the eighteenth century.

Pericles's most lasting claim to fame, and that which has led mankind to gloss over his shortcomings, is the creative sunburst of Athens under his stewardship. To provide unemployed veterans with work he dipped into the treasuries of his allies (with no real right to do so) and financed a tremendous program of public works which produced the Parthenon and the other great buildings of the Acropolis, as well as temples and monuments of supreme beauty, many of which remain to this day.

At the same time, Pericles was the patron and friend of Sophocles the playwright, of Phidias, the Parthenon's sculptor and builder, of painters and poets, of Anaxagoras the philosopher and of many sages. During his rule the leaders of Greek thought flocked to Athens, and Pericles encouraged the new ideas and intellectual challenges they brought with them. There was lively thinking in the rest of Greece, but the finest was to be found in Athens, while Pericles was alive.

Yet the new ideas had roots going back to the mists of Greek prehistory, roots in Homer (tenth century B.C.) Europe's first literary genius, whose poetry was to the Athenians of Pericles' time what the Bible was to be to Christianity.

Homer's pantheon of conniving, adulterous gods, who behaved as indiscreet mortals, may seem a perverse creation today, but it was a great advance on the religion that till then had gripped the people in their totally irrational worship of dark, irresponsible forces, dead ancestors, spirits and capricious local deities.

Homer's gods—or rather the Greek gods of the new cult of his time, to which he gave a lasting testament—at least were understandable; they behaved exactly like human beings. They could be placated, bought, flattered. They made some sense. But they did not all satisfy Homer. He did not treat them all with reverence, and in this he was essentially Greek. Greeks are incapable of reverence; that is why they profess to prize it so, and they have punished irreverence cruelly, throughout history.

Homer made fun of some gods—Zeus, for instance, Ares, god of war, Aphrodite—thereby evoking the skepticism needed to counteract miracle-mongering priests and to clear the way for rational scientific thought. Homer was on the side of Apollo and Athena, both restrained, well behaved, reasonable and honorable. He also admired Hephaistos, blacksmith-god of the artisans.

These "decent" gods, Homer used as symbols of a nobler, greater divine order, an order in which man had a choice, and was not the plaything of blind, powerful fate. "Through their own foolishness," Homer had Athena say, "men bring on themselves more suffering than is their lot. And then they blame the gods."

Perhaps more important than Homer's message was his language, a marvelously sophisticated instrument of communication, fully equipped with words to express abstract thought and generalizations. Homer also had structural brilliance. In the masterful construction of the Iliad, extraneous matter is ruthlessly pruned in the story line and the descriptive passages are never mere exhibitions of poetic virtuosity.

These then were some of the preconditions for the flowering that occurred in Athens during Pericles's life: freedom, subtlety of language—a refined tool for evolved thinking—and an existing wealth of culture that questioned belief and superstition.

There was surely another ingredient—connected directly, perhaps, with the birth of rational science in Greece: the light had something to do with shaping the Greek mind, and this the tourist can see for himself today when cruising the islands. The eye reaches sixty miles or more and is stopped not by mist but by distance. Nothing is opaque in Greece, nothing looks unlike itself. Everything is clear, lambent, stark and unmistakable.

The sea, moreover, was and is blue and glittering and almost always smooth. It had dark moods, of course, but they were predictable then as now, and never lasted long.

Across this reassuring sea, are the islands, like stepping-stones, making exploration so simple and safe that it became part of the Greek nature, and evolved into a search for fact, the basic ingredient of the early Greek scientific drive, whose methods were refined in Athens. The Greeks concentrated on careful observation, on measuring, on minute checking by experiment, always with the purpose of finding the "reason why." Nothing could be taken for granted and when they did not have enough facts, they resorted to hypotheses, to attempting, that is, an explanation of the yet unknown and uncheckable.

Starting with Thales, whose teachings were so important at the time of Pericles' birth, the Greek scientists worked out how to measure structures by measuring their shadows; how to predict eclipses. They proved that air and void are not the same by showing that water will not go in a bottle if the air is not let out—a simple trick perhaps, but no man had used it before as an experiment to actually prove a point.

They developed plane geometry, arithmetical and geometric progressions. They worked out the mathematical formulas that determine the relationship between the pitch of one musical note and of another. They knew sound is vibration. That there are forces of attraction and repulsion was established by inducing static electricity in small pieces of amber which they called electron.

Physicians of the Hippocratic school dissected bodies to discover the cause of disorders and said only charlatans would call an illness "sacred." The flow of blood to and from the heart was demonstrated. In rudimentary attempts at psychotherapy it was found that exciting some disturbed people to exhaustion, produced a sleep akin to collapse from which they woke restored. All this and more, in Pericles' lifetime; not by guesswork but by observation and experiment. The method

was unprecedented and certainly more important than the re-
sults, even though these were the foundation without which
our whole majestic scientific edifice could not have been
erected.

More impressive, however, were the hypotheses, the projections made by these Greek scientists from the few facts they
knew. The universe, they said, had to be composed of identical, infinitesimally small particles that were everywhere, and
since these were everywhere, there must be worlds other than
ours. Our world, the earth, had to be a sphere, floating in
space, and it was not the center of the universe. And on our
earth, everything was a combination of the same common
basic particles that endlessly "commingle and decompose" as
Anaxagoras said. Everything was always in flux, always changing, another sage maintained.

As for life itself, man must have evolved from other crea-
tures, probably of the sea, concluded a remarkable thinker
who studied aquatic mammals.

The Greeks did not stop with such scientific projections;
they had a word for the whole range of their search for knowledge and understanding—"philosophy," which meant love of
wisdom. And in their view there was a unity of all knowledge.
Above all, the philosopher had to examine "the reason why,"
to examine also whether what he dealt with as a scientist was
real or an illusion.

Who or what then had made "it" all, if "it" existed? Inevitably, there were then as there are now, endless arguments
on these fundamental questions. Certainly they led themselves up dead ends of logic from time to time, but on the
whole they kept a firm hold on reality, which they considered
to be ordered by a great power they variously called God or
"mind," meaning a superior intelligence.

As for man, he had a soul which could not be plumbed,

Heraclitus said. And what should be man's relation to the Universe? Homeric ethics were perfectly compatible with the world of Greek philosophy. The universe was an ordered universe and excess was the sin against order.

The Homeric ethic and the universe of the philosophers who flourished in Athens were acceptable by the men who had a full and exciting life ahead of them; but there were those who longed for a promise of something more after death. Thus there flourished in Athens at that time, a new faith which evolved from pre-Homeric ancestor worship, a doctrine of rebirth into a worse state through pollution, and rebirth into a better state through purification. This was the Orphic religion, full of secret initiations and "cleansing" rites, the so-called Eleusinian mysteries. In calamitous times especially, this faith united—in resistance against the enlightenment of a Pericles—the farmers, the squires, the frightened, those who suspected "eggheads" and the old-fashioned.

And there was much calamity for the Athenians after the disastrous Peloponnesian Wars were won by the severe and arrogant Spartans. But early in the fourth century, Athens was taken by the gentler Alexander the Great, also known as Alexander III, son of Philip, king of Macedon, and Olympias, a flamboyant princess from nearby Epirus.

Alexander inherited military genius from his father and from his mother a mystical, artistic, philosophical disposition. Prior to Alexander's birth, Olympias dreamed a thunderbolt fell on her body, from which great flames sprang and spread, before they were extinguished. Philip, his father, dreamed that he stamped his wife's body with a seal bearing the impression of a lion. On the day of Alexander's birth, a great temple at Ephesus burned down, some said because the goddess who should have been protecting it was assisting at Alexander's birth. But good news came to the family that day, too: Philip won a battle; learned that his horse had triumphed at the Olympic games; and one of his generals sent news the Illyrians were conquered. With such omens and portents surrounding his birth, it seemed inevitable that Alexander would be an extraordinary man.

As a boy, he was unhappy whenever he heard of his father's victories, fearing that the more Philip conquered, the less there would be left for Alexander to conquer. Philip declared that his son should make a kingdom for himself, because Macedonia would be too small to encompass the boy. In 343 B.C. Aristotle, the great philosopher, became Alexander's tutor and instilled in his pupil a great love of literature, and some knowledge of the sciences and medicine. Philip, meanwhile, would see that Alexander was present at meetings with ambassadors and envoys from Greece and the East—an invaluable lesson in statesmanship for the young man.

At sixteen, while Philip was on campaign outside Macedonia, Alexander subdued the hill tribes on the northern border of his father's kingdom and founded the city of Alexandroupolis. When only eighteen on an expedition with his father, Alexander led the Macedonian cavalrymen at Chaeronea who inflicted its first defeat on the famed Theban Sacred Regiment.

In 336 B.C. Philip was murdered, some historians believe at the instigation of his wife Olympias whom he had left for another woman. Possible contenders for the throne were also disposed of, including Alexander's cousin Amyntas and Philip's son by his new wife, leaving Alexander uncontested king of Macedonia.

The Greek cities Philip had defeated rose against Alexander, who sped to rebellious Thebes. When the Thebans refused his offer to spare the city if it ceased its rebellion, the Macedonians and their allies sacked Thebes, sparing only the temples and the house of the poet, Pindar whom Alexander admired. Six thousand Thebans were massacred and thirty thousand were sold into slavery. Alexander was never to forgive himself his part in this destruction and attributed whatever ill befell him thereafter, to the rightful wrath of the god Dionysus, patron of Thebes.

Alexander was kinder to Athens which he admired and showered with gifts. He then had himself elected general of all the Greeks and in 334 B.C., at the age of twenty-two, set forth against Persia, with thirty thousand infantrymen, five thousand cavalry, a superior siege train, commissary and intelligence service. Now he considered himself the evangelistic symbol of everything that Greece had wrought through the ages.

He crossed the Hellespont, pausing at Troy to make sacrifice at his hero Achilles' tomb. From there he went on to defeat the Persian army at the Granicus River in Asia Minor, after which many cities of Asia Minor surrendered to him without a fight, often welcoming him as a liberator. Wherever he went, he overthrew tyrannical leaders and installed democratic regimes. He also honored local men of letters and beloved ancient heroes.

Next, at Issus, he attacked the Persian army which had been reassembled under the Emperor Darius himself, overwhelmed the enemy and captured Darius' household. He treated them as royal guests, however, and did not take the women into slavery.

To eliminate Persian seapower, he marched on Phoenicia, taking Tyre after a seven months' siege, and proceeded to Egypt where he was welcomed as the deliverer from the Persian yoke. Here he founded the city of Alexandria, the first of seventy communities he established throughout Asia and

Africa, communities that turned out to be powerful forces for the Hellenization of the non-Greek world.

In 331 B.C. Alexander again defeated Darius at the battle of Gaugamela, then took Susa and Persepolis, the heart of Persia itself. He continued to pursue Darius, finally overtaking him near the Caspian. The Persian nobles set upon Darius and stabbed him to death because he refused to flee. In pity, Alexander wrapped his own cloak around the body of the great king and with much ceremony sent it to Darius' mother for burial with his ancestors.

From there, the great conqueror went to Parthia, Samarkand and Tashkent, and on to India where he defeated and captured the badly wounded King Poros. When Alexander asked his prisoner how he expected to be treated, Poros replied, "Like a king," and so he was.

Alexander went no farther because his troops rebelled at being so far from Greece. Thus began the long trek home, over rough terrain, with many privations which seriously decimated his troops. Back at Persepolis, in an effort to cement relations between his troops and the conquered Persians he, himself, married two local princesses and gave others in marriage to his principal generals. But once more the Macedonians rebelled, this time at seeing their erstwhile enemy treated so well. Alexander put down the rebellion by threatening that his guardsmen would no longer be Macedonians but Persians. This shamed the Macedonians who ended their rebellion and were forgiven by Alexander.

Finally he went to Babylon, despite omens that he should not do so, and while preparing for an exploratory voyage to discover a new route from Babylonia around Arabia to Egypt, he was stricken by a fever which eventually deprived him of his powers of speech. On June 13, 323 B.C., not yet thirty-three years old, weakened by disease and the many wounds he had received in his campaigns, Alexander the Great died.

This brief recital of battles and conquest hardly takes into account Alexander's lasting contribution to mankind. His was a fertilizing force in history. He started a new epoch which enlarged the bounds of knowledge and human endeavor. He gave Greek science and civilization new scope, ideas and opportunities, at the same time as that civilization was becoming the possession of all civilized men.

He refused to acknowledge the small boundaries of city-states and wanted to see them join together as one people. Once he held a town he was benevolent, and became a benefactor by the standards of the day. Before him, the most enlightened—even Aristotle—thought of the ideal state as one based on class rule and slavery; but Alexander preached that all men were born equal, sons of one Father, and he therefore asked his men to show magnanimity in victory.

Already, by the time he died, trade and commerce had begun to flow along the network of his new roads and cities and with it the Greek language—but a new Greek language, blending the many dialects of Greece into the *koine*, the common tongue. It was this new language, and the Greece that Alexander and his successors left, which was to become the teacher of Rome.

Later, along this new enlarged world, with a common language, Christianity was able to grow, with the words of the apostles and above all St. Paul's preachings and epistles which were written in the Greek of Alexander.

Throughout his short life, Alexander never forgot Athens, the intellectual capital of Hellenism, the city he respected above all others. From his booty he endowed the city and he honored it as did his successors. During the Hellenistic period, even under the Romans, Athens remained a prominent seat

of learning, the place where the ideas of the gentle philosopher Zeno, and his peers of other philosophical schools, were
to blossom. And the arts flourished, as well as commerce.

In A.D. 49 St. Paul preached in Athens and thus began the Christian era which was to see the final decline of the
ancient city. The philosophical schools remained open a few
more centuries. In the fifth century A.D. they were closed, but
by this time the torch of learning had passed from Athens to
Constantinople.

Formerly known as Byzantium, an ancient ally of Athens,
this city became the capital of the Eastern Roman Empire
under Constantine the Great in the fourth century B.C. and
was rechristened Constantinople. While in the west the Roman Empire was falling to the barbarians and plunging
headlong into the Dark Ages (with brief respites, as under
Charlemagne), the Byzantine Empire remained enlightened,
consciously Greek and run by a secular, civil service steeped in
Hellenism.

Many of the Byzantine emperors were distinguished scholars and artists; their court and capital became the center of
Western civilization and was recognized as such by Europe's
intelligentsia. Recent research has disproved the misconcep-
tions of Voltaire, Gibbon and others, who accused Byzantium
of obscurantism because its people were imbued with a deep
faith in Christianity. These critics wrongly assumed that because of its piety, the Byzantine Empire was darkly priest-
ridden whereas, in fact, many of the empire's leading clerics
were fine scholars in the liberal, classic Greek tradition.

According to contemporary experts, the Byzantines were
Europe's link with civilization and enlightenment, especially
during the Dark Ages when Byzantium preserved western
ideals and thought. Moreover, the empire was the bastion of

Europe against an endless succession of invaders—among them the Huns, Mongols, Arabs, Bulgars and Turks.

The Byzantine Empire changed in size in accordance with its military fortunes and it was often weakened by internal religious controversy and party strife. Yet, despite its weaknesses and dissensions it showed, again and again, astonishing powers of recuperation and survival.

The first great Byzantine era was under Justinian, who reconquered Italy and Africa, codified Roman law, and encouraged Hellenism. And it was under him, in the sixth century that Byzantine art and architecture entered their most glorious period. His successors lost most of Italy to the Lombards, and then the Middle East to the Arabs, but in the ninth century, Basil the First of Macedonia, founded a dynasty which gave the empire a new age of glory until Turkish invaders inflicted bitter defeats in the eleventh century.

Repeated Turkish incursions continued, one after another, battering the Byzantines, whose decline was greatly accelerated by the attack from the Fourth Crusade, which in A.D. 1204 proceeded to divide the empire into feudal fiefdoms. Fifty-five years later, the Crusaders were thrown out of Constantinople and the Byzantine Empire re-established, but thereafter its light merely flickered during the next two centuries as the Turks closed in. The empire vainly begged the awakening West for aid. Finally in 1453 Constantinople fell to the Turkish Mohammed the Second and the long and glorious Byzantine era was at an end.

Yet as it gasped for life, and even after its fall, Byzantium exercised its most powerful influence on the culture and thought of a Western Europe that was at last emerging from the Dark Ages. Byzantine artists in territories controlled by Venice, especially in Crete, put the Byzantine stamp on flowering European art, and in the sixteenth century an artist was born, whose influence is still felt on art to this day—Domenikos Theotokopoulos, known as El Greco, the Greek.

In 1456 Athens itself fell to the Turks; the Parthenon was turned into a mosque, the nearby temples into harems. Eventually the Turks used the Parthenon as a powder magazine and tore down the temple of Athena Promachos and the Propylaea (the grand entrance and ceremonial staircase) to make way for a gun battery. In 1687 the Venetians fired on the Acropolis and the powder magazine in the Parthenon exploded. The glorious temple crumbled. The Turks used some of its marble to make lime. In 1801 they gave Lord Elgin, a British diplomat, permission to carry away the Parthenon's finest sculptures, which now can be seen in the British Museum.

After almost four centuries of foreign occupation the Greeks finally won their independence in an armed uprising that began on March 25, 1821, and lasted nearly eight years before modern, independent Greece came into being. The twenty-fifth of March is celebrated as National Independence Day.

In World War I, Greece joined the Allies in fighting against Germany, Turkey and the Central Powers. Greece fought again on the side of the Allies in World War II, scoring victories against superior Fascist and Nazi forces, before the Germans finally occupied the country. In 1949 the Greeks defeated the forces of international communism which launched an all-out attack on the country. A year or so later, Greek troops won American presidential citations for outstanding bravery in Korea.

Greece today is a "Crowned Democracy," that is a democracy with a king as head of state. The powers of the various branches of the government are defined by the Constitution. The king derives his authority from the Constitution and appoints a prime minister who, with his cabinet, is subject to the approval of and is responsible to Parliament. The members of Parliament are elected by the people in secret balloting. Freedom of speech, of assembly and of the press are guaranteed by the Constitution. Greece is a member of the United Nations, the North Atlantic Treaty Organization and the Common Market.

The accomplishments of the nation since World War II have gone far beyond the reconstruction so generously helped by the United States. Greece is still basically an agricultural country but it is fast developing industry—most of it still secondary rather than primary. It has one of the highest annual rates of economic growth in the world, coupled with political and economic stability. Agriculture is being modernized; railways, highways and sea communications have been improved and are still improving. Heavy industry and secondary industries are growing—many through foreign investment— the old ones are constantly being modernized and enlarged. The expanding network of thermal and hydroelectric power plants now produces ample energy for domestic and industrial consumption. Oil refining, sugar refining and shipyards are constantly increasing their output. New projects are under way in aluminum, oil refining, petrochemicals and steel. To accelerate the rate of growth, twenty percent of the Greek national income is invested each year in development. The Greek owned merchant marine has grown, with no large domestic market, no great reservoir of capital and no industrial infrastructure to speak of, to rank third after the United States and the United Kingdom—a tremendous success story for a rocky land of only some eight million people.

RELIGION AND GREEK EASTER

For all religious groups, freedom to worship is guaranteed by the Constitution. Ninety-six percent of the people of Greece belong to the Greek Orthodox faith. The beauty and greatness of Byzantium and the role of the Greek Orthodox religion as defender of Hellenism during centuries of foreign domination explains the pervading influence of religion in Greek life.

It is a part of life to an extent rarely seen in other Western countries. I feel that the church in Greece is not only a vehicle of devotion but also a part of the nation's subconsciousness, rooted in classic purity and medieval splendor. This is best made evident at Easter, for then Greeks are at their most typical, when tradition overcomes them and dominates.

Easter is Greece's greatest festival. It is more than a religious holiday, it is a national affirmation. It is all the feasts of the villages together, and the pagan spring rites when the Greek earth is freshly green.

The ceremonies last a week, from Palm Sunday, when everyone carries from church small woven palm-leaf crosses. Fasting begins the next day and does not end till midnight the following Saturday—not quantitative fasting but qualitative. You can eat taramosalata (fish roe beaten to a paste with olive oil), clams, mussels, shrimp and kalamaria (fried baby squid).

The lamb for Easter Sunday's feast is fed its last delicacies and across the land churches compete for the best chanters. The finest village or city baker will provide the church with bread for the sacraments of Holy Week, and a supply of herbs is laid by for infusions with which the priests can gargle—for they are expected to let the rafters ring in the love of God.

I once spent an Easter at Ai-Yannis at the foot of Mount Pelion by the sea, and the whole village went to the mourning service on Holy Thursday, in a string of boats towed by a caique, to a small shrine on a tiny sea-worn rock, and here fishermen and shepherds from all over the mountain took part in the mournful service of the twelve gospels. On the way back, the villagers sang old folk poems from the wars of liberation.

On Good Friday is the burial service, a Byzantine custom. Each church builds a small mausoleum of flowers and at the appointed hour the floral tomb is carried shoulder high from every church, preceded by the cross and stars and followed by the congregation holding lit candles draped in black crepe, singing old, old hymns of death.

In Athens this is a particularly solemn occasion and uniquely beautiful, especially viewed from a tall building near Constitution Square, from which one can see the procession serpentining down the path from the church atop Mount Lycabettus, till it joins the streams of candlelight from other churches, forming a mighty river of flickering light. The streets are fragrant with the floral tombs and incense, and the solemn Byzantine chants of the massed chanters can be heard against a background of muffled military drums and keening flutes.

Saturday is a day of suppressed excitement, enervation and preparation. Eggs are dyed red, buns are baked and the special Easter soup simmers on every stove, its aroma aggravating the hunger of the fasters.

At midnight in every square, in every church in the land, the cry of resurrection rings out, not only for Christ, but also for

Greece, for the Phoenix, the national symbol, the bird which is yearly consumed by fire, yet is forever reborn. Rockets are set off on the square outside Athens Cathedral and officers fire their pistols into the air. The flame, symbolic of rebirth, is passed from candle to candle and the ceremonies are somehow more significant at midnight than in the full light of morning.

Now the fast is over and after midnight magiritsa, the traditional Easter soup, is served in every home. Made of the liver, heart and kidneys of the lamb, rice and herbs, lemon, the beaten yolk of egg, rich and creamy, it is taken piping hot, with the whole family, young and old, packed round the table. The flame from the candle brought from the church is used to light a new wick for the devotional lamp, burning before the icons.

On Easter Sunday, in backyards or open fields, the Greeks roast their Easter lamb on the spit over charcoal, while the wine cools in tubs of ice. Toasts are drunk, red egg cracked against red egg in the contest to see who has the hardest. And the whole country is gay and festive as it welcomes spring.

GREEK ART

Beginning with the sixth century B.C. and continuing for about three hundred years Greek art reached a flowering that has remained unique in the history of mankind. The seeds for these blooms had been sown much earlier.

PRECLASSIC

Fairly recent excavations in Phocis, Boeotia, the Peloponnesus, Thessaly and Macedonia lead scholars to believe that the Hellenes entered Greece long before the traditional descent of the Dorians in the twelfth century B.C. There are traces of a civilization called the Helladic, and of a vast migration into Greece at about the third millennium B.C. From the nineteenth century B.C. things quietened until the advent of the Dorians.

Heinrich Schliemann's impressive discoveries at Mycenae and Troy in the last century unearthed the remains of a civilization in a high state of artistic evolution, coinciding with the late Helladic Period (1600–1100 B.C.). This new civilization was named Mycenaean and it originated the forms which led eventually to the perfection of the classic age.

Then in 1900 Sir Arthur Evans discovered the palace of Knossos in Crete, bringing to light the even older Minoan civilization which continued to flourish during the Mycenaean period.

The most recent excitement was Michael Ventris' deciphering in 1952 of the Linear B script on clay tablets excavated at

Mycenae, Crete and Pylus—the home of Nestor, the Iliad's legendary sage. The language of the tablets, Ventris discovered, was Greek. After Ventris' tragic death in a car crash, linguists and philologists continued his studies and confirmed his findings, which would seem to add weight to the idea of the English archaeologist Wace that Greek art is one and indivisible with its preclassical phase in the second millennium, developing through various stages to the splendor of classicism.

Mycenaean art took over forms from Helladic craftsmen. Then it drew on Minoan achievements, especially in the sixteenth and fifteenth centuries B.C., the age of the pit burials in the early royal enclosure at Mycenae. Domed "beehive" tombs appeared later and are contemporaries of palaces found at Mycenae, Tiryns, Pylus and Iolcos (Volos). These palaces, though smaller and less luxurious than those at Knossos in Crete, indicate an advanced way of life, and considerable artistic achievement.

Mycenaean pottery at first was independent of Minoan influence, but its original simple linear decoration gradually gave way to elaborate designs and representations of Cretan origin.

The marvelous death masks of Mycenae, however, and the delightfully detailed swords and daggers, engraved and inlaid goblets, jewelry and armor are of a unique craftsmanship that has its own original style and is not an imitation of the Minoan.

The Dorians, rude Greek nomads, burst upon this fine blend of Helladic, Minoan and Mycenaean, in the twelfth century B.C., imposing upon it their own simple primitive tastes in art. The result at first was a deterioration of the Mycenaean strain, followed by the slow emergence during the tenth century B.C. of the first geometric period in Greek art. The patterns were austere but always reflected factors and tendencies deeply rooted in the human spirit. These new geometric tendencies mark no sudden change, for they were grafted onto the Mycenaean art.

The geometric vases of the epoch represent an enormously important phase in the history of ceramics and abundant examples exist showing the progress from style to style, from the pots of Thera (Santorini) to the masterpieces in the Athens museums, called the Dipylon vases.

These artistic developments coincided with social and religious changes. The old mysterious gods mingled with new gods which acquired human form. Neither former open-air sanctuaries nor palace shrines sufficed for the worship of the new pantheon and the first temples began to appear, fashioned after the reception halls of ancient palaces, all built in the most marvelous natural settings.

The tenth century B.C. "Megaron B" at Thermon in Aetolia (west-central Greece) is an oblong, arched edifice which must certainly have sheltered rulers before its conversion to a temple. The temple of Artemis at Sparta belongs to the ninth century B.C., while sanctuaries of Hera on the islands of Samos and Delos, and at Perachora (twenty-one miles west of Athens), all date from the eighth century and show the gradual change from palace to temple.

The numerous surviving idols of bronze, clay and stone of this transition generally preserve the Mycenaean tradition, up to the eighth century B.C., when transition at last becomes change and large statues appear, the first steps in full figure sculpture that reached its detailed perfection in the classical examples. Improvements in technique with both stone and bronze can be seen.

During the ninth and eighth centuries B.C. the Greeks spread out along the Mediterranean coast, trading, colonizing and bringing home knowledge of other cultures, morals, customs, religious beliefs, and skills, especially in pottery.

By now the pattern of Greece as a complex of independent city-states had already emerged. In this political context the stimulation of discovery and travel, the heritage from the Helladic, Minoan and Mycenaean worlds, the nature of the Greeks and of their land, all led to the classic Hellenic ideal—an integrated, intellectual edifice, encompassing politics, art, literature and philosophy, a way of life which was to last centuries without change, save in detail.

CLASSIC

Architecture dominates the classic period. From the seventh to fifth centuries B.C. the Greeks were deeply involved in research into technique and esthetics. An example of this great effort is the history of the Doric or Ionic column which Greek architects used, to create infinitely varied examples of a single style. And a feature of the architecture of these centuries is that, of all the works belonging to the epoch, no two monuments were ever built exactly alike. The temples, burial grounds, agoras, theaters, gymnasiums, stadiums, show with what intelligence Greek architects combined science and everyday life.

From the earliest Doric temples of the seventh century—the Heraeon of Olympia and the temple of Athena Pronaia at Delphi, for example—the search for something new and different went on, but always within the bounds of measure and rhythm. In the Doric temples at Thermon in Aetolia we discover painted clay metopes (spaces between beam ends), unique examples of archaic art—which is the first phase of classical art from the seventh to fifth centuries B.C. In the great panhellenic sanctuaries of the sixth century, architects began to work in the grand manner. Temples of porous stone were built on the Acropolis of Athens, at Delphi, at the Altis in Olympia, at Corinth and elsewhere.

Perfection came gradually and was reached in the fifth century B.C. with the Parthenon, the incomparable Erechtheion, the temple of Athena Nike and the Propylaea of the Athens Acropolis, as well as the temple of Zeus at Olympia, the temple of Epikourios Apollo at Bassae in central Peloponnesus, the temples of Poseidon and Athena at Sounion, of Nemesis at Thamnous (near Marathon) and the temple of Apollo on the island of Delos. This was the grand epoch of classic art, and for many it will remain the true representative of the miracle of the Greek spirit.

The Peloponnesian Wars (431–404 B.C.) brought a halt to this feverish activity but when they ended, buildings started earlier were completed. Huge theaters with perfect acoustics were built as at Epidaurus, and all over Greece splendid galleries, public buildings, stadiums and gymnasiums were erected. At the end of the fifth century, notable private homes were constructed, such as at Olynthus in Chalkidiki (northern Greece), disclosing a personal daily life centered round courtyards with peristyles, handsome rooms with mosaic floors, forerunners of those on Delos and later at Pompeii.

This climax in architecture brought with it a flowering in sculpture to adorn the buildings. Modeling reached its culminating point with the expansion of panhellenic sanctuaries, luxurious cemeteries, public meeting places, all competing in their array of statuary, works by the greatest artists of the age. Greek statues lost their motionlessness. Practically all the early works which have survived are either religious statues or funerary monuments—reliefs which decorated temples or tombs.

The first phase of classical art, the archaic, achieved the

height of its perfection in the middle of the sixth century with its marvelous *kouri* (smiling youths), the smiling maidens of the Acropolis and the pediments of the Hekatompedon on the Acropolis.

From the fifth century on, the mythical monsters which had earlier adorned temple pediments gave way to models of the human form and divine harmony begins; and this is the basis of classicism—a deep respect for man. The Greeks created works of rare perfection in which man's spiritual and physical virtues merge within a beautifully proportioned body. There are examples on the Acropolis, at Olympia, Delphi and the island of Aegina, and of course all the Greek masterpieces which adorn museums around the world—the works of Phidias, Praxiteles, Lysippus and others.

Pictorial art too was of great importance to the Hellenes who heaped honor on painters such as Apelles, Parrhasius, Polygnotus and Zeuxis, but nothing remains of their work. The only examples of painting still in existence are to be found on funerary columns, the most notable of which were discovered near Volos, and on certain wooden tablets found in a cave near Corinth.

Nevertheless, we can get an idea of classical painting from the wonderful vases of the period. From the eastern style of the seventh and sixth centuries B.C., with its decorative belts, animals and plants, vase painting passed to the black glaze made only in Athens and the plain of Attica. The technique and quality of the pottery make the vases of this period one of the most perfect examples of ceramics. Toward the end of the sixth century the red glaze vases came into being with mythological designs and scenes from private life, two techniques which continued side by side to make Hellenic workshops renowned far beyond the Mediterranean.

HELLENISTIC

From 323 B.C., the year Alexander the Great died, we enter the Hellenistic period which made a definite break with the rules and conventions of classicism. Art was permitted freedom of expression. Alexander's conquest of the East spread the Greek artistic form, while the Greeks were touched by contact with many new civilizations. From this time on, movement overruled classic immobility, passion was the mode in sculpture and some buildings became heavy with ornamentation. Yet some of the finest and most moving of Greek masterpieces date from this period, including the Venus de Milo and the Dying Gaul.

BYZANTINE

Byzantine art is an offshoot of ancient Greek art and the link between classicism and the European renaissance. Christianity gave Byzantine art new themes and approaches but classical Greece taught the principles and techniques. Like its classical progenitor Byzantine art was dominated by religious architecture. It also produced marvelous icons, painting, mosaics, miniatures. Greece is the greatest repository of these treasures.

During the Middle Ages, the Byzantines continued in an unbroken line the political, ethnic, linguistic and artistic point of view of the Hellenic and Hellenized world of Alexander the Great and his successors, who, from a cultural point of view, included the Romans.

A most important factor in the evolution of Byzantine art was the number of emperors who made determined efforts to return to classic antiquity, using ancient illustrated texts as models, but channeling artistic activity to supply the needs of imperial power and of the new religion. This channeling added abstract and mystical trends to the Hellenistic influence. The "mix" of the classical and the mystical abstract elements varied from period to period.

The most successful blend perhaps is the colossal church of Santa Sophia in Istanbul which has an astonishing airiness despite its bulk. It does not make a man feel diminished as do some of the great Gothic cathedrals. Its luminous space envelops man, including him in the splendor. In this, Santa Sophia is perhaps the finest example of Byzantine architecture. It belongs to the earliest period, fifth to seventh centuries A.D.

In the next great period, from the mid-ninth to mid-eleventh centuries, the classical Greek elements gained ascendancy under a series of artistically inspired emperors, helped by a host of cultured clerics, and a secular elite which believed it was the empire's role to revive ancient literature and the classic style.

In this period plasticity was the quality prized above all else. In painting, the figures became more supple, the landscape background had an airy perspective and lighter colors were preferred.

The pendulum swings the other way from the mid-eleventh to the end of the twelfth century and Byzantine art then begins to take on its special medieval character, with gaunt, spiritually tortured saints. Figures are flat, stylized and dry, yet drawn with a wondrous lightness and mastery of line.

From the mid-thirteenth century to the fall of Constantinople in 1453, composition became more crowded and tended to emphasize secondary elements, but pleasingly. Tall, supple figures, often borrowed from ancient subjects, are at center stage, elegantly draped and full of a delicate charm and idyllic quality, marking once more a clear swing from the medieval of the previous period, back to ancient Greek canons. This is the period of the famous series of Christ Pantocrator (the Almighty) mosaics and murals that adorn churches all over Greece and depict Christ in his maturity, aware, concerned, the eternal judge and ruler, but also the vibrant repository of the life force. Just beneath the severity of the features lies vitality.

In all these periods the Byzantines practiced the older crafts which had flourished in the ancient Greek world, adapting them to the new Christian spirit and using what would best illustrate that spirit. For this reason they neglected sculpture in the round, a technique bound with ancient idolatry. Sculpture lost its role as a public form, but private works were commissioned on a minor scale (rarely more than twelve inches high), usually to decorate imperial palaces and houses.

But relief work gave the sculptors scope and they filled the empire with exquisitely carved episcopal thrones, altar screens, gospel covers, all showing the strong classic Greek influence. And there was a sunburst of talent in the minor arts; goldsmiths, jewelers and embroiderers turned out infinitely varied, delicate, elegant art, such as beautiful copies of the Iliad, brilliantly illustrated, miracles of patience and inspiration.

Charming utensils for everyday use were lovingly wrought. Gold was often used for vases, cups and jewelry as well as for crosses, chalices and candelabra. The use of gold with enamel was particularly successful. Silver elaborately decorated was used extensively for complete dinner services.

Sumptuous textiles, especially silks, were woven in a variety of rich designs for the elaborate uniforms prescribed for court officials by the inexhaustible inventiveness of Byzantine "etiquette." But the finest textiles were used for curtains or sacred vestments to create a vivid spectacle in the church.

The Byzantine style did not die with the fall of Constantinople. It sought refuge in such major artistic centers of the period as Athos, the Meteora, Crete and Patmos. There, Byzantine art dipped into the old tradition to strengthen the beleaguered Christian faith, while enriching the Byzantine blend with new elements, developing thus important local schools, especially the Cretan, which produced a bevy of fine painters who explored the avenues of symmetrical and geometrical composition. They gave Byzantine art a new serenity in figure posture and expression. It is from this school that sprang not only El Greco, but also the men who took their art to the West and sparked the renaissance for which the groundwork had already been laid long before by the artistic influence that Constantinople exercised on Italy.

It is now accepted that the Byzantine influence gradually brought back the West to an artistic respect for the human form. The Byzantines also gave Europe great monumental composition in painting. In sculpture, the small Byzantine ivory carvings were the highly refined prototypes for the larger sculpted forms of the Gothic cathedrals. Byzantine art was the conduit that poured into Europe the values of Greek humanism that underpins what we call Western civilization.

BOOKS TO READ

Bowra, Cecil M., *The Greek Experience*. A Mentor Book, The New American Library of World Literature, New York.

Bury, John B., *A History of Greece*. Modern Library, Random House, New York.

Durrell, Lawrence, *Prospero's Cell* and *Reflections on a Marine Venus* (one vol. ed.) E. P. Dutton & Co., New York, 1960.

Herodotus, *The History of Herodotus*. Tudor Publishing Co., New York, 1952.

Kazantzakis, Nikos, *Zorba the Greek* (1953), *Freedom or Death* (1956), *The Odyssey, a Modern Sequel* (1958), *The Last Temptation of Christ* (1960). Simon and Schuster, New York.

Keeley, Edmund, and Philip Sherrard, *Six Poets of Modern Greece*. Alfred A. Knopf, New York, 1961.

Kitto, H. D. F., *The Greeks*. Penguin Books, Baltimore, 1954.

MacKenzie, Compton, *Greece in My Life*.

Miller, Henry, *The Colossus of Maroussi*. Paperback. New Directions, New York.

Murray, Gilbert, *Five Stages of Greek Religion*. Doubleday & Co., Garden City, New York, 1955.

Renault, Mary, *The Bull from the Sea*. Pantheon Books, New York, 1962.

Robinson, Charles A., Jr., *An Anthology of Greek Drama*. 2 vols. Rinehart & Co., New York, 1954.

Runciman, Steven, *Byzantine Civilization*. Meridian Books, New York, 1950.

Tarn, W. W., *Alexander the Great*. Beacon Press, Boston, 1956.

Thucydides, *Complete Writings*. Modern Library, Random House, New York, 1951.

Warner, Rex, *Pericles the Athenian*. Little, Brown & Co., Boston, 1963.

SECTION VII

USEFUL INFORMATION

*Including addresses, the metric system,
and useful words and phrases*

INDEX TO SECTION VII

ADDRESSES

INFORMATION OFFICES FOR TOURISTS IN GREECE

Athens: 6 Karageorgi Servias Street, Tel. 222.545. Omonia Square (Underground Railway Station), Tel. 525.899
Chania: Nomarchias Building, Tel. 24.76
Corfu: Arseniou Street (Laskari Building), Tel. 530
Heraklion: 25th August Street, Tel. 20.96
Igoumenitsa: Harbor, Tel. 53
Ioannina: 98 28th October Street, Tel. 80.86
Rhodes: 4 Navarchou Kountouriotou Street, Tel. 255
Salonica: 2 Komninon Street, Tel. 71.888
Volos: 32 Argonafton Street, Tel. 35.00

INFORMATION OFFICES ABROAD

Benelux: 62 Boulevard de l'Imperatrice, Bruxelles I, Tel. 13.02.06
France: 31 Avenue de l'Opera, Paris I, Tel. OPE 27.55, OPE 30.77
Germany: Baselerstrasse 35–37, Frankfurt/Main, Tel. 335.218, 335.718
Great Britain: 195–197 Regent Street, London W. 1, Tel. REG. 5997
Italy: Via L. Bissolati 78–80, Roma, Tel. 487.249, 487.301
Sweden: Grev Turegatan 2, Stockholm O Sverige, Tel. 60 65 66
U.S.A.: 601 Fifth Avenue, New York, N.Y., Tel. HA1-5777

CRUISE ORGANIZERS (*Offices in U.S.*)

Epirotiki Line: 608 Fifth Avenue, New York City
Typaldos Lines: 500 Fifth Avenue, New York City
Traveline Inc.: 680 Fifth Avenue, New York City
Greek Line: 8–10 Bridge Street, New York City
Holland American Line: 609 Fifth Avenue, New York City
Chandris Lines: 17 Battery Place, New York City

AIRLINE OFFICES IN ATHENS

Air France: 4 Karageorgi Servias Street, Tel. 238.507
Air India: 4 Voukourestiou Street, Tel. 234.027
Alitalia: 3 Stadiou Street, Tel. 233.100
Austrian Airlines: 10 Othonos Street, Tel. 232.535
BEA: 2 Amalias and Othonos Streets, Tel. 222.521
B.O.A.C.: 2 Amalias Avenue, Tel. 222.521/7
El Al: 8 Othonos Street, Tel. 230.116
Iberia: 10 Stadiou Street, Tel. 627.748
KLM: Constitution Square, Tel. 230.756
Lufthansa: 4 Karageorgi Servias Street, Syntagma Square, Tel. 228.964
Middle East Airlines: 12 Hermou Street, Tel. 234.494
Olympic Airways: 6–8 Othonos Street, Athens, Tel. 230.991
Pan Am: 6 El. Venizelou Avenue, Tel. 628.076
Qantas: 2 Amalias Avenue, Tel. 222.521
SAA-South African Airways: 4 Karageorgi Servias Street, Tel. 229.007
Sabena: 8 Othonos Street, Tel. 538.711
SAS: 16 El. Venizelou Avenue, Tel. 625.770
Swissair S.A.: 3 Stadiou Street, Tel. 237.581
TWA: 8 Othonos Street, Syntagma Square, Tel. 230.965
UAA-United Arab Airlines: 10 Othonos Street, Tel. 233.575

OLYMPIC AIRWAYS OFFICES IN GREECE

Agrinion: 1 Elia Eliou Street, Cables: Olympair, Tel. 5.50
Alexandroupolis: 206 King George Avenue, Cables: Olympair,
    Tel. 3.61, 207
Athens: 8 Othonos Street, Athens, Tel. 230.991
Chania: 34 Karaiskaki Street, Cables: Olympair, Tel. 3.74
Corfu: 18 Const. Zavitsianou Street, Cables: Olympair, Tel. 6.10
Heraklion: 25th August Street, Cables: Olympair, Tel. 3.41
Ioannina: Hotel "Palladion" Building, Cables: Olympair, Tel. 2.18
Kalamata: Sidirodromikou Stathmou Avenue, Cables: Olympair,
    Tel. 3.76
Kavalla: 84 Omonia Street, Cables: Olympair, Tel. 36.22
Kos: 2c Stefanou Cazouli Square, Cables: Olympair, Tel. 41
Kozani: 11 Triantafyllidou Street, Cables: Olympair, Tel. 3.87
Larissa: 88 Vassilissis Sophias Street, Cables: Olympair, Tel. 2.42
Lemnos: Kentriki Agora (Market Place), Cables: Olympair, Tel. 14

Mytilene: Hotel "Lesvion" Building, Cables: Olympair, Tel. 86.59
Rhodes: 27 Haile Selassie Street, Cables: Olympair, Tel. 5.31
Salonica: 2 Komninon Street, Cables: Olympair, Tel. 70.300
Samos: Th. Sophoulis Avenue, Cables: Olympair, Tel. 3.37

SHIPPING LINES SERVING THE ISLANDS

Arkadiki Lines: agent: M. Markantonakis, 1 Astingos Street, Piraeus
Cavounidis Line: 2 Posseidonos Street, Piraeus
Diapouli Line: 2 Astingos Street, Piraeus
Epirotiki Line: 2 Bouboulinas Street, Piraeus
Foustanos Line: Building Giannoulatou Square, Piraeus
Greek Coast Lines S.A.: 10 Othonos Street, Athens
Laga: 2 Astingos Street, Piraeus
Lakoniki: Posseidonos Street, Piraeus
New Epirotiki Line: 11 Akti Miaouli, Piraeus
Nomikos Line: Building Tanpy, 19 Akti Miaouli, Piraeus
Typaldos Line: Akti Tselepi, Building Typaldos, Piraeus

SOME TRAVEL AGENCIES AND TOUR OPERATORS IN ATHENS

ABC Tours: 102 Aiolou Street, Tel. 222185
Alfa Tourist Agency: 6 Hermou Street, Tel. 623326
American Express: Syntagma Square (126), Tel. 234781
Arvanti: 3 Hermou Street (126), Tel. 220383
Carayanides: 58 Stadiou Street (131), Tel. 230677
CHAT: 4 Stadiou Street (133), Tel. 223137
Creta Tours: 29 25th August Street, Heraklion, Crete, Tel. 8254
Doucas Tours: 8 Venizelou Street, Salonica, Tel. 76071
Hellas: 5 El. Venizelou Avenue (133), Tel. 222230
Hellenic Express: 4 Stadiou Street, Tamion Building, Tel. 222173
Hermes en Grece: 4 Stadiou Street (133), Tel. 237431
Horizon: 14 Nikis Street (118), Tel. 233144
Ilion: 10 El. Venizelou Avenue (134), Tel. 624415
Key Tours: 2 Hermes Street, Tel. 232520
Nicoloudis Tours: 9 Valaoritou Street (134), Tel. 629417
Olympos: 4 Voukourestiou Street (133), Tel. 237671
Varvias: 10 Karageorgi Servias Street (125), Tel. 235086

Viking Travel: 7 Karageorgi Servias Street (125), Tel. 229383
Wagons Lits/Cook: 8 Hermou Street (126), Tel. 234705

YACHT BROKERS

Alcyonides: 10 Othonos Street, Athens 118, Tel. 230.151
Archipel Club: D. Gritsis–25 Loukianou Street, Athens 139,
Tel. 728.056
Balkania: G. Priovolos–91–93 Academy Street, Athens 141,
Tel. 625.150
Constantopoulos & Son: 44 El. Venizelou Street, Athens 143,
Tel. 631.767
Delmouzos & Louys: Aegean Yacht Service–4 Kriezotou Street,
Athens 134, Tel. 631.358
Delta Maritime Co., Ltd.: 1 Streit Street, Athens 111, Tel. 233.961
Hellas Yachting: C. Nikolaidis–4 Kriezotou Street, Athens 134,
Tel. 625.698
Koutsoukelis B.: 3 Stadiou Street, Athens 125, Tel. 227.011
Leggeris C.: 4 Kriezotou Street, Athens 134, Tel. 625.698
Marine Corner: J. Kastrinakis–64 Akti Koumoundourou,
Tourkolimano, Tel. 473.796
Nautiki Ltd.: 1 Alexandras Square, Passalimani, Tel. 463.936
Propeller: E. Bouboulis–1 Akti Moutsopoulou, Passalimani, Piraeus,
Tel. 471.495
Yacht Corner: C. Bibis–36 N. Votsi Street, Tourkolimano, Piraeus,
Tel. 473.390
Yachting Cruises: N. Tsouchlos–18 Voulis Street, Athens 126,
Tel. 226.840

CAR RENTAL AGENCIES

Autorent: 73 Syngrou Avenue, Athens, Tel. 914.771
Avis: 48 Amalias Avenue, Athens, Tel. 234.713, 228.050
Bamaco Hellas Ltd.: 53 Vassilissis Sophias Avenue (op. Hilton),
Tel. 720.600
Byron: 7/9 Evelpidon Street, Athens, Tel. 817.458
Christinakis: 234 Patission Street, Athens, Tel. 875.746
Hellascars: 7 Stadiou Street, Athens, Tel. 222.230
Hertz: 12 Syngrou Avenue, Athens, Tel. 913.891
Nereus: 7 Sachtouri Street, Piraeus, Tel. 471.252

BANKS IN ATHENS

American Express: Syntagma Square
Bank of Greece: 21 El. Venizelou Avenue
Bank of the Army Share Fund: 13 Kolokotroni Street
Commercial Bank: 11 Sofokleous Street, Athens
Commercial Credit Bank: 10 Pesmatzoglou Street
First National City Bank: 8 Othonos Street
Ionian and Popular Bank: El. Venizelou and Pesmatzoglou Streets
National Bank of Greece: 86 Aiolou Street

ART GALLERIES IN ATHENS

Zyghos: 8 Omirou Street
Parnassos: Platia Karytsi (Kariti Square)
Zachariou: 7 Kanari Street (Kolonaki)
Karatza: 22 Kolokotroni Street
Pratt Institute: 22 Massalias Street
Merlin: 8 Merlin Street
Cultural Cooperation: 25 Voukourestiou Street
Nees Morfes: 9a Valaoritou Street
Kentron Praktikon Efarmoghon: 75 Patission Street
Aithoussa Technon: Plaka (Old Athens)
A.T.I.: 24 Stratiotikou Syndesmou Street
Athens Hilton Hotel (Art Gallery): 17 Vassilissis Sophias Avenue
Rhodes Art Gallery: Rhodes
Kalamae Art Gallery: Kalamae (Peloponnessus)
Hellenic American Union: 22 Massalias Street

ARTISTS OF NOTE

Ghikas,	painter	Zongopoulos,	sculptor
Tsaronhis,	"	Capralos,	"
Moralis,	"	Apergis,	"
Nikolaou,	"	Apartis,	"
Engonopoulos,	"	Pappas,	"

STORES IN ATHENS

HANDICRAFTS

There is a permanent display of Greek Arts and Handicrafts at the *National Organization of Hellenic Handicrafts:* 9 Mitropoleos Street (off Syntagma Square)

Diakosmitiki: 5 Stadiou Street (off Syntagma Square)

Syllogos Ellinikis Laikis Technis: (Association of Greek Popular Art) at 4 Voukourestiou Street (close to Syntagma Square)

Their Majesties Fund: (*a*) 2 Panepistimiou Street, 2 Voukourestiou and Valaoritou Streets (*b*) Shop at the Athens Hilton Hotel

Tsantilis: (Handwoven Material) at Aiolou and 31 Mitropoleos Streets

Tanagrea: 15 Mitropoleos and 26 Voulis Streets (off Syntagma Square)

Knossos: 4a Stadiou Street (off Syntagma Square)

Lykeion Ellindon: (Greek Women's Lyceum Club) 17 Dimokritou Street

Artisanat Grec: (A. Vassiliadis) 10 Nikis Street (off Syntagma Square)

Shops in Pandrossou Street: (close to the Athens Cathedral at Mitropoleos Square)

Sclavos: 18 Eleftheriou Venizelou Street

Arghalios: 7 Filellinon Street

Diplous Pelekys: Cretan House, 23 Voulis Street

Kalokairinos: (*a*) 3 Panepistimiou Street (*b*) 8 Voukourestiou Street (*c*) 3 Stadiou Street

Mati: 4 Voukourestiou Street

JEWELERS

Zolotas E.: 6 Panepistimiou Street

Vourakis: 8 Voukourestiou Street

Zenetos: 19 Voukourestiou Street

Katsikopoulos & Markou: 20 Ermou Street

Konstantaras Achilefs: 6 Voukourestiou Street

Katrampoulos: 24 Voukourestiou Street

Dandolos: 11b Karageorgi Servias Street

DRESS SALONS

Sistovaris-Dessès: 9 Venizelou Street (off Syntagma Square)
Tsouchlos: 8 Daidalou Street, Plaka
Papamichailof-Tsamadou: 4a Akadimias Street
Georgette: 18 Omirou Street
Marilene: (Vasso Kourtidou) 19 Patriarchou Ioakim Street
Eleni Mallidou: 11 Kanari Street (Kolonaki)
Fofi Vassiliadou: 1 Tsakalof Street

LADIES' WEAR

(Accessories, material, knitwear, underwear, etc.)
Papayanni: 47 Ermou Street
Amazon: 48 Ermou Street
Stragigiou: Ermou and Platia Kapnikareas, 3
Sinanis: 9 Ermou Street
Vogue: 3 Ermou Street
Tsouchlos: 10 Nikis Street
Horrockses: 1 Valaoritou Street
Vardas & Anagnostopoulos: 44–46 Stadiou Street
Tsitopoulos: 9b Ermou Street

LADIES' SHOES

Petridis: 9 Panepistimiou Street
Mouriadis: 4 Stadiou Street
Kalogyrou: 1d Kolokotroni Street
Petrakis: 16 E. Venizelou Street
Mavridis: 13 Kanari Street

HABERDASHERS

Bonton: 4 Stadiou Street
Strongylos: 25 Stadiou Street and 3 Panepistimiou Street
Noble: 7 Stadiou Street
Lentzos: 29 Stadiou Street
Konstandaras: 24 Stadiou Street
Arvanitidis: 22 Stadiou Street

MEN'S SHOES

Petridis: 9 Panepistimiou Street
Mouriadis: 4 Stadiou Street

Sevastakis: 57a Panepistimiou Street
Paschalidis: 52 Stadiou Street
Garyfallos: 5 Stadiou Street
Theodossiadis: 2 Philellinon Street
Bey: 43 Stadiou Street

DEPARTMENT STORES

(Minute by American standards)
Lambropoulos: Stadiou Street and 99 Aiolou Street
Dragonas: Aiolou-Sofokleous and Philopimenos Street
Athenée: 33–35 Stadiou Street
Katrantzos: 38 Stadiou Street
Mignon: 13 Patission Street

GIFT SHOPS

Tzanes: 9 Venizelou Avenue
Kalokairinos: 3 Stadiou Street
Psaros: 3 Stadiou Street
Contessina: 16 Voukourestiou Street
Scarabee: 16 Voukourestiou Street
Lori: 22 Voukourestiou Street
Mourano: 11 Voukourestiou Street
Alexandrakis: 10 Kanari Street
Mati: 20 Voukourestiou Street

TOY SHOPS

Tsokas: 52 Aiolou Street
Kastrinakis: 53 Aiolou Street
Magioros: 17 Ermou Street
Panellinios Agora: 9 Stadiou Street

LEATHER GOODS

Vienezikon: 9 Stadiou Street
Skourletis: 28 Ermou Street
Dardoufas: 4 Nikis Street
Lambropoulos: 29 Mitropoleos Street

PORCELAIN, CHINA AND CRYSTAL STORES

Akron: 26 Stadiou Street

Deros: 4 Stadiou Street
Dionatos: 23 Philellinon Street
Koumbatis: 14 Philellinon Street
Alexandrakis: 10 Kanari Street
Mourano: 11 Voukourestiou Street
Nissiotis: 9 Stadiou Street
Sgourdas: 61 Aiolou Street
Athena: Kolokotroni Square

HAIRDRESSERS

George: 4 Kanari Street
Costas Bouboukis: 16 Voukourestiou Street
Anghelos: 2 Amalias Avenue
Kammer: 11 Panepistimiou Street
Hilton: (inside the Hotel Hilton)
Antoin: 69 Acadimias Street
Alex-George: 26 Acadimias Street
Emile: 17 Acadimias Street

BARBER SHOPS

Hilton: 17 Vassilissis Sophias Avenue
Grande Bretagne: King George I Street
Athenee Palace: 1 Kolokotroni Street
Kammer: 11 Panepistimiou Street
Stini: 4 Stadiou Street

COSMETICS

Salon Arden: 17 Ploutarchou Street
Bacharias (Rubinstein): 3 Stadiou Street
Marinopoulos: 66 Panepistimiou and 2 Patission Street
Georgandas: 21 Voulis Street
Nicolaidis: 42 Mitropoleos Street
Nicolaidis: 18 Ermou Street
Yerolimatos: 9 Kriezotou Street

PHARMACIES

Marinopoulos: 66 Panepistimiou Street
Marinopoulos: Kolonaki Square, 23 Kanari Street
Marinopoulos: 20 Kifissias Avenue
Bakakos: Omonia Square

Litos: 17 Stadiou Street
Damvergis: 39 Panepistimiou Street
Gerolymatos: Inside the arcade—Spyromiliou
Lemos: 68 Panepistimiou Street

OPTICIANS

Mouzakis: 6 Stadiou Street
Kortessis: 3 Stadiou Street
Ranios: 6 Omirou Street
Marinopoulos: 66 Panepistimiou Street and 2 Patission Street
Paraskevopoulos: 4 Stadiou Street
Papadiamantopoulos: Ermou Street

GROCERIES

Vassilopoulos: (*a*) 19 Stadiou Street (*b*) "Eklekton," 29 Voulis Street
   (*c*) Platia Proskopon (near Athens Square)
Stamatis: 23 Stadiou Street
Agrotikon: 33 Panepistimiou Street
Palladion: 54 Panepistimiou Street
Pantheon: Plateia Kolonakiou
Le Gourmet: 9 Amerikis Street

METRIC SYSTEM

WEIGHTS

Grams 1000 = 1 kilogram
  kilograms 1000 = 1 ton
16 ounces = 1 pound
To obtain grams multiply ounces by 28.
To obtain kilograms multiply pounds by 0.45.
To obtain ounces multiply grams by 0.03.
To obtain pounds multiply kilograms by 2.2.

LENGTH

To obtain centimeters multiply inches by 2.54.
To obtain meters multiply feet by 0.3.
To obtain meters multiply yards by 0.9.
To obtain kilometers multiply miles (land) by 1.6.
To obtain kilometers multiply miles (sea) by 1.8.
To obtain inches multiply centimeters by 0.39.
To obtain feet multiply meters by 3.28.
To obtain yards multiply meters by 1.09.
To obtain miles (land) multiply kilometers by 0.62.
To obtain miles (sea) multiply kilometers by 0.53.

SPEED

Kilometers/hour.
To obtain km/hrs multiply miles/hours by 1.61.
To obtain mls/hrs multiply km/hrs by 0.62.

TEMPERATURE

	Centigrade
212° F equals	100° C
122° F equals	50° C
98.6° F equals	37° C
59° F equals	15° C
32° F equals	0° C
0° F equals	−17.8° C

USEFUL WORDS AND PHRASES

This little list of phrases will not make you a linguist. It will not help you understand Greek. It will merely help you order food and ask for essentials. The pronunciations are given so that each syllable is as close to familiar English sounds as possible. If you recognize an English word in the pronunciation guide, fine, use it: for instance the name Harry as in ef-harry-sto. Wherever the letter "o" is given singly try to pronounce it as in *pot* or *for*. Pronounce "th" always as in *th*ought or *th*in; "d", always as the "th" in *th*en, *th*is, *th*ough; "ks" as in doc*ks*ide; "e" by itself, always as in b*e*t, l*e*t, men. (Stress the letter or syllable in italics. Speak quickly, running the syllables together.)

GENERAL

Hello, goodbye, pleased to meet you, drink up, good health—for all these there is one serviceable all purpose greeting	Y*a*s-as
Please (to be used often)	par-ak-al-*o*
Thank you	ef-harry-sto
Yes	ne (e as in bet)
No	*O*-he
I don't understand	den kat-al-av-*en*-o
Get an interpreter, please	v*res*-te ena dee-erm-ee-*ne*-ah par-ak-al-*o*
Pardon me	sig-*nom*-ee
Please show me	d*icks*-tem-oo par-ak-al-*o*
Give me	*dost*-em-oo
I want	th*el*-o
I want this	th*el*-o aft-*o*
I am an American	*eem*-e americ*a*-nos
Where is	poo *een*-e
The U.S. Consulate	america-neek-o proks-en-*ee*-o
The tourist police	toor-ees-teek-*ee* ast-een-om-*ee*-ah
The police station	ast-een-om-eek-*os* stath-mos

Help (shout this one)	vo-*ee*-thee-ah
Help me, please	vo-*ee*-thees-ste par-ak-al-*o*
I want a doctor	the*l*-o yat-*ro*
Please take me	par-ak-al-*o* p*art*-em-e

LODGINGS

Where is a hotel?	poo tha vro ksen-o-do-*hee*
a room	dom-*at*-ee-o
better	kal-*eet*-er-o
larger	meg-al-*eet*-er-o
cheaper	ftee-*not*-er-o
a bed	kre-*vat*-ee
soap	sap-oon-ee
a towel	pet-*set*-ah
the toilet	apo-hoary-tee-ree-o
toilet paper	hart-*ee* apo-hoary-*ree*-oo
insecticide	end-omok-*tono*
Call me at o'clock (write down time)	kseep-*neest*-eme

RESTAURANTS, FOODS, BEVERAGES

I want a restaurant	the*l*-o est-ee-at-*or*-ee-o
I want to eat	the*l*-o na *fa*-o
I want water	the*l*-o ne-*ro*
I am hungry	pee-no
I am thirsty	deep-so
a spoon	koo-t*a*-lee
a plate	pi*a*to (rhymes with piano)
a napkin	pe-t*se*-tah
a knife	ma-h*ai*ry
a glass	pot-*ee*rie
a fork	peer-*oo*-nee
salt	a-*la*-tee
pepper	peep-*per*-ee
vinegar	ks*ee*-dee
the menu	me-n*oo* (the "e" as in bet)
hors d'oeuvres	mez-*ed*-ess
soup	soop-a
eggs	av-g*ah*
cheese	tee-r*ee*
meat	kre-as (the "e" as in bet)

meat pie	kre-at-*op*-eet-ah
beef	vo-ee-dee-*no*
lamb	ar-n*ee*
lamb chops	pag-ee-d*a*k-ya ar-n*ee*-see-ah
lamb innards on the spit	kok-o-r*ets*-ee
pork	hear-ree-*no*
pork chops	breez-olah
steak	beef-*tek*-ee
veal	moss-harry
fish	ps*a*-ree
clams	kee-thon-ya (delicious, but eat them only if you've had shots)
lobster	as-tak-*os*
red snapper	sin-ag-*reed*-ah
red mullet	barb-*oon*-ee
sea bass	sphere-*eed*-ah
shrimp	gar-*eed*-ess
well done	kalop-see-m*e*no
rare	sen-ny*a*n
raw	o-m*o*
baked	too f*o*or-noo
boiled	vras-t*o*
fried	tee-gan-*ee*-to
roasted	psee-to
bread	pso-m*ee*
broiled	stee-sc*a*r-rah
village bread	hoary-*at*-eek-o psom-*ee*
lettuce	ma-*roo*-lee
potatoes	pa-*ta*-tes
rice	r*ee*-zee
squash	ko-lo-k*ee*-thee-ah
spinach	spa-*nah*-kee
tomatoes	to-*ma*-tess
fruit	fr*uit*-ah
apples	m*ee*-lo
bananas	bah-n*an*-ess
cherries	ke-r*as*-yah
grapes	staph-*feel*-yah
lemons	lem-on-yah
oranges	porto-*kal*-yah
peaches	ro-d*a*k-een-ah
plums	dam*a*sk-een-ah

strawberries	fra-ool-ess
watermelon	karp-oozy
pastries	past-ess
chicken	cot-op-oo-lo
beer	beer-ah
bottled water (of the Sarira source)	sar-eez-ah
brandy	coniac
chocolate	so-ko-la-tah
coffee	ka-fe ("e" as in bet)
coffee with milk	ka-fe me gal-ah
one coffee (Greek)	en-ah met-rio
lemonade	lem-onad-ah
milk	gal-ah
orange juice	porto-cal-ad-ah
sugar	zachary
tea	tsa-ee (rhymes with rye)
water	ne-ro ("e" as in bet)
wine	crass-ee
white	asp-ro
red	kok-een-o
resinated wine	rets-een-ah
unresinated wine	are-rets-een-oto
one glass	en-ah ("e" as in men) pot-eerie
one bottle	en-ah book-al-ee
the bill please	logar-eeasm-o par-ak-al-o

BUSES, TRAINS, CAR PARTS AND GARAGES

Where can I get the bus?	poo-e-he le-of-or-ee-o
Where can I get the train?	poo e-he tren-o
Where is the station?	poo e-he stath-mo
Is the road good?	een-e o drom-oss kal-oss
Is the road bad?	een-e o drom-os kak-os
I want a service station	thel-o ga-raz
mechanic	mec-han-eek-os
a battery	bat-tar-ee-ah
brakes	fren-ah
carburetor	car-beer-rat-ter
clutch	sim-blek-tees
diesel oil	diesel-ola-do

gasoline	ven-*zee*-nee
a jack	greel-os
oil (for the sump)	mee-han-*el*-e-o
spark plugs	booz-*ya*
a tire	l*a*st-ee-ho

SERVICES AND HIRING

Where can I find?	poo tha vro
a doctor	yat-ro
a dentist	od-on-do-y*a*t-ro
a barber	koor-*e*-ah
a drug store	farm-ak-*ee*-o
a grocery	bah-*kal*-ee
a movie	cinem*a*
a restaurant	est-ee-at-*or*-ee-o
a tailor	rought-tee
This needs washing	thel-ee plee-sim-o
This needs repairing	thel-ee *dior*-thom-ah
This needs dry cleaning	thelee cath-ar-east-*ee*rie-o
This needs pressing	thel-ee sid-*er*-om-ah
I want a car	thel-o aft-ok-*een*-eet-o
I want a boat	thel-o v*a*rk-ah
I want a taxi	thel-o tax*i*
I want a driver	thel-o so-*fair*
I want a porter	thel-o ham-*al*-ee
I want a guide	thel-o ksen-ah-go
I want a donkey	thel-o gah-ee-doo-r*ak*-ee
I want that	thel-o aft-*o*
I want a haircut	thel-o koor-emma
I want a shave	thel-o ks*ee*-reez-mah

USEFUL WORDS

aspirin	aspir*in*-ee
batteries	bat-ar-r*ee*-as
buttons	coom-bee-*a*h
cigarettes	tsee-g*a*-rah
a comb	kt*e*n-nah
envelopes	f*a*-kel-la
a flashlight or lantern	eel-lek-treek-ko fan-*nar*-ee
handkerchiefs	mand-*eel*-lee
ink	mel-lan-*ee*

a laxative	kath-arctic-ko
matches	speer-tah
a needle	vel-on-nee
paper	hart-ee
a pencil	mol-eev-ee
pins	car-feets-ess
razor blades	ksee-raf-ak-ya
scissors	psal-eed-ee
shaving cream	krem-ah ksee-reez-mat-os
shoe laces	kord-on-ya
thread	closs-tee
a toothbrush	odon-dov-voortsa
toothpaste	odon-dok-rem-ah
rope	skee-nee

NUMBERS 1 TO 10 COMPARATIVES

one	en-ah
two	dee-o
three	tree-ah
four	tess-se-rah
five	pend-ee
six	eks-ee
seven	ep-ta
eight	ok-to ("o" as in doctor)
nine	en-ya
ten	dek-ah
how much	po-so
You charge too much	pol-ah zeet-at-te
a few	leeg-ah
many	pol-lah
some more	kia-lo
large	meg-gal-lo
medium	met-tree-o
small	meek-kro ⎫
short	cond-do ⎬ the "o" as in doctor
long	mak-kree

THE GREEK ALPHABET

The pronunciations of Greek letters, or combinations of letters called diphthongs is always the same. (In parentheses next to the name of some letters is the Greek pronunciation where it might vary from that taught in America or England.)

	Capitals	Lower Case	English Equivalent
Alpha	A	α	A (as in bar)
Beta (veeta)	B	β	V
Gamma	Γ	γ	Y (as in yet or yak before the letters I and E; but nearer a G before an A or O)
Delta (thelta)	Δ	δ	TH (as in that)
Epsilon	E	ε	E (as in bet)
Zeta	Z	ζ	Z
Eta (eeta)	H	η	EE (as in meek)
Theta	Θ	θ	TH (as in thought)
Iota (yacht-a)	I	ι	EE (as in meek)
Kappa	K	κ	K
Lambda	Λ	λ	L
Mu (me)	M	μ	M
Nu (nee)	N	ν	N
Xi (xee)	Ξ	ξ	KS or X (as in dockside or oxalic)
Omicron	O	o	O (as in dot)
Pi (pee)	Π	π	P
Rho (row)	P	ρ	R
Sigma	Σ	σ, ς	S
Tau (taf)	T	τ	T
Upsilon (eepsilon)	Y	υ	EE (as in meek)
Phi (fee)	Φ	φ	F

	Capitals	Lower Case	English Equivalent
Chi (he)	X	χ	H (as in Harry or hero)
Psi (psee)	Ψ	ψ	PS (as in lopsided)
Omega	Ω	ω	O (as in dot)

DIPHTHONGS (combinations of letters pronounced as one sound; always with the same pronounciation)

AI   always pronounced as the E in BET

AY   ″   ″   ″ ″ AF in AFT

EI ⎱
OI ⎰   ″   ″   ″ ″ EE in MEEK

EY   ″   ″   ″ ″ EF in DEFT

OY   ″   ″   ″ ″ OO in BOOT

There are many little accents that appear over Greek words, as for instance ἀπό. If there is more than one accent sign over a word, ignore the first. Only the second matters; it indicates which syllable to stress.

INDEX

For more entries, see the index of place names on page 232, the table of contents, and the index of useful people, shops, agencies, banks, etc. on page 339.

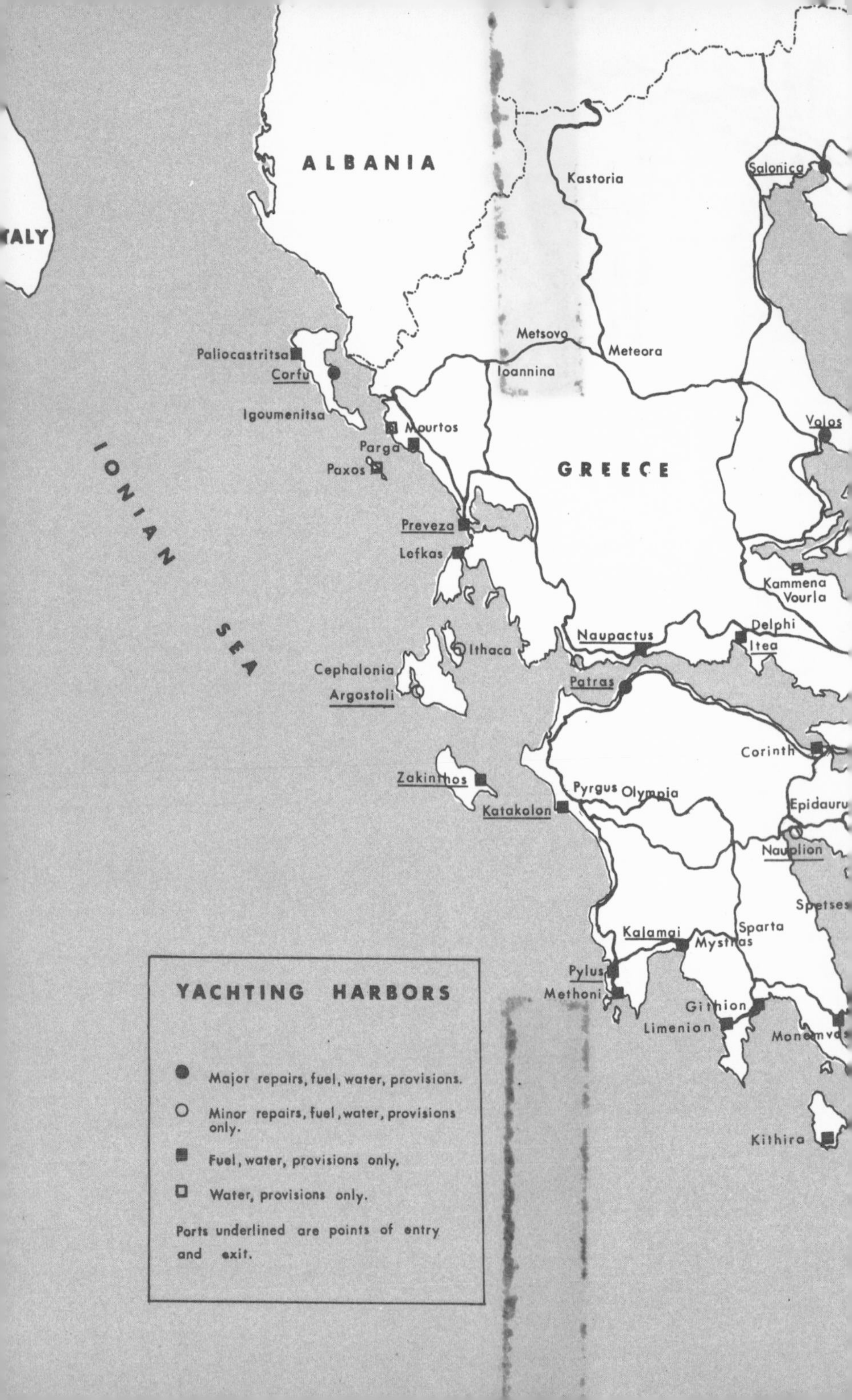
ALBANIA
Kastoria
Salonica
Metsovo
Meteora
Ioannina
Paliocastritsa
Corfu
Igoumenitsa
Mourtos
Parga
Paxos
IONIAN SEA
GREECE
Volos
Preveza
Lefkas
Kammena Vourla
Naupactus
Delphi
Itea
Ithaca
Cephalonia
Argostoli
Patras
Corinth
Zakinthos
Katakolon
Pyrgus
Olympia
Epidauru
Nauplion
Spetses
Kalamai
Sparta
Mystras
Pylus
Methoni
Githion
Limenion
Monemvas
Kithira
YACHTING HARBORS
Major repairs, fuel, water, provisions.
Minor repairs, fuel, water, provisions only.
Fuel, water, provisions only.
Water, provisions only.
Ports underlined are points of entry and exit.